A Century of Yiddish Poetry

Also by Aaron Kramer:

Poetry

Another Fountain
Till the Grass Is Ripe for Dancing
Thru Our Guns
The Glass Mountain
The Thunder of the Grass
The Golden Trumpet
Thru Every Window!
Denmark Vesey
Roll the Forbidden Drums!
The Tune of the Calliope
Moses
Rumshinsky's Hat
Henry at the Grating
On the Way to Palermo
O Golden Land!
Carousel Parkway
The Burning Bush
In Wicked Times

Translation

The Poetry and Prose of Heinrich Heine
Morris Rosenfeld: The Teardrop Millionaire
Goethe, Schiller, Heine: Songs and Ballads
Rilke: Visions of Christ

Criticism

The Prophetic Tradition in American Poetry: 1835–1900
Melville's Poetry: Toward the Enlarged Heart

Contributions to Symposia

Seven Poets in Search of an Answer
Poetry Therapy
Poetry the Healer
Paumanok Rising

Anthology

On Freedom's Side

A Century
of Yiddish Poetry

Selected, Translated, and Edited by
Aaron Kramer

Cornwall Books
New York • London • Toronto

Cornwall Books
440 Forsgate Drive
Cranbury, NJ 08512

Cornwall Books
25 Sicilian Avenue
London WC1A 2QH, England

Cornwall Books
P.O. Box 488, Port Credit
Mississauga, Ontario
Canada L5G 4M2

The paper used in this publication meets the requirements of the American National Standard for Permanence of Paper for Printed Library Materials Z39.48-1984.

Library of Congress Cataloging-in-Publication Data

A Century of Yiddish poetry.

Includes index.
1. Yiddish poetry—Translations into English.
2. English poetry—Translations from Yiddish.
I. Kramer, Aaron, 1921–   .
PJ5191.E3C46   1989   839'.0913'08   87-48007
ISBN 0-8453-4815-9 (alk. paper)

Printed in the United States of America

for my mother and father

Contents

Joseph Rolnik (1879–1955)   109
    At God's Behest   109
    My Oceans   109
    I. Raboy   110
    I Am Not Rich   111
    Incognito   112
    Heed the Moon   112
    Four Paces in Sunlight   112
Eliezer Steinbarg (1880–1932)   113
    The Clever Stream   114
    The Shirt and the Coat   115
Mani-Leib (1883–1953)   115
    On Fifth Avenue   116
    By Heavy Locks   116
    A Song About a Hunchbacked Pair of Tailors   117
    Your Grace   118
    The Lands and the Oceans   118
    Beauty   119
    My Mother   119
    Amid the White Tables   119
    Ballad of Two   120
Avrom-Moishe Dillon (1883–1934)   121
    Our Word   121
    Rain   121
    I Feel the Whole World's Hardness   122
    Till Now   122
Reuben Eisland (1884–1955)   122
    The Trees Lead   123
    Zische Landau Recites a Poem   123
Joel Slonim (1884?–1944)   124
    The Seamstress   125
Israel-Jacob Schwartz (1885–1971)   126
    Parting   126
    A Little Mother   127
    At First They Were White   128
    Precious This Soil (excerpt)   129
Moishe Leib Halpern (1886–1932)   129
    In the Golden Land   129
    The W-w-words of Murdovietz Barnuhle   130
    By Its Barrenness   131
    Up from Earth There Grows   132

11

SOVIET POETS

POETS OF THE LEFT

POETS OF THE HOLOCAUST

Preface

Although there is hardly a plethora of Yiddish poetry anthologies in English translations, several *are* available, notably Ruth Whitman's *Modern Yiddish Poetry* (1966), Irving Howe and Eliezer Greenberg's *A Treasury of Yiddish Poetry* (1969), Howard Schwartz's *Voices within the Ark* (published in 1980 and incorporating almost all of the Whitman book), and Irving Howe's *Penguin Book of Modern Yiddish Verse* (1987). To offer a new compilation, therefore, requires some sort of defense.

In at least five respects, *A Century of Yiddish Poetry* differs markedly from its predecessors: (1) Rather than focus only on the modern poets, I have given equal prominence to the extraordinary pre-twentieth-century generation from which they sprang and against which many of them turned, exactly paralleling the anti-Victorian trend in British and American poetry. (2) Rather than ignore the strongly reformist impulse in the leading introspectivist and aestheticist figures, I demonstrate that most of them, in their lives and work, were socialists or Labor Zionists, as were most of the good minor poets no other recent anthologists have included. (3) Rather than utterly banish the big cluster of left-wing poets, who enjoyed the adulation of a huge pro-Soviet audience for over thirty years, I give them as much attention as their Soviet counterparts, whom other anthologists seem to admire now primarily because Stalin martyred them, just as he would have martyred the members of the Proletpen group if he had had them in his power. (4) Although there is a good deal of overlapping, and the towering figures of the Holocaust (Grade, Korn, Sutzkever, Zeitlin, Zychlinska), as well as the Soviet giants (Hofstein, Kulbak, Kvitko, Markish), are central to the Second Golden Age, I have placed both the Soviet and the Holocaust poets in distinct categories so that the sheer magnitude of their numbers, achievements, and destinies becomes dramatically clear. Among the seventeen Soviet poets in this collection (Howe and Greenberg group seven) are those who survived their incarcera-

21

tion as well as those executed in 1952, a few victimized much earlier, and several who somehow escaped harm, most of whom eventually emigrated to Israel; among the twenty-one Holocaust poets I have included the unknown along with the famous, those who perished along with those who survived, and those who personally escaped the Nazis but whose nearest and dearest were slaughtered. (5) Rather than misrepresent the predominant form of Yiddish poetry (traditional rhymed stanzas), thus catering to the current bias against rhyme and pattern with the convenient rationale that they are impossible to replicate well, I have insisted on matching the form of a poem, because form is an intrinsic part of what is being said, and it is the translator's duty to transmit the total experience offered by a poem.

I do not claim to have selected these poets' best or most representative work; rather, I have chosen pieces that touched me and were congenial to my translating skills. Nevertheless, the total collection, combined with the biographical sketches, seems to me to transmit the history of Yiddish verse clearly enough so that I can resist offering a long scholarly thesis here. One point, however, strikes me as particularly poignant and worthy of mention. In little more than half a century, Yiddish poets moved from defensiveness in using a ridiculed "pseudolanguage," to a defiant, loving, untranslatably exquisite celebration of that very language in the teeth of its annihilation. In this respect, at least, Yiddish poetry stands alone.

Acknowledgments

Of the many people who encouraged me in the creation of this book, I will here name only three: Menke Katz, for his unflagging enthusiasm over the years and his choice of fifteen valuable poems I would not otherwise have translated; Ber Green, for a lifetime of loyal friendship and inspiration, and for six hours of intensive interviews that enriched my background in Yiddish literature, particularly with regard to the Proletpen; and Dina Abramowicz, YIVO's extraordinary librarian, whose caring has sparked my efforts and whose generous acts of service, far beyond the call of duty, merit my deepest gratitude.

Many of Aaron Kramer's translations of Yiddish poetry have been published in the following journals:

Bitterroot, Canadian Outlook, Chicago Forum, Home Planet News, Jewish Currents, Jewish Life, Journal of Humanistic Psychology, Midstream, New England Review, Ocarina (India), *Poet* (India), *Poet Lore, The Polish Review, Sing Out!*, and *Yiddish America*.

Other selections have appeared in the following volumes:

A Treasury of Jewish Folklore (1948), *Warsaw Ghetto Uprising* (1953), *Lift Every Voice! The Second People's Song Book* (1953), *"Jewish Life" Anthology* (1956), *A Treasury of Jewish Poetry* (1957), *The Jews in the United States* (1958), *A History of Jewish Literature* (1960), *Toil and Triumph: The Life of Morris Rosenfeld* (1960), *Isaac E. Ronch: Selected Poems* (1961), *The Right to be Different* (1961), *Jewish Book Annual* (1962), *Morris Rosenfeld: Selections from His Poetry and Prose* (1964), *A Treasury of Yiddish Poetry* (1969), *One Hundred Years of the Yiddish Press in America* (1970), *Songs of Peace, Freedom, and Protest: A Tom Glazer Songbook* (1970), *Anthology of Holocaust Literature* (1973), *On Freedom's Side: American Poems of Protest* (1973), *American Labor*

Songs of the Nineteenth Century (1975), *World of Our Fathers* (1976), *The New Country* (1976), *Unter Yankele's Vigele: An Anthology of Yiddish Lullabies* (1976), *Antonio Maceo: A Biography* (1977), *The Shalom Seders* (1982), *The Israel Yearbook* (1982), *Anthology of Magazine Verse* (1983), *Carry It On! A Pete Seeger Songbook* (1986), *Anthology of Magazine Verse* (1986–1987), *The Penguin Book of Modern Yiddish Verse* (1987), and *Yiddish Poetry: Freshness of the Ancient* (India, 1987).

This book was in part assisted
by a grant from the
ZHITLOWSKY FOUNDATION FOR YIDDISH CULTURE

A Century of Yiddish Poetry

The First Golden Age

Folk Songs

1

Hey, hey, hammerkin!
Come into my chamberkin!
I'll show you something rare—
iron shoes are there.
Twin horses run like lightning;
a bride and groom are fighting.
She gave birth to a chap;
first rocked him in her lap,
then in his crib; then found
a bed for him in the ground.

(Brest-Litovsk)

2

Hark, pretty girl, to whatever I ask,
and answer my questions from first to last.
Where lies a water where no fish swim?
Where stands a house and no table within?

You foolish fellow, you downright dunce!
Your noggin hasn't a grain of sense!
In deep well-water no fish swim;
when a house is empty, no table's within.

Hark, pretty girl, to whatever I ask,
and answer my questions from first to last.

Where's there a king without a land?
Where is there water without any sand?

You foolish fellow, you downright dunce!
Your noggin hasn't a grain of sense!
The king in a card game has no land;
the water of eyes is without any sand.

Hark, pretty girl, to whatever I ask,
and answer my questions from first to last.
What rises higher than a house?
What moves more nimbly than a mouse?

You foolish fellow, you downright dunce!
Your noggin hasn't a grain of sense!
The chimney is higher than the house;
the cat is nimbler than the mouse.

Hark, pretty girl, to whatever I ask,
and answer my questions from first to last.
Where's there a tailor with no shears, none?
Where's there a soldier without a gun?

You foolish fellow, you downright dunce!
Your noggin hasn't a grain of sense!
A tailor who's dead has no shears, none;
a soldier discharged is without a gun.

Hark, pretty girl, to whatever I ask,
and answer my questions from first to last.
What's deeper than the deepest spring?
What's bitterer than a hornet's sting?

You foolish fellow, you downright dunce!
Your noggin hasn't a grain of sense!
The sea is deeper than the deepest spring;
death's bitterer than a hornet's sting.

(Warsaw)

This tale was once told far and wide:
a husband parted from his bride;
he went away despite her tears
and tarried for a sea of years,
a sea of years in a land unknown
—lovely Chaneh remained alone.

At last he came to her, but masked.
"Do you have clothes or gold?" he asked.
"Do you have wealth or fancy dresses?
Do you desire a stranger's kisses?"
"I have no wealth or fancy dresses;
I don't desire a stranger's kisses."

He brought a ring, nor dull nor tiny.
It weighed two pounds, was red and shiny,
and fair as all the universe,
and worth more than a rich man's purse.
"I offer you this ring as a gift,
if you'll forget the man who left."

"Oh your ring is neither dull nor tiny;
it weighs two pounds, is red and shiny,
and fair as all the universe,
and worth more than a rich man's purse;
but it's a gift I will not keep.
For my dear husband I'll wait and weep."

He brought an apron white as milk
that washes easily as silk
and reaches to the very floor
—a hundred roubles at the store!
"I'll offer this apron as a gift,
if you'll forget the man who left."

"The apron is truly white as milk
and washes easily as silk
and reaches to the very floor
—a hundred roubles at the store;
but it's a gift you should not offer;
for my dear husband I'll sigh and suffer!"

"Blest is my being, blest my life—
that I am your husband and you my wife!
I thank you, and I thank you, Moon;
I thank you, God, for your precious boon!
I thank you, Star of the morning skies;
I thank you, God, for my wedded prize!"

(Warsaw)

4

I'm a hare out in the world, a little hare;
fright and suffering face me everywhere;
fright and suffering, suffering and fright,
hound me, surround me, by day and by night.
I'm a lonely little hare, in a wretched plight.

Winter comes, with its heavy snows;
then indeed begin my worries and my woes;
my worries and my woes begin—
no place for me to dry my skin.
I'm a lonely little hare—what misery I'm in!

I stand, stand there on the mountaintop.
The hunter hunts me till I'm ready to drop.
He hunts me down, lets loose his hounds;
they close in, and my poor heart pounds.
I'm a lonely little hare, whom grief surrounds.

They take me captive, take me so swiftly!
Onto the butcher block they lift me,
slit open this little belly of mine,
swallow me down with mead and wine.
I'm a lonely little hare, in a world unkind.

(Vilna)

5

At six I stagger
out of bed
and meet in the mirror
someone dead.
Alas, dear God,
be honest with me—
is a seamstress all
I can hope to be?

I dress while
the rooster's tuning up;
heart dry, but
no tea—not a drop.
Without great joy
I set out for work;
when I arrive,
they greet me like dirt.

I sit there sewing;
Madame, half-awake,
screams from her bedroom:
"Why are you late?"
By winter's end
my face looks wrecked.
Wages? "At Passover
you'll collect. . . ."

My mother waits
at the door for my money.
Somebody bellows:
"Not one penny!"
Alas, dear God,
take pity at last!
If You save me from sewing,
I'll pray . . . I'll fast!

(Warsaw)

6

In the front room
I'm made to know
the number I happened
to pick was low.
Alas and alack,
what could be worse?
My twenty-first birthday
falls like a curse.

In the front room
along with the rest
I'm given an order
to get undressed.
In the next room
I'm handed a gun:
my five-year comrade
in rain and sun.

Out the back door
what should I see
but a troop of soldiers
waiting for me.
Down the back stairs:
there to meet me
with lowered heads
my parents greet me.

Dearest mother,
fare you well.
Dark as your life is,
mine is hell.
Dearest father,
shed no tears.
You're rid of me
for five full years.

Dear sisters, brothers,
farewell to you all.
As you see me now,
let no tears fall.
Farewell, dear friends;

as you see me this day,
I've signed five years
of my life away.

Farewell, my bride,
my beauty, my best!
I'll miss you more
than all the rest.
Alas and alack,
what could be worse?
My twenty-first birthday
falls like a curse.

(Odessa)

7

Were I to be a rabbi,
I don't know the prayers;
were I to be a merchant,
I have no wares.

Were I to be a butcher,
I own no knife;
were I to be a teacher,
I can't read or write.

Were I to be a cobbler,
—no last to make heels;
were I to be a baker,
—no oven peels.

Were I to be a coachman,
—no horse to hitch;
I'm just a poor Jew
dumped in a ditch.

(Czimerowicz, Podolia)

Michl Gordon (1823–1890)

MICHL GORDON was born in Vilna in 1823. In addition to his cheder studies he secretly learned Russian and German and composed verses. At twenty he married the sister of the future poet Judah-Leib Gordon, whom he influenced profoundly. He was first published in Hebrew in 1846. His wife died early; he remarried and moved to his in-laws' town. During that time he began writing and reciting Yiddish poems that circulated widely, but he was advised by the literati, who had contempt for Yiddish, not to have them published. Lacking a trade and unsuited to the business world, he led a life of poverty, preferring the ill-paid post of resident tutor for some wealthy Ukrainian families. His first collection, *The Beard and Other Fine Yiddish Poems,* published in Zhitomir in 1868, opened a new chapter in Yiddish literature. Because the book appeared anonymously, a myth grew that Gordon was ashamed of his Yiddish work. He feared, in fact, the vengeance of the Hasidim, whom his verses mocked, and he ironically identified the author as "a great Hasid." A year later the only volume of a planned series of Yiddish books of general knowledge appeared: Part One of his *The History of Russia.* Almost a score of years passed before any of his new poems appeared in journals; unfortunately, much of his manuscript work disappeared. In 1884 his second wife died; five years later he was stricken by cancer. That year his *Yiddish Poems* were issued. The youthful exuberance had given way to bitter sorrow, reflecting the loss of his personal hopes and of his belief in the Christian world's "good will" toward Jews. His death in 1890 in a Kiev hospital went unnoted in the Jewish press, but recognition of his historic role began a year later with the tributes of Peretz and Frug.

MY LIFETIME

Out of my mother's womb I came
with a great sob, with a great scream.
But now I'll go into the ground,
my lasting home, without a sound.

As through an open door one comes
into the street from narrow rooms,
just so I'll calmly leave my bed
and take my rest among the dead.

The end of my short life is near;
the final hour will soon be here.
Just now begun, already done;
just now arrived, already gone.

Millions of years had floated past
before I saw the world at last.
Millions of years are yet to be,
and I will neither hear nor see.

Sometimes the ocean flings up spray:
a drop against the morning's ray;
and in a flash, with lightning motion,
the drop falls back into the ocean.

So the short lifetime that is mine;
so does my drop of fortune shine:
flung up from the eternal sea,
then back, back to eternity.

Shmuel Bernstein
(ca. 1830–ca. 1883)

SHMUEL BER(E)NSTEIN was born in Kaminetz-Podolsk, the
Ukraine, in the early nineteenth century and died in the early
1880s. His collection, *Magazine of Yiddish Songs for the Jewish People*,
first published in Zhitomir in 1869 and often reprinted, included
several translations from German and Russian and a verse tribute
to him by Michl Gordon. During the 1860s and 1870s he was a
popular contributor to the newspaper *Herald Voice*, in which he

was represented by poetry and prose as well as a serialized comedy in five acts.

FALSE HOPE

The world is large; it stretches far.
Each person follows Fortune's star;
Hope cheers him in a cheerless time:
"You'll prosper yet, your sun will shine."
She promises him hills of gold;
from one cent, thousands will unfold.
She's not unlike a spark of fire:
she'll glow, grow brighter, then expire.
In godlike form she comes to him;
he feels reborn in every limb. . . .
Thus he grows old, thus he grows gray,
thus to the grave she lights his way.

Isaac Leib Peretz (1851–1915)

Born in 1851 in Zamosc, near Lublin, Poland, ISAAC LEIB PERETZ moved to Warsaw and became its leading cultural force, writing first in Hebrew, then in the language of the common people, whose spiritual heritage he voiced in novels, plays, and a famous series of Hasidic sketches. His 1888 "Monish" was the first verse novel in modern Yiddish. His *Complete Works*, in eighteen volumes, were published in 1926. His *Selected Stories*, in English translation, edited by Irving Howe and Eliezer Greenberg, were published in 1974. Long before his death in Warsaw in 1915 he was universally recognized as one of the three giants of modern Yiddish literature, along with Mendele Moicher Sforim and Sholom Aleichem.

THREE SEAMSTRESSES

Their lips gone blue, their eyes gone red,
their cheeks without one drop of blood,
their foreheads pale and dripping sweat,
their breath irregular and hot—
    three girls sit and sew.

The needle bright, the linen—snow;
one girl thinks: I sew and sew;
I sew by day, I sew by night—
but where's *my* gown of bridal white?
    what's come of all my sewing?

I don't sleep, don't eat a crumb.
If I could save a certain sum,
Baal Ness might find—no matter who—
even a widower would do,
    old and plagued with children.

The second thinks: I stitch all day
and stitch myself two braids of gray!
My head's on fire, my temples thrum,
and my machine beats like a drum:
    ta-ta, ta-ta, ta-ta!

Folks are winking over me:
with no ring, no canopy,
there'd be fun, a love affair
lasting maybe one whole year—
    but what then? what then?

The third spits blood and racks her mind:
I sew me sick, I sew me blind;
and every stitch goes through my side. . . .
This very week he takes a bride;
    I do not wish him ill!

Eh!—what's past is past. . . ! The crowd
will come with coins to buy my shroud,
and a bit of earth somewhere.
Nothing to disturb me there;
    I will sleep, will sleep!

THERE WAS A YOUNG GIRL ONCE

There was a young girl once
who loved a lad;
the boy loves her dearly,
but both are sad:

her father is wealthy;
her lover's poor.
The millionaire father
shows him the door.

She bows to his wishes,
takes a rich groom;
the lad wilts and withers
in his lone room.

She hears he has perished
and steals outside;
she reaches his grave plot;
it opens wide.

His outstretched hands draw her
down where he lies;
she lifts back the cerement,
kisses his eyes. . . .

They open; with chill hand
he clasps his lover.
The grave shuts above them,
entwined forever.

DON'T THINK

Don't think the world is a tavern, created
to blast one's way forward by punching and clawing
right up to the bar stools, and gorge there and guzzle
while those in the rear look with eyes that grow glassy,
half-swooning, and gulp their saliva and draw in

their stomachs that twist with the cramps of the hungry.
O don't think the world is a tavern.

Don't think the world is a Market, created
for strong folk to trade with the weak and exhausted,
to purchase the virtue of girls who are needy,
to bargain the milk from the breasts of poor women,
from workmen their marrow, from children the pale smile
—the guest that appears on their faces so seldom.
O don't think the world is a Market.

Don't think the world is a jungle, created
for wolves and for foxes, for theft and for swindle,
the heavens—a drape, so that God will not notice,
a fog—so that none can behold what your hands are,
a wind—so that every wild outcry is smothered,
an earth—that will soak up the blood of the slaughtered.
O don't think the world is a jungle.

The world is no tavern, no Market, no jungle!
Here everything's weighed, all is carefully measured!
Not one drop of blood, not one tear, unrecorded;
no spark that's snuffed out in an eye is glossed over.
From teardrops come rivers; from rivers come oceans;
from oceans—a tempest; from sparks—a great thunder.
O don't think there's no Court of Justice! . . .

MY MUSE

No, my Muse is not a flower;
in no meadow is she found;
not a butterfly, that kisses
every blossom on the ground.

No, my Muse is not a songbird;
trills nor sweets are in her nature.
She's an aged Jewish woman
—shriveled up, an ugly creature.

41

A deserted wife, with orphans
scattered half across the world;
and a pauper, from whose mouth
curses fly and screams are hurled.

Morris Winchevsky (1855–1932)

MORRIS WINCHEVSKY, known the world over as the *Zayde* (Grand-father) of Yiddish proletarian poetry, was born in 1855 in a Lithuanian village. His family moved to the capital, Kovno, where he received advanced rabbinical training, but he rebelled and became a bank clerk. Taking a post deep inside Russia in 1874, he made contact with the revolutionists who had come from the universities to carry on propaganda among the peasants. In 1877 he held a bank post in Koenigsburg, Prussia; here he saw the first socialist newspaper for Jews, edited by Aaron Lieberman. When Lieberman was arrested in 1878, Winchevsky became editor. A number of his poems of protest appeared in its pages. He was soon arrested and deported. After a short stay in Paris he settled in London. There, to reach the tens of thousands of Jewish factory workers, he turned from Hebrew to Yiddish. With William Morris and others, he founded the British Social Democratic Federation. He wrote a revolutionary pamphlet, *Let There Be Light*, and edited a socialist weekly, first called *Dos Poilishe Idl* (The Polish Jew) and, afterward, *Di Tsukunft* (The Future). In 1885 he helped found the first Yiddish labor daily, *Der Arbeiter Freint* (The Work-ers' Friend), which circulated as widely in the United States as in Britain. Here were published his fighting songs and "London silhouettes." In 1894 he came to America and continued, in Boston and New York, to edit socialist journals. He also produced a valuable autobiography. In 1924 he visited the Soviet Union, receiving a tumultuous welcome everywhere. He contributed to the *Morning Freiheit* throughout his later years, and on his seven-tieth birthday the *Freiheit* published his collected works in ten volumes. He died in 1932.

THREE SISTERS

In England there's Leicester—the city;
in London there's Leicester—the square;
and daily three sisters, three pretty
young sisters, are known to be there.

The youngest is out selling flowers;
the second cries "Laces!" all day;
the oldest comes by in dark hours
and bargains her body away.

The younger ones look at their sister
not hatefully, not with a frown;
all three curse a world that is twisted;
all three curse the street and the town.

And yet, when those two—after hours—
return to the hole that is "home,"
they moisten the laces and flowers
with tears that will never be known.

IN RAIN, IN THE WIND AND THE FROST

What can they be doing—two waifs—on the street,
in rain, in the wind and the frost?
with cold little fingers, and wet little feet,
with blue little lips, and with pale little cheeks?
How far is their home—are they lost?
Their home?—only I am their home, says the street,
in rain, in the wind and the frost!

And where can two children be going so late,
in rain, in the frost and the wind?
No friends? and no parents who lovingly wait?
Orphans? Too bad! Am I seeing straight?
No doubt of it—one of them's blind!
The street answers: I'm their friend, early and late,
in rain, in the frost and the wind.

And why are they suddenly standing so still
in rain, in the wind and the frost?
Too young to go begging, and too poor to sell;
for stealing they've neither the strength nor the will.
Who'll feed them? Who'll throw them a crust?
Ah, this time the stone-hearted street keeps still;
the rain, too, keeps still—and the frost.

MY VOW

A good many years ago, while I was rotting
in jail, at a tyrant's command,
and while, like a corpse, I was being forgotten
by lover, and laughter, and friend—

I uttered an oath once, the holiest oath:
to battle for truth and for rights;
to give up my comfort, to give up my youth,
to give up my days and my nights—

as long as a man can be chained like a slave,
as long as the world is a jail,
as long as the toiler, from cradle to grave,
hears only a curse and a wail.

Yes, many years back, in the dark prison hell,
divided from brother and bird,
I uttered this oath in the gloom of my cell,
—and night was the witness that heard.

IN BATTLE

When the drums of liberation
shall at last begin to sound,
you may find me at my station
on the bloody battleground.

And my brothers, I shall lead them
not from a commander's post;
only with my songs of freedom
shall I move the mighty host.

For, beside the ammunition,
at that hour—hot and grim—
we'll be needing, in addition,
an inspired battle hymn.

I HEAR A CRY

A cry of anguish comes to me:
a pitiable sound.
It seems to start up suddenly
from regions all around.

Far off I hear it, then close by;
I hear it everywhere—
and ever louder grows the cry,
until it rocks the air.

I ask the planets in their spheres,
I ask the earth and sky:
"This cry of anguish in my ears—
what does it signify?

"Is it the final shriek of pain
that dies out and grows dumb?
Or does this 'oh!' and 'ah!' proclaim
a birth that is to come?"

"It is a birth—a birth sublime!"
the wind at once explains:
"Long past her time is Mother Time;
these are her labor pains. . . ."

A BROOM, AND WATCH ME SWEEP!

Enough! I will not sow again
for idle hands to reap!
I never will bow low again.
A broom, and watch me sweep!
Hand me a broom! I'm through with them,
I'll sweep them off the earth!
Yes, yes—that's what I'll do with them:
one whisk is all they're worth!

They wore my heart and soul away;
my sweat became their jewel.
The crumbs I earned they stole away,
and rode me like a mule.
The black hoods cannot harm me now—
the curses *they* can keep!
The titles don't alarm me now—
a broom, and watch me sweep!

Sholom Aleichem (1859–1916)

SHOLOM ALEICHEM was born Solomon Rabinowitz in Pereyaslav,
the Ukraine, in 1859. He first wrote in Hebrew, but in 1883, the
year of his marriage, he turned to Yiddish with an autobiographical love story. He adopted his pseudonym to disguise his
identity from the Jewish intelligentsia, including his father, who
held Yiddish literature in contempt. Moving to the Kiev region,
he produced many novels, critical essays, and poems, and in 1888
founded *Di Yiddishe Folksbibliotek,* a brilliant literary annual whose
two volumes represent a turning point in the history of Yiddish
literature. His prodigious and immensely popular newspaper
work did not keep him from poverty, and in 1906, appalled by the
pogroms in Kiev, he moved his large family first to Lvov, then to
Geneva; he went on to New York where promised financial back-
ing did not materialize and his new plays failed. To raise funds, he

undertook a lecture tour of Russia during which he collapsed and nearly died of tuberculosis. In 1909 the entire Jewish world celebrated his fiftieth birthday. His works soon appeared in Russian and Hebrew. A second visit to the United States in 1914 proved fatal. Acclaimed again, but without financial aid though publishers grew wealthy from sales of his masterworks, he was forced into a devastating series of lecture tours and died in May 1916. Hundreds of thousands attended his funeral. Of his carefully revised complete writings, only twelve of the forty volumes appeared during his lifetime, nor did he live to see his finest stage works produced. Since then he has been universally acknowledged as one of the world's supreme literary masters.

EPITAPH

Here lies a simple Jew, who wrote
in sort of Yiddish-German style
for women and for common folk;
his task—to make them smile.

A whole life long he hurled his wit
against the world's great wickedness;
the world felt none the worse for it;
but he was in distress!

Precisely when the crowd guffawed
and split their sides in greatest glee,
he ailed—none knew of it but God—
aside, that none should see.

Simeon Frug (1860–1916)

Born in 1860 in Bobrowi Kut, Cherson, one of the first Jewish agricultural colonies, SIMEON FRUG established a formidable reputation as a Russian poet in the tradition of Lermontov and

47

Nekrassov. He was invited to settle in St. Petersburg, where he contributed to the leading Russian periodicals. In response to the pogroms that swept the Ukraine in 1881, he began writing Yiddish poems. One of his most famous songs, "Have Pity," was provoked by the 1903 pogrom in Kishinev that also inspired the masterpiece of his friend Bialik. His *Complete Writings* (1910) were published in New York in three volumes, with a foreword by Reuben Brainin; two years later his works in Russian appeared in six volumes. He died in Odessa in 1916.

SAND AND STARS

The moon is aglow and the stars are afire;
the hill and the valley take night for their cover. . . .
The little old volume lies open before me;
I read it, I read it a thousand times over.

I read the dear words, so well loved and so sacred;
their promise sings forth unto me:
"My people, you'll be like the stars in the heavens,
like sand on the shore of the sea. . . ."

Not one single word, O Creator Almighty,
not one will be lost of your pledges sublime;
your holy decrees shall at last be enacted—
all comes in its place, in its time.

Already fulfilled is one promise you made us:
it's something I know and I feel;
for we are become like the sand of a wasteland
that's crushed under everyone's heel.

Yes, God, it's the truth! We've been driven and scattered,
like sand and like stone to be mocked day by day;
but what of the stars, so bedazzlingly splendid—
the stars, God, the stars—where are they?

SPRING SONG

It's warming up, it's waking up—
the plowland decked in green.
The first brave kernel lifts her head,
surveys the lovely scene.

She feels the fresh and frisky wind,
the day that brightly breaks.
She's magnetized toward heaven's light
and, like a child, awakes.

Enough of crouching deep in earth
away from life and light
all through a winter's dreary spell—
gray noon and starless night!

Spring up, you golden stalks of grain,
and fill yourselves with sap!
Pour forth, oh fresh young force, and flood
the plowland's greening lap!

Spring's on the move. He flashes, roars. . . .
Rolled back and put to flight
is winter's long and dreary spell—
gray noon and starless night!

IN A WINTER'S NIGHT

Our grandmother sits with the sock in her hand.
The lamp flickers low. From her knitting
rise animals, giants, and birds without end,
that worry the wall with their flitting.

Our grandmother's silent: the stories she knows
were all of them told before summer.
Her heart hides a venomous serpent of woes,
and nothing can wrestle it from her.

Outdoors it is frosty; outdoors there's a storm;
the snow covers footpath and meadow.

49

There hovers a lonely and sorrowful form
as slow and as still as a shadow.

The aged one sits in the lamplight, bent low,
and softly she whispers, she sighs.
One tear, then another—forever they flow
and light up the gloom in her eyes.

Morris Rosenfeld (1862–1923)

MORRIS ROSENFELD was born in 1862 in the province of Suwalki, Poland, into a family of fishery workers. He wrote his first poem, in Yiddish, at fifteen. By 1882 he had married his childhood sweetheart and had left for Amsterdam, where he spent three months as an apprentice diamond cutter. In 1883, after six months in a London factory, he went home to Poland but soon left permanently and settled in London, where he became a sweatshop worker and socialist. He moved to New York, where the *Folks-zeitung* published his revolutionary poem, "Dos Yohr 1886." In 1888 he became a contributor to *Der Arbeiter Freint* and issued his militant first collection, *Di Glocke. Blumenkette* (1890) consolidated his position, but he had to keep working in a sweatshop, where his health deteriorated. Occasionally he traveled, singing and reciting like a troubadour of the Middle Ages. In 1894 he founded a weekly, *Der Ashmodai* (Asmodeus). *Dos Liderbuch* (1897) came to the attention of Harvard's Leo Wiener whose volume of unrhymed translations was published as *Songs from the Ghetto*. During the next few years Rosenfeld lectured at Harvard, Wellesley, and Radcliffe. Translations appeared in French, German, Czech, Rumanian, Polish, Russian, Hebrew, Hungarian, and Japanese. In Europe he was feted by royalty and heard great actors recite his poems. But when his gifted son died at sixteen, a stroke nearly finished the poet, leaving him feeble and almost blind. *Naiste Shafungen* appeared in 1912, simultaneously with the nationwide celebration of his fiftieth birthday. *Dos Buch fun Liebe* was issued two years later. A period of abuse by new-wave critics and poets followed. When a rumor started that he was dead, he had the rare treat of reading extraordinary eulogies. He died in 1923.

THE TEARDROP MILLIONAIRE

It's not a tuning fork of gold
that sets my throat to sing,
nor do my melodies unfold
to satisfy a king.
The groans of slaves, when they are tired,
awake my bitter songs;
it's only then that I'm inspired:
I reckon up their wrongs.

And this is why I pine away,
and half-alive I linger—
what wages can the workers pay,
what pittance to their singer?
They pay with tears for every tear—
that's all they can afford:
I am a teardrop millionaire,
and weep upon my hoard.

A TEARDROP ON THE IRON

Oh, cold and gloomy is the shop!
I press and press and never stop.
My heart is weak, I cough and groan—
my chest is heavy as a stone.

I cough and press and dream and doubt;
my eyes well up, a tear drops out.
The iron glows—my little tear,
it seethes, and does not disappear.

I have no strength, it's all used up.
My fingers let the iron drop.

And still the tear seethes on and on
as though it never will be gone.

My heart is heavy—and my brain
is wracked; I ask in grief, in pain:
"Oh friend in need and sorrow—say,
oh tear, why don't you boil away?

"Oh silent tear, oh silent tongue,
will others like you come along?
Are more of my hot friends to fall,
or will you be the last of all?

"Are you the herald, to proclaim
that there are more from where you came?
I want an answer—tell me, friend,
when will the lamentation end?"

Still other things would I have asked
the fiery tear of my unrest—
but all at once began to pour
tears without measure, more and more;
and it was very plain to see
how deep my well of tears must be.

MY PLACE

Don't look for me where myrtles green!
Not there, my darling, shall I be.
Where lives are lost at the machine,
that's the only place for me.

Don't look for me where robins sing!
Not there, my darling, shall I be.
I am a slave where fetters ring,
that's the only place for me.

Don't look for me where fountains splash!
Not there, my darling, shall I be.

Where tears are shed, where teeth are gnashed,
that's the only place for me.

And if your love for me is true,
then at my side you'll always be,
and make my sad heart sing anew,
and make my place seem sweet to me.

TO MY BELOVED

How good to look at you again,
my love, my joy, my one bright dream!
You come now, and you come in vain
to be with me at my machine.

There's steam and smoke and madness here—
there's no place for a guest to stand.
I can't so much as touch you, dear,
for I have hired out my hand.

Come to me later! Come at night—
for then, my darling, I am free.
My spirit wakes, my heart grows light,
the flame of love revives in me.

I'll sing as I have never sung,
the moment that your face appears;
and every word upon your tongue
shall turn to music in my ears.

I'll greet you then in such a way
as I would now, if I could dare.
Then all my troubles of the day,
my inmost wounds, will be laid bare.

And you will have my kisses all,
and tears enough—you'll have those too.
Whatever good is in my soul
I'll offer as a gift to you.

But now, beloved, you must go.
Love has no business in a shop.
I can't so much as touch you—no!
My life starts when the treadles stop.

CORNER OF PAIN AND ANGUISH

Corner of Pain and Anguish, there's a worn old house:
tavern on the street floor, Bible-room upstairs.
Drunkards sit below, and all day long they souse.
Overhead, the pious chant their daily prayers.

Higher, on the third floor, there's another room:
not a single window welcomes in the sun.
Seldom does it know the blessing of a broom.
Rottenness and filth are blended into one.

Toiling without letup in that sunless den:
nimble-fingered and (or so it seems) content,
sit some thirty blighted women, blighted men,
with their spirits broken, and their bodies spent.

Scurfhead struts among them: always with a frown,
brandishing his scepter like a mighty king;
for the shop is his, and here he wears the crown,
and they must obey him, bow to everything.

MY LITTLE SON

I have a son, a little son,
a youngster mighty fine!
and when I look at him I feel
that all the world is mine.

But seldom do I see him when
he's wide awake and bright.
I always find him sound asleep;
I see him late at night.

The time clock drags me off at dawn;
at night it lets me go.
I hardly know my flesh and blood;
his eyes I hardly know. . . .

I climb the staircase wearily:
a figure wrapped in shade.
Each night my worn-faced wife describes
how well the youngster played;

how sweetly he's begun to talk;
how cleverly he said,
"When will my daddy come and leave
a penny near my bed?"

I listen, and I rush inside—
it must—yes, it must be!
My father-love begins to burn:
my child must look at me! . . .

I stand beside the little bed
and watch my sleeping son,
when hush! a dream bestirs his mouth:
"Where has my daddy gone?"

I touch his eyelids with my lips.
The blue eyes open then:
they look at me! they look at me!
and quickly shut again.

"Your daddy's right beside you, dear.
Here, here's a penny, son!"
A dream bestirs his little mouth:
"Where has my daddy gone?"

I watch him, wounded and depressed
by thoughts I cannot bear:
"One morning, when you wake—my child—
you'll find that I'm not here."

SHOOT THE BEAST!
(written for the Molly Maguires shot down in a Pennsylvania strike)

Don't spare the bullets! load your gun
and shoot the hungry miner dead!
A miner's life is seldom done
the same as other folks'—in bed.
A miner's life—what is it worth?
This year or next—let it be finished!
He is a creature of the earth;
you kill a corpse; you won't be punished.

Why should a miner fear the tomb?
Has daylight ever glowed for him?
—a man who toils in total gloom
and hears the great walls caving in!
A miner flinch at dying? No!
Just load your gun, and shoot away!
The ground's his country—let him go,
not bother us another day!

What does he need, down in the mine,
this slave whom sunlight never knows?
A home in which the sun can shine?
A higher wage? A suit of clothes?
Oh shoot away, don't spare the lead!
It's safe to shoot a miner dead.
Oh shoot again, in case you missed him!
No man will hear, no god assist him.

THE LION

Why do you throw *me* bones, and cram
your bellies full of beef?
What do you really think I am?
A dog with trash-can teeth?

A dog that bums around all day
and sleeps in halls at night,

and when a bone is flung his way
gives thanks at every bite?

A kitchen dog that humbly chews
at rotten scraps of food,
and has to lick the Master's shoes
to show his gratitude?

Be careful! I'm a lion, sir!
Don't play your games with me—
for all I have to do is stir,
and mincemeat's what you'll be.

I know each foot of forest ground—
since birth I've fled the hunter—
my roar strikes terror miles around:
you recognize that thunder. . . .

Don't think, because I hush again,
there's nothing in my head—
one day I'll break the cage, and then
you'll all be lying dead.

WHAT IS THE WORLD?

And if it's no more than a bedroom, our earth,
and life but a dream, but a slumber—
I also am ready for *my* few years' worth
of dreams that are good to remember.

Let *me* dream of luxury, dream of delight,
like those with the world in their keeping.
I want to see eyes that are loving and bright,
and have no more nightmares of weeping.

And if it's a grand celebration, a ball,
where all are invited as brothers,
then I, too, should sit in the banqueting-hall—
my portion as large as the others'.

I, too, am well able to eat what is good;
a choice bit of meat gives me pleasure;
the blood in *my* veins is as red as the blood
of those who are swollen with treasure.

And if it's a garden, surrounded by trees,
where all kinds of roses are growing,
I want to go freely wherever I please,
no sentries to keep me from going.

I'd like to find garland of flowers to wear
instead of these thorns that have crowned me—
I want to go strolling, my love always there,
with myrtles and laurels around me.

And if our world's nothing but bloodshed today,
where bondmen rise up in resistance—
no wife and no children can keep me away;
I won't watch the war from a distance.

I'll leap into battle—I'll make myself brave,
and fight for the slaves like a lion;
and if I am hit, and the field is my grave,
I'll know how to laugh—though I'm dying!

WALT WHITMAN (America's Great Poet)

Oh, thou, within whose mighty poet-heart
two fathomless abysses intertwined:
the deepness of the pure, blue heavens and
the softly cradled deepness of the earth;
within whose heart arose the sun, the moon,
and where, in all their bright magnificence,
stars without number blazed, whole worlds of stars;
within whose heart the buds of May awoke,
and where the harsh voice of the thunder sang
beside the twitter of the nightingale;
within whose overwhelming chant one feels
the pulse of nature, its omnipotence;

immortal bard, I honor thee: I kneel
upon the dust, before thy dust, and sing.

David Edelshtat (1866–1892)

DAVID EDELSHTAT was born in 1866 in Kaluga, Russia. At twelve
he wrote a Russian elegy for a young doctor loved by the poor.
Soon afterward his family moved to Kiev. In 1880 he was
wounded in a pogrom. Befriended by a group of radical students,
he left with them for America in 1882, hoping to establish a farm
colony. But he found himself in a Cincinnati sweatshop. One of his
revolutionary poems in Russian was published in London's *Arbeiter Freint,* but Winchevsky rejected a second poem with the
request that only Yiddish work be submitted. Within weeks after
mastering the new language he produced two of his most beloved
songs, "In Battle" and "My Testament." His verses were welcomed
by New York's *Judische Volks-Zeitung* and *Warheit.* Enraged by the
Haymarket frame-up (Chicago, 1886), he joined the anarchist
movement, and in 1891 he was appointed editor of its newly
founded paper, *Di Freie Arbeiter-Shtimme.* He left Cincinnati and
established his "headquarters" in New York, writing and editing
after a full day in the sweatshop. A few months later he was
discovered to be tubercular and entered a Denver sanatorium,
where he died in the fall of 1892.

TO THE MUSE

Muse! is that you knocking again
at the door of my heart's bleak room?
Turn back, my child—you knock in vain—
my heart is crowded with gloom.

I'm sick and weary—see for yourself.
How could I sing tonight?

And how could a song of sorrow help
my people in their plight?

The world is tearing me limb from limb:
it's savage and depraved.
My song is no more than a sexton's hymn
over an orphan's grave.

I never learned how to polish my rhymes,
how prettily thoughts can be dressed.
The bloody dramas of these times
were staged within my breast.

Great is my sadness. A venomous snake
resides in your wretched singer.
She sits in my brain, asleep and awake;
she's writing now . . . with my fingers.

Stop knocking, Muse, at the door of my heart!
No lamps of hope are alive;
it's crowded with tears, and terribly dark.
—Go to the poets who thrive!

to them who know about golden noons,
who've reached the rapturous isle;
and me, with my fetters and my wounds,
leave me alone for a while!

MY TESTAMENT

Oh comrades mine, when I am dead
carry our banner to my grave:
the freedom-banner—flaming red
with all the blood that workers gave.

And there, the while our banner flutters,
sing me my freedom-song again,
my "Battle Song"—that rings like fetters
around the feet of workingmen.

And even in my grave that song,
that stormy song, will reach my ears,
and for my friends enslaved so long
there, too, shall I be shedding tears.

And when I hear a cannon sound
the final siege of want and pain,
my song shall trumpet from the ground
and set the people's heart aflame!

MY FINAL WISH

Death doesn't scare me—all I dread
is dying on a sickroom bed.
There is one thing I wish for most:
to die in battle at my post!

Not like the weak, exhausted slaves
whom hunger whips into their graves—
no! but with my banner high,
my rifle blazing, let me die!

Not showered by a few late tears—
no! but with freedom in my ears
roaring the tyrants' epitaph
let me die proudly, with a laugh. . . .

FROM MY JOURNAL

I wrote till the blood of my heart was drained,
and now the inkwell's dry;
not a single drop of blood remained,
not a single tear have I.

The vampire world sucked all I had—
and now that I am spent,
I sit here spiritless and sad,
alone in my poor tent.

My people—I loved you not like these
with their fake philosophic airs,
who pat their paunches, and live in ease,
as though they were millionaires.

Oh, no! the sufferer's every sigh
resounded in my breast
and turned into a battle cry:
"Revenge for the oppressed!"

The blood of slaves rained down upon
my blooming April vine—
wherever tears of slaves might run,
they met with tears of mine.

I drowned my own pain in the sea
of mankind's greater pain.
The holy sparks of liberty
within me turned to flame.

Leon Zolotkoff (1866–1938)

Born in Vilna, Lithuania, in 1866, LEON ZOLOTKOFF attended a
Russian school; at seventeen he moved to Paris, attending lectures
at the Sorbonne for two years while he worked at various jobs such
as printing. His first poems, in Russian and Hebrew, described the
poverty of the Jewish immigrants in Paris. After a brief return to
Russia, he moved on to London, buying the small print shop in
which Winchevsky's *Arbeiter Freint* was published. His first Yiddish
poem, "Lullaby of a Worker's Wife," appeared in its pages in 1886.
He was drawn into the revolutionary movement, and in 1888 he
co-authored a *Socialist Passover Haggadah*. The same year he settled in Chicago. Initially active as a socialist orator there, he
eventually gained a law degree, established various journals, became a leading conservative editor and publisher, and, in 1898,
helped found the Knights of Zion. He wrote voluminously in the

decades that followed—novels, plays, historical works, and a daily column. An autobiographical novel, *From Wilno to Hollywood,* appeared in English translation in 1932. He died on Long Island six years later.

LULLABY OF A WORKER'S WIFE

Sleep, my child, my joy, my light;
enough of your tossing and turning!
You still can't know your mother's plight
or feel how her tears are burning.

Seven years without a sigh
I lived with your poor father;
he wove in the factory, and I
patched our torn clothes together.

Over the machine he bent,
and earned an honest living;
no gay times for him—each cent
into my hand was given.

Something happened once at work—
to think it, makes me shiver—
an accident—some crazy quirk—
his hand was gone forever.

Ach, where's a man with such a loss
to make a bit of money?
And the millionaire, the boss,
won't give him one more penny.

Like a beggar-man he goes—
it's driven me half-wild—
and seeks compassion for his woes,
a crust of bread for his child.

You can't guess your mother's plight
or feel how her tears are burning;
sleep, then, child, my joy, my light;
enough of your tossing and turning.

David Goldstein (1868–1931)

DAVID GOLDSTEIN was born in 1868 in Suwalki, Morris Rosenfeld's region of Poland. At fourteen he emigrated to England, slaved in a sweatshop, and embraced anarchism. After three years he moved—first to New York, where he joined the anarchist Pioneers of Freedom, then to Philadelphia, whose Knights of Freedom he represented at the 1889 New York conference of anarchists and socialists gathered to establish a newspaper. He later lived in Boston. In a continuous struggle for survival, he worked for some years as a tailor, then operated a newsstand, and later tried to run a coffeehouse. His poems of social content began appearing in 1887. *Winter Flowers,* a collection of his verse, was issued in 1916. From then until his death fifteen years later, his name and work sank into almost total neglect.

I TOLD THE SEA

Deep in the gloom of night I brought
my sorrow to the sea.
He lay that hour lost in thought,
yet listened to my plea.

And now he bears my grief about
and bellows in despair.
I listen to his anguished shout
and stand struck dumb with fear.

HUNGER

And withered be my hand if I should plead
with you for the poor bit of bread I need.
Unto my palate may the tongue stick fast,
within my throat the word die unexpressed,
and may my bowels be gnawed at, long and deep,
as if by hungry worms that never sleep.

I'll firmly shut my lips, I'll go unfed,
and will not take from you your beggars' bread.

Then softly, quietly, my lad
asks me: "You look so pale, so sad?"
and whispers slowly, whispers hushed:
"Good poppa, I don't beg for much:
if there's some bread . . . a bit for me. . . ."
(It costs him pain, that modest plea.)
A tear comes to my eye; my son
sees it, and does not plead again.

Yehoash (1870?–1927)

YEHOASH, whose real name was Solomon Bloomgarten, was born in 1870 (or 1872) in Wirblau, Lithuania, and studied at the Yeshiva of Volozhin. He emigrated to New York in 1890, soon after his first poems had been published in Peretz's *The Yiddish Library*. Tuberculosis drove him to a Denver sanatorium for the decade of 1900–1910. In 1907 he began work on a posthumously published translation of the entire Old Testament into Yiddish, probably his greatest achievement. Soon after his return to New York his Hebrew-Yiddish dictionary appeared. This was followed by *The Teachings of the Fathers* and *Fables* (both 1912), *In Sun and Fog* (1915), the seven-volume *Writings* (1916), the ballad *Solomon's Ring* (1916), and *In the Web,* a two-volume compilation (1921). He died in 1927.

IN THE SEA

In the sea a wave rolls on—
in the open sea, my son;
and who is to detect it?

In the sea, since tides were known,
every instant crests a throne;
comes a storm wind, blowing wild,
kings it for one minute, child;
and who's to recollect it?

AMID THE COLORADO MOUNTAINS

I

High black mountain peaks conspire
to enclose the orb of light.
Through the clouds that billow densely
day's last flames defy the night. . . .

Unfamiliar shapes and colors
soon emerge and soon recede.
Great hands hidden in the mountain
shift the scenery with speed. . . .

But the valleys soon lie lifeless,
as the twilight fires fade—
for what audience, there, westward,
is the night-light drama played?

II

Beyond the peaks a thunderstorm
is ready to commence.
The black clouds, like attacking knights,
come on in regiments.

It flashes forth! The blades unsheathe,
a savage sorrow howls
and more than once reverberates
from the abyss's bowels. . . .

Already every dale can feel
a gruesome tumult rise.
And on my face the first warm drop
has fallen from the skies. . . .

So I too am anointed now,
and feel at home with cloud
and titan-peak, with lightning-flash
and thunder roared aloud.

III

The quiet evening hour arrives
with streaks of gold and purple,
and summer-day and summer-night
are now a loving couple. . . .

The mountains loom up blue and large,
the vale grows small and darkens,
and there's a soundless melody
somewhere, to which one hearkens.

Like incense rises toward the sky
a scent of meadow flowers.
The world grows calm and holy in
the soft glow of such hours.

ON AN IMMIGRANT SHIP

The waves in agitation
rush on; a mist hangs thick.
A ship splits the black water;
one light moves on the deck.

A handful of sad figures,
tears in the eyes of a few;
amid them a makeshift coffin,
in the coffin, a—God knows who. . . .

He was a Jew, one supposes;
nobody knows where he's from. . . .
Someone offers a Kaddish;
and just as soon as he's done

the coffin is lowered slowly. . . .
The sea can't wait to be fed.

The silent company scatter
and think no more of the dead.

Only the Jew who said Kaddish
over the body, swears
that deep from the rushing billows
an "Amen" answered his prayers.

WOOLWORTH BUILDING

Home winds a remnant of the craziness of day,
the eyes aglow and feverish, the faces clay. . . .
Few wheels now—one car where there were twenty;
over the asphalt, ponderous and empty,
a heavy wagon rolls.
Evening falls
like a dead fly on the knot of blent
wire and mortar and cement. . . .
The roar becomes a murmur, as in sleep
a gasp through gritted teeth
after a smothered cry. . . .
And high above all spires that scrape the sky,
alone, erect, and straight—behold
the temple of the god of iron and gold!

CAIN'S CURSE
(On the Victims of the Triangle Fire)

Come all you high priests at the altars of Mammon
who have for an instant—and just for an instant—
forgotten the Devil-God whom you serve,
to offer, with hearts unsoftened,
one brief, stingy tear
for a hundred coffins—
you all who keep count and figure and reckon,
from early till late,
the gold that you've got and the gold that you crave,

and have in the bustle of greed and the chase
forgotten the groan of your trampled-on brother
and smothered the voice of your own soul as well—
come all, and assemble amid the dark rows of
a hundred extinguished lives,
and into those eyes that are glazed now
look deep—to the cold-yellow marrow
where just a few hours ago
the buds of the future were sprouting
and nests of warm hope were atwitter—
look deep and then lift up your hands
to the heavens, to on high,
and say it so loud
that your soul has to hear it,
that your conscience, stone-deaf, has to hear it—
and say, if you dare,
if you can:
"Not we did the spilling of blood,
and we're without stain!"
If your tongue is unable to move,
benumbed by a nightmarish horror,
by dread of the Eye
that sees through the cosmos—
of the Hand that will reach,
with its doom,
to the best-hidden crannies,
for the best-hidden sin—
may then, from the eyes that are glazed now,
a lightning glare forth
and burn its black seal
across your spirit—
may then the stilled whites of those orbs
awake you at night from your eiderdown slumber—
and when, at dark windows, you'll press to the pane
your forehead exploding with fever,
then may you behold not the stars
in the skies but those eyes . . .
and may the hoarse night wind
hair-raisingly rasp you
—a curse. . . .

TO MORRIS WINCHEVSKY (on His Fiftieth Birthday)

O good, devoted grandpapa,
old youngling, child of fifty Mays,
who, more than you, have merited
the laurel wreath of love and praise?

Who, from the swamp of life, have come
like you: untarnished, true as gold?
Who serve as well the great Ideal
that you so gallantly uphold?

Who else, like you, have lived their dream
year in, year out, and day by day,
and strictly weigh—on duty's scale
and truth's—what they both do and say?

Who, in the frost of life, like you,
have kept the spark of heaven strong?
And in a world that ages soon,
who—in their age—like you, are young?

O good, devoted grandpapa,
to you the loveliest flower is due.
But only thorns grow all around;
how then can it be picked for you

when in our fields the poison-weed
sprouts forth and blossoms everywhere,
and at each step I take, a grave
returns my melancholy stare—

when crisscrossing inside the brain
that great black spider lies in wait
which weaves and snarls the senses in
a net of curses and of hate?

O good, sweet-hearted grandpapa,
no flowers now—the time is wrong.
But yours should be the finest flower;
to you belongs the loveliest song.

70

SUBWAY

An invisible hand has closed a door
and pressed inside a heap of people:
part submerged on benches,
part hanging onto white rings.
The limelight falls
on thin, transparent fingers
minutes ago at the typewriter;
on hard, heavy hands
sweated from the workshop;
and on mother-of-pearl gloves. . . .
And the heap sways
back and forth, back and forth,
in a worn, extinguished rhythm,
as if bewailing a corpse. . . .

The heap shakes,
and falls together in a pile
congealed.
And the invisible hand
pries open a door. . . .
Smiling, a thin young girl pushes her way
into the clump,
with a bunch of lilacs pinned on her jacket.
And the heap again begins to sway,
worn, extinguished,
as if bewailing a dead one,
and amid them the thin girl
with the bunch of lilacs. . . .

Anna Rapport (1870?–?)

According to N. B. Minkoff, ANNA RAPPORT (or Rappaport) was
born in Kovno, Lithuania, in 1870. Other sources, however, give
1876 as her birthdate. If they are right, this niece of a famed

71

Dvinsk rabbi was fourteen when she left for the United States in 1890, taking her mother's maiden name (Ziff) and becoming a sweatshop worker. Bayonne, New Jersey was her home from 1897 to 1905. Later she lived in Massachusetts and settled in New York in 1912. Her first outburst of poetry appeared in the *Arbeiter Tseitung* and the *Folks-Advokat* over a five-month period (1893–94). For nine years thereafter she published nothing; then, from 1903 to 1909, she was again productive, contributing poems to the *Tsukunft* and *Forward*. Later she withdrew from Yiddish literature, but maintained her early radicalism as a staff writer for the *Socialist Call* (1911–17).

RESURRECTION (1905)

The back of our brother lifts higher and higher;
he bends to his master no longer.
The limbs of the Jew, which were buckling and breaking,
grow straighter, and prouder, and stronger.

His head, which was bowed to the earth, sees around it
horizons all opening wide.
His face, which was spat upon even by children,
is lit up and glowing with pride.

No crawling, no licking the hand when it beats him;
he knows he has rights of his own:
to live, to create, to consider, to struggle;
no more does he feel like a drone. . . .

He uses his powers of mind and of body,
nor is he affrighted by death.
He fights against hunger, he battles for freedom;
he fights to the very last breath.

And where he's allowed to move freely, one sees him
and hears him as never before.
He carries the banner of truth and of justice;
the Jew that once was, is no more!

Joseph Bovshover (1872–1915)

Joseph Bovshover was born in 1872 into a rabbinical family in Libovich, Russia. He gave up his talmudic studies while yet a child and took a job in a flour factory. After emigrating to New York, he became a fur worker and wrote his first sweatshop songs. He joined the anarchist movement and met Edelshtat, whose death he elegized the following year. He soon began a series of prose studies on the nature of poetry and on such poets as Heine, Emerson, Whitman, and Edwin Markham. He also wrote English poems, published under the pseudonym "Basil Dahl." His translation into Yiddish of *The Merchant of Venice* was performed by Jacob Adler with great success in 1898. He also supplied prologues for Yiddish productions of Schiller and Hauptmann. In spite of his literary success he went hungry. A rich brother made a futile effort to "establish" him as a grocer. At twenty-seven his melancholia had developed to such a point that it was decided to place him in a mental hospital, where he remained until his death in December 1915. In 1918 his reputation began to be reclaimed as the Soviet Jewish press paid tribute to him and published his work. A collected edition of his poetry and prose had been issued by the *Freie Arbeiter-Shtimme* in 1911.

TO MY BROTHERS

If I am the lyre,
then you are the strings.
You waken my voice
and tell me to sing.

For every new song
I thank you alone—
without you I grow
as silent as stone.

If I love you no more,
and suddenly tire—
no music again
shall leap from the lyre.

THE FLOWER ISLAND

When I was a boy I imagined an island:
a green-covered island where wildflowers bloom—
designed by the magical paintbrush of Nature
with many bright colors, with rarest perfume.

That dream of my childhood, aglow in the darkness,
commanded my heart like a magnet of gold;
and—seized with desire—I searched through the heavens;
I sought among clouds for my dream to unfold.

Since then I have known many summers and winters,
and now I could curse at my silly young brain—
I wasted my time in the clouds, in the heavens;
I looked for my island in vain, all in vain.

Right here upon earth, where my poor mother bore me
to bow before masters, to cringe at their power,
right here is the island of now and forever
—if only the thorn could be plucked from the flower!

TO SING OR TO CURSE

There's a little wind that rushes
through my fiddle's every string,
and it whispers, and it murmurs:
"Sing a song in praise of spring!"

There's a little flame that rushes
through my heart's vibrating strings,
and it flickers, and it urges:
"Curse and damn the tyrant kings!"

IT IS A DREAM—YET TRUE

I dreamt a lambkin lay
along the riverbanks.

74

Beside her stood a wolf
who growled his hungry thanks:

"How well I did, to break
the little creature's neck!
And now her flesh will make
a perfect midnight snack."

He opened wide his mouth
and tore at her; he feasted
with hearty appetite—
nor would the bones be wasted!

But all at once his lamb
was neither dead nor dying:
she rose up from the grass
transformed into a lion

and flung the frightened wolf
so fiercely to the ground,
his hide was smashed, his limbs
lay scattered all around.

* * *

I start up from my sleep—
the morning sun bursts through.
I slowly look about—
it was a dream . . . yet true.

MOTHER AND DAUGHTER

A mother's at the washtub;
her daughter stands there, too.
They wash and scrub together
until the clothes look new.

All week at home the mother
does everything herself.
The girl has only Sundays
to stay at home and help.

The mother's thin and feeble,
her skin a sickly hue.
The daughter is a flower
that fades for want of dew.

The mother loves her daughter,
but she herself's half-gone.
The daughter loves her mother,
and helps the wash get done.

And in the small apartment
I watch the weary pair.
It really is quite common,
but more than I can bear.

TO THE WIND

Carry, oh wind, upon your pinions
the fevered message of my lyre—
though it is coal-black on the surface,
beneath it you can see the fire. . . .

Wherever human hearts are beating
—be they the foulest or the best—
there must you bring my burning message
and blow it deep inside the breast.

And if you find the blood is frozen,
awake it, as you wake the sea;
and make it seethe, and make it angry,
and wake the flame of liberty!

RESOLVE

On and on I must and will,
though the world loves standing still.
It's the fate of Man to know
much of bliss and much of woe.

76

Care has often found my bed;
more than once my breast has bled.
All my sorrows I concealed,
and by now the wounds are healed.

Like a lighthouse I shall loom
in this world of grief and gloom,
blazing through the midnight skies
till my sleeping brothers rise.

TO THOSE IN POWER

I come like a comet newborn, like the sun that arises at morning;
I come like the furious tempest, that follows a thundercloud's
  warning;
I come like the fiery lava, from cloud-covered mountains
  volcanic;
I come like a storm from the north, that the oceans awake to in
  panic.

I come because tyranny planted my seed in the hot desert sand;
I come because masters have kindled my fury with every
  command;
I come because Man cannot murder the life-giving seed in his
  veins;
I come because Liberty cannot forever be fettered by chains.

From earliest times the oppressèd have waked me and called me
  to lead them;
I guided them out of enslavement, and brought them to
  highroads of Freedom;
I marched at the head of their legions, and hailed a new world at
  its birth;
and now I shall march with the people until they unfetter the
  earth!

And though you may choke me and shoot me and hang me—
  your toil is in vain!
No dungeon, no gallows can scare me—nor will I be frightened
  by pain—

77

each time I'll arise from the earth, and bedeck it with weapons of
doom,
until you are finished forever, until you are dust in the tomb!

Abraham Liesin (1872–1938)

ABRAHAM LIESIN was born Abraham Wald in Minsk, Byelorussia,
in 1872. One of the founders of the Jewish Socialist Labor Party
("Bund"), he published his first collection, *Modern Poems,* illegally
in 1897. In danger of arrest, he left Russia the same year and
settled in New York. From 1913 he edited the great New York
literary journal *Tsukunft* (Future). His last years were embittered
by the effort of the *Forward,* which owned the journal, to termi-
nate it. Aided by his colleague, B. Vladeck, he held on. One week
after Vladeck's death in 1938, Liesin died too, before his stirring
elegy—as appropriate for himself as for his friend—appeared in
print. His three-volume *Songs and Poems, 1888–1938,* illustrated
by Marc Chagall, was published the same year. An autobiography,
Memories and Pictures, was issued in 1954.

RUSSIA

There weeps within your borderless green stretches
a craving without end;
O country of both dreams and patches,
great is your punishment!

Your wreck lies frozen mute when sun prevails,
or in a blinding snow;
O land of wolves and nightingales,
who hears your cry of woe?

Broken and bound, under thatched roofs in millions,
each buried in his hut;

O land of martyrs and of villains,
are you alive or not?

THE GODDESS
(from *The Statute of Liberty*)

From afar the land shows greenly;
a new world swims into sight.
At its threshold waits the Goddess
glowing in a new sun's light.

At the border of the ocean,
on a granite pile she stands
brown-arisen from the water,
and she beckons and enchants.

With a far-off gaze, and holding
high the torch of liberty,
like a proud, bold titan-dream she
stands between the sky and sea.

Like an epic song of daring,
strong bronze beauty set alone,
she extols the wonder-city,
miracle of steel and stone.

At the border of the ocean,
to the wanderer she seems
like a wondrous incarnation
of the world of his best dreams.

Heaven blossoms down upon her;
playfully the sunlight glows;
round her feet she curls the sea foam,
and the wave tells what it knows.

On her often falls the shadow
of a dark and savage cloud;
thunder rolls, the sea awakens
and insanely cries aloud.

But she does not hear or notice,
always proud and always slender,
full of thought and aspiration,
full of magic, strength, and splendor.

THE SPIDERWEBS
(from *The Statue of Liberty*)

So proudly she stands with the crown on her head,
surveying the billowy scene,
and high, ever higher, she raises her torch
and dreams her magnificent dream.

And thirstily over the torch and the crown
the spider takes shelter and weaves;
as soon as his webs are completed, he waits
and sucks out each life he receives.

He drinks and he thinks that for his sake alone
the torchlight so luringly spreads
that draws every fly from anear and afar
to him where he waits in his webs.

Benjamin Rosenblum (1872–1902)

BENJAMIN ROSENBLUM, one of eight children, was born in Grodno
in 1872. Their father died young and the family then moved to
Brest-Litovsk, where the fifteen-year-old poet became a lock-
smith's apprentice. After arriving in the United States in 1891, he
worked at various trades and suffered severe poverty while study-
ing first in the agricultural school at Woodbine, New Jersey and
later at Rutgers, from which he received a degree in civil engi-
neering. His first poems were published in *Der Arbeiter Freint* in

1892, his year of greatest creativity. Several of his Hebrew poems were also published. After graduating from Rutgers he got a good city job in Brooklyn, but a serious intestinal condition resulted in his untimely death in 1902.

AT THE CEMETERY

Night arrives, and wrapped around her
is a pitch-black coat.
I go wandering through the graveyard,
lone and lost in thought.

I recall the freedom-fighters
lying in the ground,
and I count the graves—so many—
scattered all around.

Count and count, and grow confused, and
reckon them once more.
Ach—in vain! The graves are countless
filled in freedom's war.

Hushed, bewildered, I embrace, I
kiss each cold gray stone.
Blind with tears I stray and stumble,
wretched and alone.

But my spirit's eased and lightened
when I look around
and behold a flower blooming
up from every mound.

Nahum Babad (1872–1903)

Even more tragic perhaps than the fate of Rosenblum was that of
NAHUM BABAD, also born in 1872 and orphaned early. As a boy he
wrote Russian poetry. Leaving Bessarabia at seventeen, he toiled
in a New York factory for two dollars a week. Simultaneously he
took evening courses. His first Yiddish poems and sketches appeared in the labor press in 1891. More Russian than Jewish in his
upbringing, like Edelshtat, he, too, chose to write in Yiddish for
the sake of reaching the immigrant masses, and some of his songs
also achieved wide popularity. Like Edelshtat, he developed tuberculosis after a few sweatshop years. In 1893, in a futile effort to
avoid his hero's fate (Edelshtat had died at twenty-six the previous
year), he went west. In San Francisco he worked for a Russian
immigrant newspaper, published new poems, and translated for
the English press. Later that year he returned to New York.
Debilitated by five more factory years, he again left for San Francisco in 1898 and died there in 1903, shortly after completing his
medical studies. His prose works include *The History of America*
(1895), *Heinrich Heine* (1900), and a condensed popular edition of
the U. S. Constitution (1902).

TO THE POET
(written ten months before Edelshtat's death)

Don't cry, I beg you, unfortunate brother;
wipe off your tears, tell your pain to depart;
see how your songs of unhappiness smother
all my young hopes and cut open my heart!

Dreadful afflictions have drained and distressed you,
each day a hell to confront and survive.
Parasite creatures have whipped and oppressed you;
life's been a war to stay barely alive.

And on your fiddle, so old and so broken,
moaningly, sighingly, quaver the strings;

nothing but bitter laments has she woken;
nothing but ballads of sorrow she sings;

but I, I am young and my life's just beginning;
the bright world invites me to come take a look.
My heart wants to fight and to wager on winning;
let me, I beg, at least dream of good luck!

Hear with what pleasure the birds are all singing
in murmuring forests, in blossoming fields!
See how the children are dancing and springing!
Everything's gay, and what vigor it feels!

Sing me, like them, of the spring that breathes sweetly;
winter's still distant—forget it, forget!
I want life to thrill me and fill me completely
—since I am young, since there's time for me yet.

LOVE

I was young. My visionary heart
beat time with all the world in harmony.
The pangs of others tore my soul apart,
and others' joy became my melody.

And when Love, so ravishing, so young,
would softly, sweetly, beckon me to her,
I answered: "No, I cannot heed your song
while life's great battle seethes outside my door!"

I grew old . . . exhausted, pale and weak—
a sick shade of the "I" I was before,
with eye all bleary and with shriveled cheek . . .
and creep along, a striding man no more.

Stricken to the heart, I open wide
thin arms unto my Love, my beautiful,
and cry: "The door is open—come inside!
o bring some joy to every silent wall!"

Vain the pleading, foolish all my cries. . . .
Her answer kills the hope to which I clung:
"Love comes but once, can't stay—and when youth flies,
she flies with it—she flies to someone young."

Chaim Nachman Bialik (1873–1934)

Born in 1873 in Radi, the Ukraine, CHAIM NACHMAN BIALIK made
a profound international impression with "The City of Slaughter," a Hebrew poem provoked by the Kishinev pogrom of 1903.
He lived for some years in Odessa, where *Grief and Wrath,* a
Yiddish collection, appeared in 1906. After the 1917 revolution
he lived in Moscow, pursuing his studies in the Hebrew poets of
medieval Spain. In 1921 he left for Berlin, where he founded the
Dvir publishing house, which he continued in Tel Aviv after
settling there in 1924. That year he published his translation of
Schiller's *William Tell.* In 1926 he made a long sojourn in the
United States. His translation of *Julius Caesar* appeared in 1929.
Two years later he visited Poland. He died in 1934 in Vienna, but
was buried in Tel Aviv.

SEA SONG
(from Yehuda Halevi)

I've deserted all my loved ones,
on my house I've turned my back;
I'm entrusted to the sea now:
waft me, sea, to mother's lap!

And you west wind, ever-faithful,
drive my vessel to that shore

which my heart, with eagle pinions,
has so long been searching for.

Bring me safely to my harbor,
then fly back to those I love;
greet them tenderly, and tell them
how much happiness I have.

WHEN I WOULD WEEP

When I would weep with a deeper emotion,
then am I drawn, as a cloud to an ocean,
closer to you, to my suffering brothers.
One special tear, of the bitterest grieving,
deep in your deeps may be silently craving,
craving my poems—a tear of my mother's!

What of *your* tears still unfallen, still welling,
agonies told and still more that need telling,
torments and woes that—like choked, hidden sources—
hollow out rocks, seep through sepulchers, wander
deep in the earth, where like blindworms they blunder
—till they dry up in their courses.

Let them explode, all those tears you're withholding!
Let them more easily, freely, come rolling!
Maybe, who knows, God will someday surprise us:
maybe the dark times will end for us, brothers;
maybe we too will be happy, like others,
those on whose lives the sun rises.

And, as a keepsake of now, of these horrors,
there may be left you a second "El Nares,"*
he who'll set heaven and earth on their ears.
Blessed is he, be he blest through the years,
he whose bright voice makes immortal your tears,
holy, two-thousand-year shedding of tears!

---

*The Psalmist, who authored "By the Waters of Babylon."

THE FINAL WORD

I was dispatched to you by God:
he saw you bowed beneath the rod;
he saw how soon you rot and drop,
how day by day you shrivel up,
how lax and limp your hand has grown,
and gone the power that was your own—
and God recalled you to his thought,
and unto you I have been brought.

And thus and so to me God spoke:
"I can't do more—*you* smash the yoke! . . .
Tear from their heart a sob, a cry.
Shoot forth a teardrop from their eye.
Heavy and bitter be the tear,
the last groan horrible to hear,
so horrible—the earth will shiver
and shake the evil off forever."

God's word I could not disobey.
I went, though stones were in my way.
One feeling only, one desire
had set my blood and bones afire:
I felt you were encoiled by snakes
and for your grief not one heart breaks. . . .
What drove me on was your despair.
I thought my help was needed there.
God punished me: within my breast
he placed a heart that will not rest,
that's twisted by the pangs of others,
that burns when hell consumes my brothers. . . .
I heard that life was hard for you;
I thought you felt, I thought you knew
and mutely on your tears you choked,
for aid, for solace prayed and hoped—
no time to lose—I'll be there soon,
I'll lift your spirits, heal each wound,
and when you bleed I too will bleed,
and run to bandage those in need,
and, where one must, my tongue will wash
the blood from every dripping gash.

86

I'll comfort, badger, weep, awake—
and won't allow defeats to tame you.
I'm on my way—and for your sake
I bring a message to enflame you.
I have been graced by God with spirit—
this soul of mine you shall inherit.
God forged in me a dauntless fire
that rips up peaks and does not tire,
that will not let me stoop or cower
and looks grim evil in the eye.
God granted me a tongue of power
as piercing as a piercing cry—
it will be iron, if you're stone;
if you are iron, it will be steel.
I come! As soon as I am known,
you'll rise, and end your long ordeal!

Now I am standing at your door—
my tongue of power is no more.
There hangs on me a heavy night—
extinguished is my spark, my light.
I met with mocking and disgrace;
you shut your door against my face—
the hand of God you've shaken off,
and at the word of God you scoff.

But know, you miserable folk—
no longer do I offer hope. . . .
I have a word, a dreadful word,
to drive you out when it is heard,
to make your light of day grow dark
and shoot a poison through your heart,
envenom every bite you eat,
embitter every slice of bread,
and make your life more bleak than bleak,
and not allow you to drop dead. . . .
Comfort's a word you'll never hear.
I've burned the soul that held you dear
and torn my bond with one and all. . . .
My zeal lies broken in the mud—
I shall besoil you with my gall
and shall besmear you with my blood. . . .

87

And God commands me:
                    "Now go buy
a pot down there from some poor potter,
and hurl it with your loudest cry
that all may hear the words you utter:
'This is the way you'll all be broken!'
Not one tear more, not one word spoken. . . .
Bow your head deeply, and grow dumb—
the day goes; it will come, will come."

Isaac Reingold (1873–1903)

ISAAC REINGOLD (pseudonym for Isaac Toomim) was born to a Hasidic family in 1873 near the Ukrainian city of Lutsk. In 1889 the family settled in a Woodbine, New Jersey, colony. Disowned after quarreling with his father about religion, Reingold left for the Midwest. Aroused by the social protest of which Chicago was the center, especially in the wake of the Haymarket frame-up, he worked in the sweatshops of Baltimore, Philadelphia, Milwaukee, and Chicago, reciting his incendiary songs before workmen's clubs. At nineteen he eloped with a sixteen-year-old girl, whose intensely religious father refused for years to recognize their marriage, even after five children were born. A frequent contributor to Chicago's *Teglicher Yiddisher Kurier* and the anarchist weekly, *Freie Arbeiter-Shtimme,* whose editor David Edelshtat had just died of tuberculosis, Reingold also managed—despite frail health and a thirteen-hour day at the machine—to publish several issues of *Reingold's Lieder Buch* and *Der Lieder Magazin,* as well as a book of poems, *A Bintel Blumen.* Stage stars such as Bessie and Boris Thomashefsky commissioned him to adapt the Broadway hit songs of the day to Yiddish verses that depicted immigrant life. He also provided the libretto for *By the Waters of Babylon.* In a 1902 visit to New York he made a powerful impression on its Yiddish literati, but a year later he died of the same heart ailment that was later to end a son's life at nineteen. In the decades that followed, his name virtually passed from memory. In 1952 his family published *Selected Poems.*

I AM A JEW
(excerpt)

Although I feel the world's distress
is tearing me apart,
the anguish of the Jew—alas—
lies closer to my heart.
I sing for peace, for freedom too;
yet first and last I am a Jew;
the song of mine that rings most true
I'll dedicate, with tender hand,
to Zion, to my fatherland.

O Zion! fling aside your sorrow,
let your pain be dumb;
delights will climb your wall tomorrow
—your belov'd ones come!
Should the way be doubly hard,
should each mile be blocked and barred,
fists of hatred beat the drum—
still they come! they come!

THE SOLDIER

Close by where the battle is fought
a man stands alone, lost in thought,
in thought, and so worn and so wan—
it is a young infantryman.

By sorrows unshared, unrelieved,
his poor heart is pressed and aggrieved.
It is for his love he is yearning,
back home—but what hope of returning?

At home are his room, and his girl:
the love of his heart, his whole world.
She waits, strong in faith, day by day—
but should she have faith? . . . who can say!

The lead flies so densely around,
the men drop so still to the ground:
a moan and a silence, that's all. . . .
Who knows? maybe *he* is to fall!

"O fighter! You lunge to the strife.
You fight, and too soon lose your life.
You fight, and win lands for your lord;
but answer me: What's your reward?

"Will someone recall later on
this victory here, that you've won?
Will one of the rulers—say who!—
just *one,* shed a teardrop for you? . . ."

Such questions are murmured, are weighed,
and then—all at once—a grenade!
Whatever he sees, he sees red;
the young man of battle—falls dead.

THE POET'S WILL

My final bewildered days under the sun,
they hurry and hover, delay and drive on.
They're hasting and hovering, flying and driving—
an end to my suffering, struggling, and striving.
Death stands at my pillow; he'll soon set me free—
he's pouring his poisonous drops into me.
I see him, I feel him throughout my sick body;
he beckons me, shows me a grave that's all ready,
and tells me: Now listen! This warning's my last.
Record what you own; make your will—make it fast!
Confess (a few pages); decide on your heirs;
before it's too late, settle up your affairs!

O Death Everlasting, you savior from pain,
I cannot escape you, nor is it my aim.
I'm sick and bent double; I'm wretched and lonely;
with thousands of eyes I am seeking you only!
But why make a will? Have I lands? have I chattel?

some prize over which my survivors would battle?
What's there to decide on? What's there to record?
No goods have I gathered, no wealth have I stored.
What fortune would come to a miserable singer,
a poor Jewish poet who's dying of hunger?
You mock me! You laugh at my squalor, it's plain!
O Death Everlasting, who breaks every chain. . . .

But wait, there is one thing I *do* have—oh hear it!
a precious commodity, precious—I swear it!
I've harvested, winnowed it all my life long;
it is my full yield: a few pages of song.
These sorrowful stanzas that clamor and weep
I leave for my suffering brothers to keep.
But if my poor legacy gives them no pleasure,
let those who say Kaddish inherit my treasure;
and if it's a prize no one wishes to save,
then let it be buried with me in the grave,
because, if my song is no longer of worth,
at least it has earned a few handfuls of earth.

Jacob Adler (1874–1974)

JACOB ADLER was born in Dinov, Galicia, in 1874. At fifteen he left
for America and became a shop worker in New Haven. His first
pieces—two proletarian poems—appeared in the *Forward* in 1897.
After that he contributed to dozens of publications here and
abroad. His humoresques, especially "Yente Telebente" and
"Moishe Kapoier," brought him immense popular acclaim. His
early works include *Memories of My Home* (1907) and *Happy Moments* (1914) as well as two collaborations: *Dreams and Reality*, with
Joel Slonim (1909), and *The Yiddish Bandit*, with Moishe Nadir
(1910–11). From 1912 through 1919 he edited a nonpartisan
weekly, the *Brownsville and East New York Express*. Apparently, after
three volumes in 1933, he produced nothing in book form. He

ultimately retired to South Gulfport, Florida, where he lived until 31 December 1974—three weeks past his one-hundredth birthday.

THE MACHINE WORKER

Weary and shaking,
every bone breaking,
home he comes aching,
home from the shop;
hungering, thirsting,
brooding, and bursting
with rage he keeps cursing
the hell of his job.

He damns every demon
who whips into screaming
the men and the women,
sweat-soaked through and through,
who're snipping and sewing
with tears ever flowing
not thinking or knowing
of anything new. . . .

He prophesies ill then
to all who take children,
grow rich as they kill them
—each boy and each girl.
The poor mothers languish,
they groan and they anguish—
too deep is the pang which
they're paid by the world.

He hates every stitcher
who makes others richer
while he, spineless creature,
sinks deeper in debt;
who holds out a skinny
fool's hand for a penny—
whose food, when there's any,
is marah on bread. . . .

He hates the poor dunces
who, robbed of their senses,
sit tongue-tied in trances
and welcome the rod . . .
who've no joys to share in,
whose breasts have grown barren,
till, coughing and tearing
their lungs, they spit blood.

Avrom Reisen (1876–1953)

Born in Koidenev in 1876, AVROM REISEN began writing verse at the age of nine. He was soon corresponding with Peretz, in whose anthology *The Yiddish Library* (1891) his work first appeared. After his mother's death and the family's dispersal, he taught in various towns; in Minsk, he began portraying the hard life of his people in both stories and poems. While serving as a musician in the Russian army in 1895, he befriended other writers and became an active promulgator of Yiddish as a national language, producing two anthologies, *The Twentieth Century* and *European Literature*, and translating Hebrew masterworks into Yiddish. He moved from city to city, including Vienna, Paris, and London. In 1904, to avoid war service, he left Russia for good. Along with Peretz, Nomberg, and Asch, he worked on the newly founded Warsaw paper *The Way*, and he was an influential delegate to the historic 1908 language conference in Czernowicz, at which Yiddish was officially adopted as a national language. Thereafter, in Cracow, he edited *The Yiddish Word* and *Art and Life*, and in Vilna collections of his prose and verse were issued. In 1912, a twelve-volume edition of his works appeared in New York; two years later, on his third visit, he decided to settle there. He made The Bronx his home, and it was there that he died in 1953, revered for hundreds of superb lyrics and stories.

THE FIRST IMMIGRANTS
(The Trip to America)

I

It was aboard a foreign ship
we came unto this land;
across the flood our fate was in
a foreign captain's hand.

The vessel roughly rocked herself,
first one way, then the other;
hard dreams they dreamt, the few who slept
—cradled by such a mother.

II

A new, a foreign land—what sort
of people will we find?
Many of us had left a wife
and helpless babes behind.

A bit of garden, a poor hut,
a father white as snow. . . .
And there were several whose hearts
endured another woe.

III

How long, each wondered silently,
will we be on this ship?
A sailor laughed when someone dared
to ask about the trip.

Night turned to day, day turned to night
—a long, long night—before
the good ship's captain sighted land
and brought us safe to shore.

FROM CHEDER

My heart is afraid
like that of a boy who has left
his cheder on a winter night and has

parted from all his singing classmates
and stands alone in the market place.
A frost-black winter night.
There! he still hears the echo of their ballad;
there! his eye still catches the last shimmer
of light from the paper lanterns;
but soon it is all gone—no beam, no sound!
Alone, alone, he heads for home. His home is far!
And his chum has taken back the little lantern. . . .
He walks and runs . . . the wind pursues him
and his little legs are buckling
and his child-heart grows afraid and pounds. . . .

HOPES

Ah, hopes of mine—revive and grow!
Awake once more, once more.
Chill is the ever-thickening snow,
but from the bird's throat, ballads pour;
winter's a time he does not know—
ah, hopes of mine—revive and grow!

A WINTER SONG

Frolic, frolic, winds of malice!
Lord the lands and seas!
Break the branches, fell the forest,
punish whom you please!

Drive the warblers from the woodlands,
banish them afar;
those without the strength to flee you—
slay them where they are!

Rip the shutters off the houses,
shatter every pane!

95

If one lamp still flickers faintly—
quick! put out its flame!

Frolic, frolic, winds of malice!
Now's your time to play.
Long will last the rule of winter;
summer's far away. . . .

TO THE HAMMER

Oh hammer, good hammer, crash down!
Strike harder, give blow after blow!
There isn't a crumb in the house,
no—nothing but trouble and woe.

Oh hammer, dear hammer, crash down!
The clock will strike twelve before long;
my eyes are beginning to close—
oh help me, dear God, make me strong.

Oh hammer, sweet hammer, crash down!
Strike harder than ever, be swift:
by morning the shoes must be done,
the landlady's daughter's fine gift!

Oh hammer, good hammer, crash down!
Don't slip and fly out of my hand!
You're all the provider I have;
without you my life's at an end. . . .

HIS WORKS OF WONDER . . .

Great must be His works of wonder
if the world's not yet gone under,
if one man is left whose woes
have not made him tear his clothes,
if there's one man walking now
without ashes on his brow.

And if Nineveh's bright spires
still are unconsumed by fires,
if the sun still flames afar
and at night each lustrous star,
if no voice, as used to speak,
prophesies from vale and peak—
if He sees, with lips locked fast,
even Himself He has surpassed.

WORLD SORROW

I wandered through the quiet field—despair
prodded me on and on—until
at last I listened and stood still:
the sorrow of the world was in the air.

There was no sound; yet someone, I believed,
was walking quietly around;
and crowded was the air with sound,
and quietly the earth, the whole earth, grieved.

Night came. On high the moon hove into view—
how, or where from, I do not know.
She stood there, tremblingly aglow,
and I imagined she was grieving too.

And all that's been endured, from first to last,
the agonies of every age—
rode past in quiet pilgrimage,
and floated past, reverberated past.

IN A DARK TIME

All the sepulchers have opened
in the ancient burial ground:
every dark and evil figure
has arisen from its mound.

Guard yourselves, you who are living,
from the specters in the streets:
smile no more—one doesn't jest with
dead men in their winding sheets.

Mightier than living giants
are the corpses: every glance
from their sockets through your heart will
pierce and puncture like a lance.

One of them—I recognize him—
Rome's dictator of ill-fame;
he cuts down the youngest trees and
sets the loveliest shrines aflame.

The Inquisitor's among them—
that familiar face returning. . . .
Quiet, children, hush your learning!—
He might earmark you for burning. . . .

Even in secret do not murmur
as Marranos used to do,
for the spy behind the paling
has been resurrected too.

TO A SNOWFLAKE

And if you are a snowflake
you ought to drop
on the top
of a peak
and there forever glow.
But oh, your fate is bleak
if you'll come down
here in this town. . . .
They'll soon make mud of you
and after that—you're through!

THE PAIR

On a dirt road—bleak and gray—
a man and woman make their way;
Hunger is she,
and Death is he.

On they struggle—arm in arm,
as if to keep each other warm;
the two are old—
they feel the cold.

Death calls to his ladylove:
"Come, my dear, delicious dove,
my joy, my pretty,
into the city!

"There's a new day just begun:
people scurry, rush, and run. . . ."
Her voice is surly:
"It isn't early!"

"True," says Death, "we'd better speed;
there'll be work for us, indeed!
The air is full:
they call! they call!"

And through many a winding lane
softly, softly come that twain
without a word—
unseen, unheard. . . .

EIGHT

Eight live there,
and only two beds.
When night comes, where
do they lay their heads?

Three with their father
and three with their mother—

three with their mother
all tangled together.

When night comes,
they get ready for bed;
it's then she delivers
her plea to be dead.

She means it sincerely,
nor is it surprising:
cramped quarters, but private,
the last room one lies in.

NIGHT

Sometimes when darkness
covers the ground,
the busy world rests
and utters no sound.

To look at the world
is then my delight,
for everything's sweet
and everything's right.

Down many a street
I secretly roam
and once in a while
look into a home.

It seems to me then
the father am I
of all these poor souls
who barely get by.

It saddens me then
to turn and be gone,
leaving them here,
my children, alone. . . .

THE PROMISE

I promised myself that I never
would long for good fortune and bliss,
but give up my life forever
to man in his grief and distress.

Though later, at many a party,
I mingled with holiday folk,
and sang, and my laughter was hearty—
the promise I never broke.

TO MY PEOPLE

Now, in the darkest age of man, I cannot say a
consoling word to you, my miserable folk.
I cannot see as far as did the sage Isaiah
nor match the lamentations Jeremiah spoke.

The visionary power Ezekiel was given,
has not been mine; I hear no voices in the air;
it seems to me that there is nobody in heaven;
it seems to me that heaven is altogether bare.

Don't think, my people, I'm a little man and cannot
send forth my spirit, soaring, as the prophets could.
If even they were living now upon this planet
they'd understand no more than I have understood.

And even He Himself, the Lord of all creation,
if He were truly seated on His heavenly throne
and all His countenance a raging conflagration—
in horror He'd put out His flame, and turn to stone. . . .

THE CALL

So miserable is whatever I look at;
and everything's guilt-ridden, every road crooked;

and everyone's terrified heart has turned cold—
ah, come to me, vision—unfold, unfold!

Unfold, vision, now, as of old, like a flame,
in dark, lonely vales to the prophet you came.
Descend like an angel, a blaze from the skies;
pour fiery beams on my heart and my eyes.

Is this then a better, a holier time?
Are Nineveh's lanes without sin, without crime?
I'll carry your torch—I'll obey your command—
wherever you send me—by sea or by land.

And should the wild tempest play havoc with ships,
I'll thunder at them from the watery deeps.
I'll wrestle and wrangle with wave and with wind
to come and wreak justice on those who have sinned.

IN DAYS OF CLOUD

In days of cloud
"Hush!" is the rule;
what we're allowed
befits a fool.

Cut my heart's wall;
take out all brightness,
and take out all
that smacks of greatness.

Lift it on high
through gloom, through night;
say this: that I
brought hope and light.

THE LAUGHTER

Tears had lost the power of stirring—
all the gates were bolted tight;

one, however, comprehended,
and that one man laughed outright.

Like a prophecy it happened
under midnight's gloomy cloud.
Led off to their execution
one among them laughed aloud.

When at last he had been halted
by his executioners,
from the wall his roar of laughter
sounded through the universe.

—All has passed in perfect order,
and the reckoning's been made;
but his laughter falls like thunder,
making those who hear afraid. . . .

Without tears he took their bullets—
we inscribe it on the page. . . .
Like a sign, a curse, his laughter
will resound from age to age:

Till the end of time your Love's a
mock, your Power a disgrace.
Woe to the conqueror whose victim
bursts out laughing in his face!

FROM ONE SIDE OF THE WORLD

From one side of the world, the sun—
and from the other, clouds come wheeling;
one side makes ready for Messiah
and on the other, slaves are kneeling.

Between them stands Humanity
half joyful and half dumbly frightened:
one side would swallow all the world;
the other wants it to be brightened.

Which way shall Man stretch forth his hands?
there, where the beams of daylight beckon?
or shall he turn his countenance
to where the smoke and powder thicken?

Which way? Man, ponder for a while:
shall dawn or darkness fall behind you?
shall you approach Messiah's fire,
or shall the smoke and powder blind you?

Chaim Roisenblatt (1878–1956)

CHAIM ROISENBLATT (pseudonym of Chaim Rosenbluth) was born
in Podolia in 1878. At thirteen he emigrated to the United States
and became a sweatshop worker. His first poems, published in
1900, were influenced by Morris Rosenfeld; but Frug, Reisen, and
Yehoash soon inspired a richer lyricism, the music of Poe and
Oscar Wilde reshaped his technique, and he turned to symbolism,
thus earning recognition from Di Yunge (The Young Ones) as a
pioneer of their aesthetic movement. His collected poems appeared in 1915. A year later he became editor of the *Detroit Weekly,*
in which he featured the work of Di Yunge. From 1921 until his
death in 1956 he was a leader in the Yiddish cultural life of Los
Angeles, incorporating western scenes and lore in such collections
as *Adam's Children* (1944), *On the Shortest Day of Autumn* (1953), and
Twilight, issued a year after his death in 1956.

AMERICA
(excerpt)

The spirit of John Brown and Jefferson,
Lincoln and Paine, has wandered on this earth.
Upon our soil and underneath our sky

Walt Whitman sang of man and God and sea,
and Emerson—of light and bliss and mirth,
and Poe—of love and death and lonely sorrow;
and, children of the old world, you and I?
Upon the shores of this fair continent
we've put up our new tent.
Long have we roamed, and it was late, late when we came;
but the land still is large, is free:
new cities will be built tomorrow.
The sun above us will unfurl his flame,
and long, long will the white days linger on.

AT THE JUBILEE

(For the jubilee of *Di Freie Arbeiter-Shtimme,* with which Joseph Bovshover had been closely associated. Bovshover was then in a mental hospital.)

A vacant chair, a glass of wine
before it—bubbling to the brim.
Invited is a precious guest,
but we are not to be with him.

And vacant will remain his chair,
and full and undisturbed his cup.
Within a gloomy castle's walls
an evil wizard mews him up. . . .

The deepest melancholy drapes
his window, and conceals his sun
that sheds its rays on the white world
just as his own bright spirit's done. . . .

Long through his skull, like great black crows,
his fantasies have wheeled and whirled;
and from the darkness they look down
upon his desolated world. . . .

A chair, and at the table's head
a wineglass, bubbling to the brim.
Lechayem! lift your glasses to
the absent guest, and drink to him.

I'M A WATER CURRENT

I'm a water current, born
of a mountain, lost and lorn
in the midst of high, bare rocks within some deep and unknown
   valley.

Willows, with a lonely tune,
sway above me night and noon,
and I've been assaulted by a dismal melancholy.

Till unto the boundless sea
God Himself will carry me
and disperse my molecules amid that rolling tide of glory.

To the billows, tower-high,
to the storm winds bounding by,
God Almighty, what shall be my story?

The Second Golden Age

Joseph Rolnik (1879–1955)

JOSEPH ROLNIK was born in Zhokhovitz, Byelorussia, in 1879, the son of a miller. He first came to the United States at the age of twenty, supporting himself by selling newspapers on the street. He then spent four years in England, returned to Russia in 1904, and finally settled in New York in 1908. Though published by Di Yunge, who recognized him as a precursor of aestheticism, he remained aloof from all groups. His early volumes include *On the Dark Road* (1913), *First Ennui* (1922), and *Poems* (1926); among his later works are *A Window to the South* (1941) and *Selected Poems* (1948). A quarter century after his death in 1955 his widow issued an enlarged *Selected Poems* in a bilingual Tel Aviv edition.

AT GOD'S BEHEST

At God's Behest! Then let Him lead me
whereto He will and how He will. . . .
I won't put up a fight, but like a
child I'll follow and keep still.

On mountain peaks, in deep abysses,
with eyes wide open—and yet blind,
into the lair of beasts: the Father
leads—the child comes close behind.

MY OCEANS

Ever tranquil are my oceans.
Far from land my vessels drive.

When the moment is propitious
they will all arrive.

Over tranquil lanes God leads them;
where they're headed God can tell.
Why, then, do I need to worry?
All will turn out well.

I. RABOY

I and the poet Isaac Raboy,
next door neighbors are we.
Sometimes I go in to him,
sometimes he comes to me.

Between us—me and him—are just
some panels plastered white.
We hear each other walk about—
he left, I right.

On Henry Street, twenty-five years back:
we were one family then. . . .
"The Earlier Age" is what we're called
today, by younger men.

A word-stable is where I toil;
he works at mink and sable.
He is thoroughly left, and I've
a somewhat rightish label.

We talk things out like good old friends;
our words are plain and true—
though I'm a wee bit right, and he
is left-wing, through and through.

* * *

And as we remember Levin's Cafe,
five steps down, there seems
to be a warm and delicate dew
dissolving over our limbs.

And as we remember our boyhood homes,
he Rishkon and I Mir,
hand in hand my rightness and
his leftness disappear.

My father had a watermill, his
a horse-drawn cart. Around
and around in water turned our wheel,
and his turned on the ground.

We talk about Sabbath and workdays,
of mouth-watering treats:
what holiday feasts are in our pots,
and what his village eats.

We talk things out like good old friends;
our words are plain and true—
though I'm a wee bit right, and he
is left-wing, through and through.

I AM NOT RICH

I am not rich; I have one garment
for home and street and house of prayer;
on holidays, when greeting God, and
when I bargain at the fair.

The dust of summer settles on it,
the mud of an October day,
the gutter's splash—and all my scrubbings
can wash not one small spot away. . . .

At funerals and celebrations,
in these same clothes. Not rich am I.
And with my every stain I'll enter
the kingdom of the Lord on high.

INCOGNITO

Every day there comes an hour:
I remove each royal garment,
take in hand my wander-staff, and
leave behind my own apartment.

Over streets and marketplaces,
fenced-in homes, I take my passage;
every boy lets fly a stone, and
each dog sends a nasty message.

Alien doorknobs burn me, scald me;
sharply pointed pellets gore me—
wandering incognito has been
done by other kings before me.

HEED THE MOON

Heed the moon and let her teach you
to go silent through the town
so that no one hears your footsteps,
no one writes your message down.

Heed the moon and let her teach you
to endure alone at night
and behind each cloud that passes
for awhile be lost from sight.

Heed the moon and let her teach you:
in the high nights of the month
let your banishment from heaven
be your test of strength.

FOUR PACES IN SUNLIGHT

I don't need to range far and wide.
I'm pleased with only

112

a hundred good paces to ride
for me and my pony.

I need no broad streams to command.
This makes me richer:
a brook, that will water the sand,
for me and my pitcher.

I don't need a palace. Where two
bright crossroads throng,
four paces in sunlight will do
for me and my song.

Eliezer Steinbarg (1880–1932)

Born in Lipkan, Bessarabia, in 1880, ELIEZER STEINBARG taught
himself Russian and German. In youth he became a village
teacher in Bessarabia and Volhynia. He began writing poems in
1902 but withheld from publication until 1910. He admired Bialik
profoundly, corresponding with him and translating his work. For
his part, Bialik planned to publish Steinbarg's fables, but World
War I intervened. Settling in Czernowicz in 1919, he swiftly became a prime figure in Rumanian Yiddish culture, lecturing
widely, editing the anthology *Kultur,* and working for the socialist
papers *The New Life* and *Freedom.* In 1920 he co-edited Bucharest's
The Awakener. He led Czernowicz's Yiddish School Union, orga-
nized a theater studio and a children's theater, for which (1920–
28) he adapted many biblical and folk legends, as well as Peretz
stories. His first book was *Aleph-Beis* (1921). In 1928 he left to
direct a Yiddish school in Rio de Janeiro, returning to Czernowicz
two years later. He died in 1932, while preparing a volume of his
fables for publication, and was buried in the children's corner of
the cemetery. Volume 1 of *Fables* appeared later that year. Volume
2 was issued in Tel Aviv in 1956. Although his work has been
favorably compared with that of Krilov and La Fontaine, it nevertheless remains largely uncollected or altogether lost.

THE CLEVER STREAM

Said a river: "All streams flow
to the ocean! Only there they go!
I don't get it! Do they find the earth too small?
too few routes? too few parched realms where rains don't fall?
where men faint for just one drop? Say: wouldn't it be better
to run *there,* than make the ocean wetter?
Rushing, roaring on! No time to stop and ponder
even in that moment when the sun goes under
tranquilly!
No! I will not go with them! I'll find a new road now;
and I vow:
even if the sea-god, even he,
sends me word: *I'll give you all*
my rare pearls, the siren too,
she who crazes you
with her call—
this time No! I'll hear not one thing he can say!"
And the stream began to coil and cut his way
over woodlands,
well-baked mudlands,
acres bare and tawny-colored
(he's no dullard!)
—everywhere he came they blessed him;
with delight each pebble kissed him.
But forever
coiling, cutting through, the river
kept exploring till he came
unto Pharaoh's desert land
where the sun's an oven, endlessly aflame.
And what happened to the stream?
Ask the sand!

* * *

Look for new paths—yes, why not?
But don't end up in some desert blazing hot.

114

THE SHIRT AND THE COAT

Hush, bell! Tie the tongue up in your throat—
someone's talking there!
Who? Shirt picks at coat:
—I am clean, not one iota anywhere
of a speck, a smudge of dirt!
God forbid! a speck is sick! declares the shirt.
You should really be embarrassed!—I?
Before whom?
—Before me, of course! I'm white; you're black as doom.
Not for nothing, brother, do I lie
closer to the heart! black's mud; but white—now there's a hue!
—That may well be true,
(says the coat) and yet
you are near the heart, fool, to absorb its sweat!

Mani-Leib (1883–1953)

MANI-LEIB, whose family name was Brahinsky, was born in 1883
in the Ukrainian village of Nyezhin. His father was a peddler, his
mother sold vegetables, and he himself became a shoemaker.
Active in the revolutionary movement, he left Russia for London
in 1904 and published his first poems there. A year later he settled
in New York, where he led the aestheticist rebellion of 1907 and
was published in its journal *Shriftn.* In 1918 *Poems, Jewish and
Slavic Motifs, Ballads,* and *The Song of Bread* were published. *Clever
Little-Tongued Lad* and *Little Flowers—Little Garlands* followed four
years later. In 1930 *Miracle After Miracle* was published, and his
children's biography of Mendele Moicher Sforim appeared in
1936. He died in New York in 1953. Two years later his widow
Rachel Veprinski prepared his two-volume *Songs and Ballads* for
publication, and in 1961 his *Sonnets* appeared in Paris.

115

ON FIFTH AVENUE

On Fifth Avenue, behind a white wall,
behind a white wall on the thirteenth story,
girls sew and wait in a sorrowing pall
for the evening bell that does not hurry.

In a swamp of hours the bell is asleep.
In the stones of the walls the day malingers.
And the needles weep; and it's wounds they beweep;
and a rustle of silk in girlish fingers.

White silk, blue silk, violet and rose;
and thinly, deafly the needles are weeping.
And on windowpanes, in the pallor of woes,
in hot pillars of dust the sun goes creeping.

And the needles weep; and it's wounds they're wailing;
and a rustle of silk in the hands of girls.
And in noon's deep wounds the day lies ailing
over hands of girls, in the stone of the walls.

BY HEAVY LOCKS

By heavy locks the factories stand shut and barred;
hammer and saw no longer grate along the ways.
On stoop and corner, bridge and boulevard,
the hungry warm themselves on balmy days.
And back of heavy bolts—with naught but hunger—
the Hate in them stirs mute, its black wings ever stronger.

And through the streets so many women walk by night
with eyes afire like the neon signs on high.
And limousines, as soft as girls' heels, and as light,
in mantles of blue smoke move timorously by.
And from each little pane, through each thin mirror,
Fear flutters its black wings—the lonely Terror.

116

A SONG ABOUT A HUNCHBACKED PAIR
OF LITTLE OLD TAILORS

In the heart of New York, in that city of stone,
the day with quick footsteps comes noisily on
and drives through the district, like cattle in flocks,
the laboring hosts to their toil in the shops.

Gray factory buildings, from bottom to top
now open their black mouths all hungrily up
and swallow the masses, and suck them all dry,
and spit them back out on the streets by and by.

And only some old ones, some small bits of bone,
remain on the sidewalk now, lost and alone,
sucked dry by the factories long before now,
allowed by old age prematurely to bow. . . .

And here on Broadway, at the end of a street,
a pair of old tailors have happened to meet,
a hunchbacked old tailor-pair, tiny and poor,
thinned out and dried out, skin and bones, nothing more.

Once wielders heroic of needles and shears,
they sigh heavy sighs for the sake of those years;
their words are not tearful, their words are not gay,
but gall, bitter gall, is in all that they say.

Ech, brother, remember how grim and how green
we slaved at the wheel of the monster machine?
The rakers we raked, in distress we grew thin,
and all for the rich was the gold we raked in.

Remember, and afterward came the great fights
for bread and for freedom, our two precious rights;
and gathering into one fist all our powers,
like heroes in war, the first triumph was ours.

The stones of the street, that were covered by dust,
are stained even now with the blood that we lost. . . .
This brought the oppressor—because we had bled—
to cower before us in terror and dread.

—Yes, brother, we lived through a turbulent age!
Our battle remains for the younger to wage—
young vigor, young blood—it's our war they inherit,
but something's not so . . . and not so is the spirit.

And we—who were first—are forlorn and alone,
forgotten, neglected, completely unknown.
We're kept now not only away from the strife,
but even from living a workingman's life. . . .

What's left but to put on our packsacks and plead:
"The hunchbacked old tailors—oh help in their need!
Once wielders heroic of needle and shears. . . .
A few little breadcrumbs! Consider their tears!"

YOUR GRACE

Not in the gray dust of your wisely worded pages,
and not in your blest tombs that have outlasted ages,
but on the unbending brow where your great doom is traced,
have I beheld your grace.

And in my mother's eyes, so old and ripe with anguish,
when, clasped, her thin hands speak their soft hosanna language
before her Sabbath candles on my young one's face,
have I beheld your grace.

THE LANDS AND THE OCEANS

The lands and the oceans, the cities and places,
the words and the smiles and the faces—
they left me and went to a valley one day,
some valley that's far away.

I see through a shimmering mistiness only
the eyes of a child: sad and lonely—
a pair of black lambs that don't know where to go,
somewhere in a world of snow.

118

BEAUTY

Poor, devout, unknown to waver,
pure through every grief and groan,
I belong to you forever,
spotless white bone of your bone.

In the yoke of common duty
I do as the least must do,
but in suffering for beauty
I am set apart from you.

Beauty on this planet roaming
weeps disgraced from place to place,
yet I bring a vessel foaming
in the Word's sheer loveliness.

MY MOTHER

My mother is a beautiful, pale woman,
and she's white as a dove's wings;
the hair like snow—down from her bonnet
drop two thin strings.

And always in her black silk garments
she is festively arrayed;
on a gold chain on her heart, her bridal
medallion is displayed.

And eyes my mother has: green eyes, green meadows
and a sun at rest;
and when she looks into the eyes of someone,
that someone knows he's blest.

AMID THE WHITE TABLES

Long I sat amid the tables decked in white,
looking into eyes, engaging in debate;

119

and those other eyes I had forgotten quite
till the kind old waiter leaning toward my ear
with a quiet sadness and a smile of cheer
guiltily confided to me: Late. . . .

—So, a good! . . . tomorrow I'll again be here.
Streets, and night. A fog blew in through every bone.
Streets. And from the fog there swam at me two dear
eyes: those other eyes, aflame through teardrops flowing;
and like stars, twin stars, forever guiding, glowing,
they escorted me, a small me, home.

BALLAD OF TWO

Away from the noise and the house went the pair.
He'd laughed to the girl with a rose in her hair;

the girl, as it happened, was one she despised—
so both left their friends with the briefest goodbyes.

As soon as the door was behind them, the gray
that sat in her eye sent a yellowing ray:

a long, rusty knife from right under her bonnet,
whose blade she pulled out with his heart's blood upon it.

And over their footsteps a silentness glided
between these two strangers whom hate had divided.

Ahead of them lay in a frosty white glow
a snow-streaming night and a carpet of snow

and lanterns of white, and with steps that were swift
they moved with the snow, and behind them they left

two straight rows of steps that soon separately ran:
the steps of a woman, the steps of a man.

Avrom-Moishe Dillon (1883–1934)

AVROM-MOISHE DILLON (family name Zhurovitsky) was born in 1883 in a village near Grodno. His family moved to America in 1904, adopting the maternal family name of Dillon. His early poems appeared beginning in 1910 in such journals as *Shriftn* (New York) and *Renaissance* (London). He was a leading member of Di Yunge. *Yellow Leaves,* a 1919 collection, was illustrated by Zuni Maud. A year after his death in 1934, friends issued his *Poems.*

OUR WORD

No, our word is not yet dead,
though the sky's already red
and the sun dies overhead—
no, our word is not yet dead.

Though it wither here and there,
still our word will bloom up fair
in another soil somewhere—
and our word will grace the air.

Meanwhile drive the dread away
and the ghost along the way
lurking at the edge of day:
dread and darkness and dismay.

RAIN

Against whose fate is it the rain explodes?
Perhaps it's against mine the rain explodes,
or else against the fate of a blind hunchback
who drags himself along some dusty roads?
perhaps a dog, a soul transformed, which roams the roads?
Against whose fate is it the rain explodes?

121

I FEEL THE WHOLE WORLD'S HARDNESS

I'm sleeping in the park, all bunched-up on the stone-hard
   ground;
I feel the whole world's hardness—hard as stone.
The autumn sky is hanging darkly over me;
the park, emaciated, is my cover and my home.

I'm sleeping in the park, all bunched-up on the stone-hard
   ground;
somebody black bends down, in black he covers me.
I feel upon myself the blackness of the black, hard world.
More fierce, more fierce, more lone, o my aloneness, may you
   be!

TILL NOW

Till now I've not been known by any person,
and none will know me to my dying day;
and so I'll leave this place with woes that worsen—
and so in grief and pain I'll pass away.

And maybe I'll find rest "in the blue yonder,"
and maybe there it will be worse:
weary-headed, once again to wander—
wander, and at every step to curse.

Reuben Eisland (1884–1955)

Born in 1884 in Great-Radomishl, West Galicia, REUBEN EISLAND
began writing Hebrew poems at sixteen. In 1903 he emigrated to
America and turned to Yiddish poetry a year later. Like Mani-
Leib, with whom he founded Di Yunge in 1907, he was a factory

122

worker. In 1915 he edited the journal *Literature and Life,* and from 1918 he worked for *The Day.* He translated four volumes of Heine's prose as well as the *North Sea* cycle. In 1920 he produced a novel, *Without a Fatherland.* His first book of poems, *From My Summer,* was issued in 1922. With Mani-Leib he edited the journal *The Island* (1925–26). A second collection, *The Song of the Stag,* appeared in 1944, and *From Our Springtime,* a compilation of essays, was published in 1954 in Miami Beach, where he died the following year.

THE TREES LEAD

The trees lead to a distant view,
and, alongside, the lane is blue.

And, bluish as a fairy tale,
a town gleams in a misty veil.

And half-decided, without aim,
I go wherever goes the lane.

I'll heed the summons of the trees
and leave behind all memories

and have no thought of what's to be,
but let the blue light beckon me.

ZISCHE LANDAU RECITES A POEM

He rocks his blond head forward,
then back he lets it rock,
and under heavy lashes
there is a misty look.

Lips sensually murmur
and give the subtlest twitch
—as young men speak of women
by whom they've been bewitched.

123

Two fingers come together—
a ring. With slow gyration
the ring takes flight—a whisper,
and then an incantation.

The blue eyes smile and pertly
light up; then all at once
a word flies like an arrow
of high intelligence.

Now comes a sharp-toothed stanza
that bites forth the lip's blood;
the tongue tastes words, deciding
whether their wine is good.

He rocks his blond head forward,
then back he lets it rock.
The hunted word's been captured;
it glitters in his look.

He rocks his blond head forward,
then back he lets it rock.
O rock me, rock me, rock me,
O my not-here good luck!

Joel Slonim (1884?–1944)

JOEL SLONIM (originally Slonimsky) was brought to this country by
his parents from Drogitzine, near Grodno, at the age of two,
probably in 1886. He went through school and college in Chicago.
Although his first published articles and poems were in English,
he soon began producing Yiddish poetry as well, inspired by his
father, a fine linguist whose special love was Yiddish and whose
favorite poet was Rosenfeld. Slonim became managing editor of
the militant *Warheit,* and later served for twenty-five years as chief
political reporter for the *Day,* in whose Sunday edition his poetry

was regularly featured. He was also Secretary of the Department of Docks under Mayor Walker. As his newspaper's Albany correspondent during the administrations of Smith, Roosevelt, and Lehman, he became their friend and unofficial adviser. His interview with Wendell Willkie on the plight of Europe's Jews won wide notice. At the same time, Slonim helped found the YKUF and was a member of its presidium, co-founded the left-wing Writers and Artists Committee, and contributed poetry to *Yiddishe Kultur*. Inexplicably, no collection of either his prose or poetry was ever issued. He died in 1944.

THE SEAMSTRESS (1905)

I've been a seamstress very long;
the years have fled away;
my back is hunched and lame by now,
my hair is turning gray.

Each day, when morning still is dark,
I take my place and sew;
and thus I sit till late at night
and stitch—a life of woe.

I was a beauty long ago!
my songs were bright and gay.
A deathly voice, the rattling cough,
sings out of me today. . . .

I've been a seamstress very long;
the years have fled away;
I ornament a world with clothes,
myself—with hair turned gray. . . .

I sit like this the whole year through,
head bowed, without a spark;
and every stitch—the needle flies—
sticks deep and drains the heart. . . .

And every stitch, it drains the heart;
my eyes can scarcely see—

oh, not long shall I flicker here—
Death's hurrying for me! . . .

Israel-Jacob Schwartz (1885–1971)

Born in 1885 in the province of Kovno, Lithuania, ISRAEL-JACOB
SCHWARTZ first published his Bialik translations and his own poetry in 1906, the year of his emigration to America. Soon he was
translating Shakespeare, Milton, and Whitman. In 1918 he settled
in Lexington, Kentucky, which he celebrated in his Whitmanesque
1925 masterpiece, *Kentucky*. His *Anthology of Hebrew Poetry* appeared in 1942, his *Early Years* a decade later. He spent his last
years in Miami and died in 1971.

PARTING

We said goodbye to our ancestral home—
a storm wind drove us here across the foam.
One left a father's grassy grave, another
looked for the last time on an aged mother.

But in the heart of each the grief was fierce,
and each one silently suppressed his tears;
packs on their shoulders, children at their side,
on alien streets their memories never died.

One brought a bit of homeland earth he'd kept;
a prayer book in which grandfather had wept;
a silent pain, the grief of generations,
an echo of deep sighs and lamentations.

Like shoots torn from the tree on which we'd grown,
we got to work erecting our new home;

the old roots there, the young heart split in two,
between them the Atlantic thundered through.

And like a young tree that will somehow sprout
up from the hard, cold mountain-rock, without
a mother's lap, yet grasping toward the sun,
so was our time of blossoming begun.

And years ran by. New juice came streaming now
through the young sapling's every branch and bough.
Its root dug ever deeper in the ground,
and with new melodies its top was crowned.

A LITTLE MOTHER

Once a bit of an orange tree, wretchedly small,
up the side of a hill somehow managed to crawl;
there it stopped, stuck its thin little roots in the ground,
and astonished it stood taking in every sound.

Then along flew its angel, one night or one noon,
hit its back with a sunbeam, as if to say: Bloom!
and the sapling obeyed and its buds began growing,
and the sun warmed its body and soon set it glowing.

And because of that grow and that glow, something burst
on its thin little arms—green and tiny at first;
pressed and pressed, as the nuts do with all their young might,
just as hard as unripe little nuts, and as tight.

But the dew sent its coolness, the sun sent its rays,
and the juices inside of them started to play;
they grow swollen, grow plump—with a sweet-smelling rind,
and like apples of gold in the redness they shine.

On the hillside the mother, two feet from the earth,
takes delight in the burden of gold she's brought forth;
she's accomplished her mission and brightens the place
like a redly branched flower unique in its grace.

127

AT FIRST THEY WERE WHITE

At first the round things were completely spotless, white,
the snowballs that the bush had newly grown—
as the young maiden's breasts are white and round
when Sin, to her, is something still unknown.

Later, in August, they took on a rosy tint
—the sun had kissed them hotly with his beams—
as the clean, tender face of a young maiden
is rosy in the first love of her dreams.

And now they're standing altogether dusky-brown,
and still are dreaming about rose and white.
Drooping their brown heads toward the yellow grass,
quietly they sway in the quiet light.

PRECIOUS THIS SOIL
(excerpt)

Precious already this new soil has grown;
fresh, and as fruitful as any I've known.
Virginal soil, so compliant, whose grass
kisses, refreshes my feet as they pass.
Attar of apple comes out of her deeps;
tender the touch of her breeze on my cheeks.
Blood has not fallen to hallow this ground;
far is the slumber my father has found.
As for my child, though, he's fed at her breast:
bright in her light, by her blessedness blest.

Moishe Leib Halpern (1886–1932)

MOISHE LEIB HALPERN has been called by Irving Howe "perhaps the most original poet in Yiddish." Born in 1886 in the Galician village of Zlochev, he moved to Vienna at twelve. Here he studied and wrote German poetry . His first Yiddish poem, composed in 1907, was rejected by a Lemberg editor as "too beautiful for a beginner." He left for the United States in 1908, stopping at Czernowicz en route to participate in the world conference that gave Yiddish equal status with Hebrew as a language for the Jewish people. In 1912 he became editor of the Montreal *People's Journal*. For years he wandered in poverty from city to city, working at a great number of trades. In New York he became a leading member of Di Yunge, all immigrant workers by day who devoted their lives to creating a poetry based not on the social rhetoric of their predecessors but on the innovations of Rimbaud, Baudelaire, and Rilke, among others. His books include *To New York* (1919) and *The Golden Peacock* (1924). Two additional books appeared shortly after his death in 1932.

IN THE GOLDEN LAND

—But would you believe, mother, if you were told
that everything here is transformed into gold,
that iron and blood make this gold, shiny bright,
yes—iron and blood, all day long and all night?

—My son, from a mother one does not conceal;
a mother can see and a mother can feel.
I think: in that country of gold, even there,
the bread you've been given is less than your share.

—O mother, dear mother, would ever you dream
that bread here is dropped into ocean and stream
because so much grain is coaxed up from our earth
that often it loses the gold of its worth?

—I don't know, my son, but it makes my heart crack.
Your face has the look of a night grim and black;

129

your eyelids hang drowsy, half-open at best,
like those of a person who's yearning for rest.

—O mother, dear mother, you surely must know
of subways that rush through the ground to and fro.
At daybreak the train drags us all out of bed,
and back to our homes late at night we are sped.

—My son, I don't know; but I'm pierced through and through.
How young, when you left, and how healthy were you!
It seems our goodbye was just hours ago,
and now I must see you again, looking so!

—The blood of my heart, must you drain it this way?
You don't sense my torment at all that you say?
What's wrong, dearest mother, what's making you cry?
Do *you* see, as I do, a wall dark and high?

—How *can* I help crying, my son, when I see
that you have forgot about God, about me?
Your very own life is a wall that will stand
blockading your way in your new golden land.

—You're right; we're apart, and apart we'll remain.
A great golden chain . . . and a great iron chain. . . .
In heaven, for you waits a bright golden throne.
In *this* golden land waits a rope for your son.

THE W-W-WORDS OF MURDOVIETZ BARNUHLE AT THE GRAVE OF A LODGE BROTHER

Even above the heads of people hale and ruddy
as bears—says Murdovietz Barnuhle—
Death's great black angel-wings are flapping loud already,
as 'round a carcass rotting in the sun
the flies are all buzz-buzzing.

At least the flies—Hell take them—let themselves be driven
away—says Murdovietz Barnuhle—

but what's a dead man's wife and children to be given?
One might as well slice up for them, like bread,
the corpse—the dreary bumpkin.

But it may come to pass that by tomorrow morning—
so says Murdovietz Barnuhle—
within our bodies too there'll be a frenzied swarming
of worms—as topsy-turvy as the words
of one who's lost his senses.

So what, if blood is gushing from these eyes of ours!—
so says Murdovietz Barnuhle—
if, just the way it happens when a man devours
a heaping bowl of caviar, the heart
is all at once on fire!

But how long can you go on howling for a dead one?—
so says Murdovietz Barnuhle—
Woman, go home! and put a caftan on, a red one—
and try to find a husband for yourself,
a father for your children.

We can't—Hell take it—change the world, though it's a horrid
affair—says Murdovietz Barnuhle—
and weeping, patting each poor orphan on the forehead
with more a heavy bearpaw than a hand,
he gives a penny.

BY ITS BARRENNESS

By its barrenness
and by the hoarse, inhuman roar that came from there,
one judged the place to be a wilderness
and that an ancient lion creeps
around a rock, because he's stricken, and
because he seeks a spot
appropriate for lying down and dying.
But in reality it was a town of empty streets
in which a crazy fellow, on his hands and feet,
incessantly crept round and round

131

a dwelling place whose walls had half come down,
and that which dragged a-clanking after him
was no more than a tin can on a string
that had been fastened to his belt behind him.

UP FROM EARTH THERE GROWS

Up from earth there grows a thing, which stands and greens into
    a tree.
There are certain other things the tree begins to bear:
green ones, blue ones, yellow, red, and brown—
these we call a plum, an apple, and a pear
and stretch ourselves tiptoe with bits of body—known as hands—
and heap our baskets full with all the sweet things we pull down,
and carry them in trucks and trains to every marketplace in
    town,
and there the finest of our wares is sold
to those who're fat and who can pay in gold;
for silver they can buy the wares
that here and there already have a few brown spots;
for copper, they can take what rots,
what the worm already shares.
And anyone who wants to get some free,
for him we leave a dunghill—he
can share his pickings with the famished mouse, who peeps
out of her wretched hiding-place and weeps.

ABIE CURLEY, HERO OF THE WAR

Abie Curley, hero of the war,
with medals flashing on his chest, and with his crutches,
lowers his left eyelid when he cries.
Yesterday, however, on a Wednesday,
in the deep of night he had himself a ball—
got ahold of seven live frogs and ate them.

Seven times I thought it was nothing at all
except the night wind crying in my garden.

Yet I did not so much as trouble to inquire
why he should cry.
Perhaps it grieves him
that all his trumpeting fails to inspire
my flowers.
They're made of stone—that was the way I dreamed them up.

But strange as this may be,
not the night wind—Abie Curley cried!
Each time, after he had eaten
one of the seven live frogs,
he mourned her death.

Now in the sun he sits again
and waits for his young friends, the kids,
to come and say "Good morning!"
He's fond of them.
The warmth they bring reminds him of his wife—
that madcap Barla.
Laughing, she gave him a bite on the chin once.
But that was in the days when he still had his concertina.

And a peacock feather on his bright green stovepipe hat,
and pants that fitted snugly,
and boots—
like a looking glass they sparkled in the sun.
Hey, my Barla!

Abie Curley dare not reminisce about delight,
for he shrieks
and then, in a coughing fit, he'll spit out blood.

However, Abie Curley's not an angry fellow;
all he closes is his left eye
when he weeps
with medals flashing on his chest and with his crutches.

BREAD AND FIRE

The sack is ready: rows of ripening rye unfurled—
enough for everyone who labors in the world.

But since it's gold the landlord barters for his rye,
empty in every poor man's house the sack must lie.
And since the villager has children to be fed
and since they're hungry and without one crust of bread—
it's not surprising that the man obeys his need
and comes to town and steals the bread on which you feed.
And since the golden showpiece that so brightly lies
across your belly cannot help but catch his eyes—
it's not surprising that he steals the chain as well.
Because of gold, his life has long since been a hell.
Because of gold, in fact, one time he even planned
to go at night and kill the owner of the land;
but since the landlord knows what dangers may befall,
a watchdog's in his yard, a sword is on his wall.

The axe is ready. Nice and sharp, but what's the good?
To chop down trees for everyone in need of wood.
But since the lord needs forests for his hunt, one must
put down the axe and leave it in the shed to rust.
And since the villager has children going bare,
and since the oven's ice, and not one log is there—
no wonder, Jew, that it's to you the man will come
and hack your door, your shutters down, to heat his home.
And, Jew, if you stretch forth your hand to stop the blade,
don't hope the man who swings the axe will give you aid.
And when you're lying on the ground, hands butchered, dead,
and when your blood along the ground runs fire-red—
no wonder if the man lifts back his weapon, Jew,
and, like a piece of timber, splits your head in two.
And since your screaming baby has a head, no wonder
if with one final blow he hacks the head asunder.

WHO IS

Who is the rider there, that spurs
and spurs his horse and never stirs?
—Be still, my blood; be still, don't cry:
the rider riding there is I.

At midnight in a field half-won
who's blocked the road that he must run?

134

—Be still, my blood; be still, don't cry:
the rider riding there is I.

And since around him all is black,
why does the rider not turn back?
—Be still, my blood; be still, don't cry:
the rider riding there is I.

Anna Margolin (1887–1952)

Born in 1887 in Brest-Litovsk, ANNA MARGOLIN studied in Odessa
and Warsaw and at the age of nineteen came to the United States
for the first time. She became Chaim Zhitlovsky's secretary and
was a professional Yiddish journalist under her real name, Razel
Lebensboim. She worked briefly in London and Paris, then in
Warsaw (1910–11). In London she was befriended by the great
anarchist theoretician Piotr Kropotkin. Returning to the United
States in 1914, she gained prominence as a writer on the role of
women, contributing regularly to the Yiddish daily, *The Day.* She
made her poetic debut in 1922, a year later published an anthology, *The Yiddish Poem in America,* and won acclaim for her 1929
volume, *Poems.* With her husband, the Hebrew novelist Moses
Stavsky, she lived for some years in Palestine, but returned to New
York, where she died in 1952.

MOTHER EARTH

Mother Earth—trodden, sun-bathed,
dark slave and mistress
am I, O dear one.
From me, the lowly, the drear one,
you flourish forth: a mighty stem . . .
and like the sun's flame, like the sky's eternal diadem,
among your roots, your boughs I wind

in a silence long and blind.
Half waking, half asleep I lie—
and seek, through you, the lofty sky.

THE GANGSTER

In the tenement door, where down the flight of stairs
the darkness explodes a streetlamp's eye,
his head, as if in a halo, appears.
The eyes of metal on his stony face,
devoid of memories, globular and bright,
have—in their hungry emptiness—
devoured the street and each who passes and each auto light.
He lifts one shoulder—does it smooth and sharp—
a scrape, a bow, the cool stiletto in his pocket.
The street lies ready like a golden harp,
and his wild fingers cannot wait to pluck it.

GIRLS IN CROTONA PARK

As in a faded picture
girls have woven themselves
into the autumn dusk.
Their eyes are cool, the smile untamed and thin.
Their clothes are lavender, old-rose and apple-green.
Dew runs in their veins.
They're stocked with bright and hollow words.
Botticelli loved them in a dream.

IN THE CAFE

With smoke, like masks, we cover up our faces.
A joke, a shoulder twitch, a weary stare.
False words flare up, then fade and leave no traces.
Have I offended you, my dear?

We all keep vile, cold masks upon our faces,
spout irony to cloak the fever, wear
a thousand smiles, guffawings, and grimaces.
Have I offended you, my dear?

Nahum Yud (1888–1966)

NAHUM YUD (pseudonym for Nahum Yerusalimchik) was born in
Bober, Byelorussia, in 1888. Beginning as a Russian poet, he
turned to Yiddish when he moved to Warsaw. In 1916 he settled
in New York and was soon being published in such journals as
Tsukunft, Kunds, and *Shriftn,* the organ of Di Yunge. His fables
and songs became extremely popular and were widely reprinted.
Among his books are *Fables* (1918), *Poems* (1924), *Fables* (the 1924
edition, vastly expanded and illustrated by the left-wing artists
Zuni Maud and Yosl Kotler, among others), and *Radiant Moments,*
published by the Workmen's Circle in 1932. For many years he
was on the staff of the *Forward,* whose Sunday edition regularly
featured one of his fables or poems. His sixtieth, sixty-fifth, and
seventieth birthdays were widely observed. A longtime resident of
Brooklyn, Yud died in 1966. A posthumous collection, *The Blessed
Hour,* was issued in 1973.

A WINTER SONG

In a snowy field somewhere
a wolf howls long and loud;
the wind wafts his despair
through forests hushed, in cloud.

Here too, in the desert of stones,
in the world's prime uproar of steel,
I frequently hear the moans
of hungering wolves in the field.

137

Amid bright celebrations,
in the din of the echoing street,
rise silent lamentations,
slinks an evil hate.

No snowy fields are in view,
and it's not so gloomy at night,
but here in these stone-woods too
Hunger displays his might.

Bent double, men go squirming
whom anguish and spite overwhelm.
Men's eyes are wolfishly burning
here too, in this golden realm.

LIKE THE EYES OF WOLVES

Like the bright eyes of wolves
on a road in the night—
so the days of my life
lead the way with their light.

From afar circle round,
circle round with their glow
all my sorrowful days
over acres of snow.

Like the bright eyes of wolves
in a forest at night
is the flash I receive
from my world: cold and bright.

Celia Dropkin (1888–1956)

Born in Bobroisk, Byelorussia, in 1888, CELIA DROPKIN received an education in both Russian and Yiddish and taught in Warsaw until she and her husband emigrated to New York in 1912. Her first poems were in Russian; she turned to Yiddish in 1918, and contributed significantly to such journals as *In Zich* and *Tsukunft.* Her first book of poetry, *In a Hot Wind,* appeared in 1935. In later life she became a painter as well. Three years after her death in 1956, *In the White Wind,* a collection of her stories, paintings, and poems (selected by H. Leivick), was published by her five children. The social themes omitted from her poetry were powerfully projected in her stories.

AT THE WINDOW

Standing at the window with head bent
from the fifth floor of the tenement,
I became pensive, a memory rose,
and the sidewalk seemed so close, so close.

The gentle, gray eyes of the sidewalk knew me,
and like a warm bed, like dear arms, she drew me.
The sidewalk was so close, so close . . .
and a memory of my warm childhood bed arose.

I suddenly craved sleep—like one possessed.
Do I dare hope this day will bring me rest?
I bent still further, further, and unto
my rest, so yearned for, like a bird I flew.

MY GUEST
(excerpts)

You're welcome, you're welcome, my guest;
drop the burden by which you're oppressed;

get undressed, take your rest
in my radiant nest;
wash your hands, wash your feet;
here's my table, come eat;
still your hunger, your thirst,
on my breast, on my breast.

. . . .

You are a spider, I a fly.
How cunningly your spiderweb is spun!
There's no escape, were one to try. . . .

The hues, mother-of-pearl, ensnare my eye
—that shimmer on your net of sun.
I flutter through, prepared to die!

H. Leivick (1888–1962)

Leivick Halpern, who took the pseudonym H. LEIVICK to avoid
being confused with M. L. Halpern, was born in Igumen, Byelorussia, in 1888. Often arrested for socialist activities from 1906
on, he spent four years in a Moscow prison and in 1912 was
sentenced to lifetime exile in Siberia. He escaped, traveled across
Europe, and reached America in 1914. Here he became a leading
member of Di Yunge, along with Mani-Leib, Zische Landau,
Moishe Leib Halpern, and Reuben Eisland. He co-edited a literary journal with the great novelist Opatoshu and produced several verse-plays, most notably *The Golem* (1921). Years of hard
work led to tuberculosis, and he spent three years in a Denver
sanatorium. Among his early books are *Under Lock and Key* (1918),
Fallen Snow (1925), and *Through Seven Deaths* (1926). A *Complete
Works (1914–1940)* was issued in two volumes. After the Holocaust
he produced a series of extraordinary works, including *I Did Not
Go to Treblinka* (1945), *The Wedding at Fernwald* (1949), and *Job's
Epoch* (1953). *A Leaf on an Apple-Tree* (1955) was followed four

years later by *Songs of the Eternal* and *In the Baths of the Tzar*. He died in New York in 1962.

SACCO AND VANZETTI'S WEDNESDAY
(published in the *Morning Freiheit* on 21 August 1927, one day before the execution; excerpts below)

Boston, Mass.
Mid-August.
Agony time.
Day gone.
And night comes on.
Night comes on and bites
a first tooth
into the risen moon.

Boston, Mass.
Wednesday.
Sacco and Vanzetti's Wednesday.

Over the keys of
a typewriter whirl
the nimble fingers
of a girl—
correctly,
exactly, V-E-R-D-I-C-T, period,
S-E-N-T-E-N-C-E, period,
D-E-A-T-H.

(For seven years
already
instead
of bread
Sacco, Vanzetti
have eaten
death.)

And behind the chair
of the fatal room

there stands prepared,
not as before inside a mask,
not as before with rope and ax,
but frilled—perfumed—
hands manicured, just like the typist's hands—
his pocket graced with watch and fountain pen—
there stands prepared the gallows-gentleman.

(For seven years
a dancing hand
instead
of bread—
death.)

I know you won't give ear to my appeal,
and yet I must cry out;
I also know that in these days
it's useless to shout the age-old shout:
"Alas!
Your heart is harder than steel,
and your brow is of brass."
Today one must speak more simply, clearly;
today each word must blaze:
Boston, Mass.—
The whole world cries: You'll pay the price,
it will cost you dearly.
Wrap yourself, Judge, in your robe of black;
hide, Professor, under your proud cap;
smile, Governor, in the sense of your might;
only you three are sober on this night
intoxicated with blood-red agonies,
this hour, when even the dungeon keys
cry: Executioner, hold back!
But Boston answers:
—Die!
.   .   .
Sacco and Vanzetti
are fresh off the boat;
howl, Johnsons,
the yellow hate in your throat!
Sacco and Vanzetti
are poor Italians;
howl, all

142

you Nordic stallions!
And the world cries:
—United States,
what a banquet
Boston awaits!
Tonight she'll eat
with jaws long ready
the roasted meat
of Sacco and Vanzetti.
. . . .
Eleventh hour,
twelfth—
no further delays to be won,
nothing, nothing further to be done.
Humanity's cry has choked on itself:
the moon is gone, is gone, is gone.
She lies extinguished, burnt to ashes, on
the dread electric chair of dawn.

CLINK-CLANK

Clink-clank goes the dance,
for my feet are fettered tight.
Black bread in my hand, I take
first a dance step, then a bite.
Teacup in my hand, I take
first a dance step, then a drink.
Guard advances, guard withdraws—
I can read him wink by wink.

Never does he know my dance—
still, a thousand eyes adore:
head on head, a woods of hands—
hands keep crying: "Quick and more."
Now from underneath the bed
someone who was hidden creeps,
strikes the bars and beats the drum:
"Higher! higher, you!" he shrieks.

Higher, higher leaps my dance;
I'll be sitting here for years;

when I tear out one gray hair,
soon a second one appears;
so I tear out two, then three,
and a dance for every hair;
so my feet dance on and clink
with the fetters that they wear.

MINE

Departed from one house and into the next!
Wherever I come, I shall be a good guest.

Withdrawing, I'll turn neither doorknob nor key,
and no one at all will look backward at me.

Whichever the town I approach—is my town;
and hearing my footstep they'll each know the sound.

The clothes shall be mine howsoever I'm clad,
and whatever nourishes me is my bread.

Whenever I come, it will be the right time.
Wherever I lie down—that bed will be mine.

IF THE ROAD'S LONG

If the road's long,
gird your loins—one has to be strong.
If your shoes clap,
keep on slowly—one doesn't look back.

If you are fettered,
no stone on which chains can be shattered,
what's to be done?
Go in chains—one must keep going on.

If you need rest,
weary too grows the punishing fist.

144

If you lie down,
lie calm on the earth and sleep sound.

WHAT'S HE DOING HERE?
(from the *Spinoza* sequence)

A sickroom! What's he doing here,
the Amsterdam philosopher?

I stare—no doubt: the one I see
is he, is he.

Full lips. Long nose. The man's whole face
as if museumed under glass.

The lungs work hard in his sick chest;
a hacking cough won't let him rest.

Three hundred years—gone in a flash.
Upon his lip the blood is fresh.

Three hundred years of moonbeams glow
on face and cushion. Flow and flow.

Bright soul, I touch you. Wake up! Rise!
and grace me with your eyes.

MY FATHER USED TO CALL IT "CHTSOS"

Midnight. My father used to call this hour "Chtsos."*
I envy it with a great envy. Fifty years,
letter by letter, everywhere I go it goes:
The Exile of Shekinah, as he chanted it in tears.

Chtsos is midnight study and prayer to commemorate the destruction of
Jerusalem.

I do, it seems, as he did: I exclaim my grief
for ruined villages and for their guiltless slain.
I clamp my mouth shut, like my father, teeth on teeth.
Just one thing's missing: his red beard aflame.

That fiery beard of his has vanished with the wind,
and I've been no more lucky with a beardless face;
the *chtsos*-lament, by which the two of us are twinned,
at last arises in the light of childhood days.

And fifty years from now, will my sons also ache
for me? will they perhaps then yearn with the same yearning?
at night will they too, tremblingly devout, awake
and feel at least a line or two of mine still burning?

If so, O Lord of Time, hear me and grant thy grace:
allow my sons a little mercy, I implore thee:
as chalk is stricken from a slate, wash off, erase
these monstrous nights of mine, the nights of nineteen-forty.

IT WAS THE DAY THAT LOST ME

It was the day that lost me;
what found me was the night.
A *chtsos*-song came and blessed me
from bright white years of light.

And words once more are humming:
"My son—my end and aim—
your outcry is becoming
a world-arousing flame.

"Praised be your fires that gather
to make the morning shine!"
A son has found his mother;
what more has he to find?

Zische Landau (1889–1937)

Born in 1889 in Plotzk, Poland, of a famous rabbinical family, ZISCHE LANDAU was orphaned early and emigrated to the United States in 1906. Here he worked as a house painter. The year he arrived his first poem was printed in the *Jewish Daily Forward*. Five years later he was among the leaders of Di Yunge. He died early in 1937 in New York. His collected comedies, *Nothing Happened,* and a collected edition of his poems in three volumes, appeared later that year. A decade passed before his brilliant translations from world poetry were published in book form.

IN A DAWN HOUR OF JULY

Just like the face of Baal Shem at his prayer,
the world beams in a dawn hour of July.
A gold and violet light lies everywhere
and sends your first step greetings from the sky.

Your daughter piggyback. You stride and stride.
No longer do your eyes just look. They soar.
And suddenly a new thought stirs inside:
Your life has meaning—never sensed before.

Your daughter babbles something. You go and go.
It's good to stride so in the dewy grass.
It's good that in your every limb you know:
there's meaning in the world, and happiness.

SOME WORDS THERE ARE

Some words there are, words wonderfully slight.
You scarcely say them, and your heart grows light.
But never do you say them; till, one day,
when you yourself are unaware of what you say,
they fall quite nonchalantly from your tongue.

You do not even know of it; the time is long
before you see that something wondrous has occurred.
You say such things that none who know you ever heard;
you see such things that never passed before your sight;
and everything you touch is sheer delight, delight, delight—
oh words, words, wonderful and slight.

A LITTLE PARK, WITH FEW TREES

A little park, with few trees growing;
a wooden house sits humbly there,
on which appears a painted raven—
it all has such a childish air.

And on the wall there hangs a tablet,
and from the tablet you will know
here lived in eighteen nine and forty
the poet Edgar Allan Poe.

The name, the raven, wake within me
a memory of years before.
And since one is allowed to visit,
I let myself approach the door.

In a kimono red as scarlet
a woman's looking through the pane.
I'm so repelled by red kimonos
that in a flash I'm out again.

To stand outside suits me much better:
I clasp my hands, and focus all
my thoughts upon the roof's brown shingles,
and on the cottage's white wall.

Within my mind are mixed together
a verse of Poe's, a word, a rhyme.
Where have I heard them, come across them?
I feel they're from a distant time.

And yet, in dream and fact, they soothed me
and frightened me to my heart's core.

All this was only yesterday.
But will it come back? "Nevermore."

THE SONG OF THE WHITE GOAT

White as the name of my mother,
and pure as the moon's hue,
fresh as thawtide weather,
I come to be with you.

Of slender words I fetch you
horizons stretching far.
A trembling silk I get you
from where the green fields are.

The queen of the old story
strides with me through the land;
the white goat, without hurry,
picks grasses from my hand.

My peacock's wings, long folded,
are goldenly outspread.
The night lies safely bolted,
and safely chained lies Dread.

THE COUNTRYSIDE, BRIGHT-GRASSED
AND SPACIOUS

The countryside, bright-grassed and spacious,
has made my house smell fresh and sweet.
I leave the world of walls behind me
and near the door I take my seat.

Across the field the ducks go waddling,
and now they dive into the lake;
I lift my head up to the heavens
to see if rain's about to break.

It is, it is! . . . how fresh the air grows!
how cool, how deep becomes the air!
Unhurried, I approach the postbox
to see if any mail is there.

A. Glanz-Leyeles (1889–1966)

A. GLANZ-LEYELES (pseudonym for Aaron Glanz), was born in
Vlotzlavek, Poland, in 1889 and was brought up in Lodz. He went
to London at the age of sixteen and attended London University.
Four years later he emigrated to New York, where he completed
his studies at Columbia University. From 1914 his prose appeared
regularly in *The Day* under his real name; he signed his poetry
with his pseudonym. *Labyrinth*, his first book of poetry, appeared
in 1918. A year later, with N. B. Minkoff and Jacob Glatstein, he
founded the introspectivist In Zich movement and its journal *In
Zich* (Within One's Self), which he edited for twenty years. His
collections of poetry include *Rondeaus and Other Poems* (1926), *For
You, For Me* (1932), *Fabius Lind* (1937), *At the Foot of the Mountain*
(1957), and *America and I* (1963). *World and Word,* a book of essays,
was issued in 1958. He died in 1966.

SHADOWS

In the whiteness of my window shade
two plunderer-birds are fighting.
Crooked, murderous beaks
bury themselves
in the softness of neck and head.
Infuriated, thirsty beaks
lock in a death-dance.
Victory's sweet!
Now he wheels in arrogant triumph,
and the beaten lies beak up.

But soon she lifts herself
and the battle seethes once more.

Uncanny.
Winning and losing.
Delight and death-fright
in the noiseless fight
and the lurk of night.
Outside my window stand the trees:
serious, silent, musing.
Their young branches, chattering leaves,
rock themselves, shake themselves,
stir themselves, wake themselves,
in each flirting little breeze
of the fresh spring night.

SPANISH BALLAD

Pepito comes a-marching, Pepito heads for France;
he flees, with hosts of Spaniards, the shattered Spanish lands.

Pepito falls and gets up, gets up and falls again—
Pepito is already a four-year-old young man.

His mother fell, not ever to get up and go on,
but up he stood—Pepito stood up, her own, her son.

The lad has been familiar with war his whole life long;
air raids are his companions—he knows their savage song.

His little friend Juanita split into two one day,
two half-Juanitas—quiet and very still they lay.

Quiet and still: what is it? A long-tailed Night who'll crawl
from pitch-black woods and drag off her trophies one and all.

But those who *can* keep moving, with mother or alone,
must do what all are doing, must run, must stagger on.

When asked where he is heading, he promptly says "To France";
Pepito's heard and answered that question more than once.

151

"To France, from whose wide heavens no bursts of fire fall
without the slightest warning, to catch you in the skull.

"Where up to now the hateful have had no time to kill
old people, mothers, children—to strike them down at will."

That's what his mother told him as Barcelona bled;
but she could not awaken when those around her fled.

Pepito came to think, as he marched without his mother,
that brother has for ages been murdering his brother;

as soon as he's a grown-up, destruction is his joy;
he only cries and trembles when he's a little boy.

"When I'm a man," Pepito decides, "all strong and grown,
I'll fly the biggest airplane that ever has been flown.

"And hundreds upon hundreds, the angry bombs will drop;
and homes will be aflame from their bottom to their top.

"When I become a man, a commander with a gun,
I'll murder everybody—and none will move, not one."

Pepito heads for France; he gets up and falls again.
Pepito is already a four-year-old young man.

Ber Lapin (1889–1952)

BER LAPIN was born in 1889 in a village near Wolkowicz, Grodno
province. When he was six, his family left for Argentina. Four
years later the death of a sibling uprooted them again. At the age
of thirteen Lapin was on his own, wandering about Russia. When
he was fourteen his poems began to appear in print. He spent
several years in Vilna, then in the United States, and again in
Argentina, finally settling in New York in 1917. Here he helped

edit Chaim Zhitlovsky's *The New Hope* and worked as Zhitlovsky's secretary. His poems frequently appeared in *Shriftn* (1925–28). With B. J. Bialostotsky and Z. Weinper he co-edited *Oifkum* and was later a contributor to *Yiddishe Kultur*. His books of poetry are *Lonely Paths* (1910; Vilna), *Portents* (1934), *New Poems* (1940), and *The Full Pitcher* (1950). A dedicated lifelong translator, his *Russian Lyrics* was published in 1919; his versions of Shakespeare's sonnets, to which he had devoted eight years, appeared in 1953, a year after his death.

HANDS

My piece of bread's not big enough
to break in half.
Millions of stretched-forth hands beseech
a crumb for each.

At home—as in a dungeon barred—
the bread is hard;
one piece—may it, by miracle,
suffice for all!

Whole worlds—outdoors a silent cry
seeks the scorched sky:
In such great misery, respond
to each one's hand!

BROTHER!

In slashing thrusts, in flashing comets,
in one word let it all sound forth;
from hillocks—hills! from boulders—summits!
from two opposing poles—the North!

Take shortcuts to far destinations;
the world now runs its final race.
Use words that won't die through mutations;
create a truth Time won't replace!

153

"Brother!"—it's here, the cry of Abel.
Come, let's plant brotherhood worldwide!
I won't sit at the banquet table
if even one slave's kept outside!

Jacob Stodolsky (1890–1962)

JACOB STODOLSKY was born in Parisov, in the district of Shedletz, Poland, in 1890. In early youth, severe differences with his Hasidic father drove him to the sordid factory world of Warsaw, where his class consciousness awoke and he became a strike organizer. Later, while in the Russian army, his comrades disguised him and smuggled him into Lemberg. There he led an anarchist group, and continued his activities in Paris, where he developed an abiding love for French culture, particularly its poetry. Still an anarchist when he reached the United States in 1912, he came under the influence of Dr. Zhitlovsky and became a Jewish nationalist. In 1919 he joined the Inzichists (introspective poets), bitter adversaries of Di Yunge (Mani-Leib, Moise Leib Halpern, Zische Landau, and the rest). His work appeared in the journal *In Zich* in 1919, and a year later in the anthology of that name. In 1944, with Menke Katz and William Abrams, he edited the journal *We,* and for some years co-edited the *New York Weekly.* Almost to the time of his death in 1962, he sporadically issued a periodical of his own, *Our Horizons,* featuring his extremely modernist poems. During those last years he owned a Yiddish bookstore. His volumes of poetry include *Her Light* (1933), *Light Before the Shutters* (1938), and *Dr. Chaim Zhitlovsky* (1941).

DEBS

Depressed I stand before the prison walls
my hands stretched forth toward him.

Out of his eyes the light that falls
is clear
and golden
as with those completely unbeholden
to their conscience;
and like the clink of gold, that drops
to the floor from a glass vase,
so onto my heart there falls from his lips
the intimate word:
Comrade, comrade, comrade;
and I ask:
Aren't the wings of my spirit flying
over the caged man's head?
Or is my courage dying
in the hour of dread?
O champion chained,
I build you a monument
of my pain.

Fling open the gates of your prisons
and set all the criminals free—
how much you'll resemble them!—
and lock us all in,
all of us,
till the rose-red ideas that swim
in our veins
will puncture, as if with strong fists, all
the prison walls!

Leib Neidus (1890–1918)

Born in Grodno, West Byelorussia, in 1890, LEIB NEIDUS wrote
poems in Hebrew and Russian, as well as Yiddish, from the age of
ten. Later he fixed on Yiddish and his first collection, *Lyrics,* was
published in 1915. The same year he was expelled from school
because of his socialist activities. Two more books, *The Awakened*

Earth and *The Pipe of Pan,* were issued in 1918. Later that year he died of heart disease. *Intimate Melodies* appeared the following year, and his collected works, including many translations of French, German, Russian, and English poetry, were published from 1923 through 1928.

I LOVE THE FOREST

I love the deep forest that drives on and on
and pushes itself toward a sky bathed in sun.
O no, not the woods, but the path set apart
that's cutting its way to the forest's deep heart.

I love the small path that has little to show
but moss and whatever poor wildflowers grow.
O no, not the path, but the lonely abode
to which one is led by the serpentine road.

I love the old house that is verdantly crowned,
that curtains of sheltering branches surround.
O no, not the house, but the girl whose dear face
is found in that house, in that quietest place.

LILIES

On a river—lilies, lilies white, are dying.
Over them for one last time the wind is sighing;
once more for their sake the beams of heaven shine;
and they drink the evening dew for one last time.

Quiet waves come in a rush to greet their grieving;
over them the butterflies lament their leaving;
souls of flowers circle round, and piously,
tremulously, bid farewell on bended knee.

In the west the colors curb their twilight riot;
somewhere with a sigh a shadow stirs the quiet;

and the grass accompanies him, sigh for sigh.
On a river—lilies, pale white lilies, die.

ABROAD

Entire nights (don't ask the number!)
I had a wealth of woes and dreams . . .
hungered for you, as a boat hungers
for the cool billows of the stream.

I hungered as a lock of hair,
dark, woman's hair longs for a flower;
as heaven's blueness longs to share
the fables tolling from a tower . . .

yearned, as an empty crib is yearning
for someone's tremulous repose;
as mirrors crave the unreturning,
as the beginning craves the close. . . .

Eliezer Greenberg (1890–1977)

ELIEZER GREENBERG was born in 1890 in Lipkan, Bessarabia, birthplace of the poets Eliezer Steinbarg, Jacob Sternberg, and Moishe Altman. In 1913 he emigrated to the United States and attended the University of Michigan, ultimately settling in New York in 1927. For some years he contributed to the *Freiheit, Hammer,* and *Signal* as well as to the journals of the opposite camp. *Streets and Avenues* appeared in 1928, followed by *From Everywhere* (1934), *Village of Fishermen* (1938), and *The Long Night* (1946). He also produced monographs on M. L. Halpern, Jacob Glatstein, and H. Leivick. From 1951 to 1954 he served as vice-president of the Yiddish PEN Club. With Irving Howe he later edited anthologies of Yiddish fiction and poetry in English translation, and for several years he served as editor of *Tsukunft*. His final collections were *Eternal Thirst* (1968) and *Remembrance* (1974). He died in 1977.

REALITY AND WORD

The word itself is open, small;
has neither friend nor foe; its role
is not to punish or console;
it looks truth in the face—that's all.

But, planted in the stanza's earth,
the word shoots up and blossoms forth
loaded with life-juice—only then
does it become life's partisan.

STAMMERERS IN ALL THE TONGUES OF THE WORLD

We've quickly learned to stammer
in all the tongues of the world,
yet are deaf and dumb to the sound of our own tongue!
Even stammerers learn
to control their stammering,
to hide how nature went wrong.

At conferences everywhere
our expertise in strangers' holy ways and days
astounds the crowds who hear it.
There, in all tongues, we stammer—
yet are deaf and dumb
to the worth of our own spirit!

But should, on that day of days,
long-dreamt,
the real world-congress come about,

158

where every nation, large or small,
will speak in its own tongue
of its own spiritual gift—
O Jewish daughters, sons who've cast yourselves adrift,
O stammerers in all the world's tongues:
in what tongue other than Yiddish
does Jewish laughter so deliciously ring out?
in what tongue other than Yiddish
are Jewish sobs so bitterly torn from the lungs?

Mark Schweid (1891–1969)

MARK SCHWEID was born in Warsaw in 1891. His verse was first
published when he was sixteen. After graduating from Warsaw's
Theatre School in 1911, he settled in New York, where he performed on the Yiddish stage, ultimately starring at the Morris
Schwartz Art Theatre and, from 1926, on the English stage as
well. His first collection, *Amber Shoes* (1921), was followed by *To
God and to People* (1923) and *I'll Make Tea* (1926). From 1946 he was
a major staff writer on the *Forward*. His collected poems were
issued in 1951; four years later he produced a biography of
Peretz, whom he had known in youth. He also authored, adapted,
or translated about fifty plays, all of which were staged, and
translated novels from Polish, Russian, German, and English. He
died in New York in 1969.

THE MILKY WAY

On the Milky Way are seven narrow footpaths;
at the crossroads sits a shepherd and he plays.
Close behind the shepherd a young queen is standing
in a soft white veil that hides her yearning gaze.

On the seven footpaths seven knights have blundered;
each is clad in armor and his sword is keen.
And he would have found his right road without trouble
if the crossroads weren't blocked by the white queen.

MOIDEH ANI

Moideh ani lefonecho*. . . . God, don't frown—
see what's happened to Thy child on alien ground. . . .
Hard years, wandering here and there—
I no longer know the prayer.

Moideh ani lefonecho. . . . A clean bed,
food, and peace, have pushed the prayer out of my head;
bitter times I've had to taste,
so my prayer has been replaced.

Moideh ani lefonecho. . . . Come to greet me.
Crooked were the paths on which I went to seek Thee.
I'm still young and blind to dangers,
and can be seduced by strangers.

Ephraim Auerbach (1892–1973)

EPHRAIM AUERBACH was born in Beltz, Bessarabia, in 1892. At sixteen he was published in the local Russian paper. His first Yiddish poems appeared in Vilna in 1909. In 1911 he wrote and was published in Warsaw. The following year he joined the pioneer settlers in Palestine, but when the First World War broke out, he was expelled by the Turks along with other Russian nationals and evacuated to Alexandria. Here he joined the Jewish

---

**Moideh ani lefonecho* means "I confess to thee."

Legion and fought at the Dardanelles. Wounded, he emigrated to the United States in 1915. *On the Threshold,* his first collection, appeared the same year, to be followed by *Caravans* (1918), *The Red Thread* (1927), *Our Old Source is Pure* (1940), and *The Tents of Jacob* (1945). From 1948 to 1950 and again in 1954 he served as president of the Yiddish PEN Club. His last book, *Between the Covers of a Book,* was published in 1968, five years before his death.

YELLOW LEAVES

Do not trample yellow leaves;
tree still sings in every vein.
In each leaf the life still breathes,
and, torn off, it still feels pain.
Do not trample yellow leaves.

Do not break the twisted twigs.
They still have the gift of crying.
Naked, each for life still begs
with the instinct of the dying.
Do not break the twisted twigs.

THE FIRST BUILDER

In the daylight hours he dug a well.
In the night he served as sentinel.
By the donkey's and the jackal's keen
he was nourished, nibbling bits of dream.
He sparked fires on the peaks of mountains,
drank flame as others drink at fountains,
with the thirst of winning back his land.
—Who built here first, is with us yet,
with his happiness and his regret,
and he spans the earth that once he spanned.

161

B. J. Bialostotsky (1892–1962)

Born in 1892 in Pumpian, Lithuania, B. J. Bialostotsky started writing Yiddish poetry at the age of ten and was first published in 1909. Two years later he emigrated to the United States and went to work in a Pittsburgh sweatshop. Later he studied at City College, New York. In 1914 he became a Poale-Zionist. He helped found the Yiddish school movement in the United States, was himself an outstanding teacher, and co-edited the first children's journal in Yiddish, *The Children's World*. His first book of poems, *Along Broadway,* appeared in 1920. From 1922 he was a regular contributor to the *Daily Forward*. From 1927 through 1932, along with Z. Weinper and B. Lapin, he edited the journal *Oifkum* (Upsurge). *Poems and Essays,* in two volumes, appeared in 1932. He translated Byron's *Hebrew Melodies* in 1946, edited the *David Edelshtat Memorial Volume* in 1953, and produced *Dream and Reality,* a book of essays, three years later, to be followed by *Song to Song,* his collected poems, in 1958. He died in 1962. *Yiddish Humor and Yiddish Clowns* was published the following year.

AUTUMN

Dawn creeps about, stark naked, on all fours.
The threshold, wrapped in fog, sleeps at the door.

Tree clawed asunder—clayey, heavy house—
vanished away, old Father Summer's voice.

Dawn, stretching forth his hand—so veined, so white—
tears a last leaf to keep his shame from sight.

Fall. Nothing sprouts or flies. The sun remains
behind a cloud: what use would be her flames?

So—naked, Dawn goes creeping on all fours
and hugs the steps—a bastard at the door.

POOR PEOPLE

Poor human beings, the children of labor,
feet caked in mud, faces dirty and worn—
year in, year out, you go on, somehow happy—
feet caked in mud, faces dirty and worn.

Mines tunneled through, highways ploughed and smoothed
    over,
shoulders caved in, hands impossibly swollen;
suns keep declining, and new ones keep rising—
shoulders caved in, hands impossibly swollen.

Calmly you sleep through the nights, as if butchered;
children keep striking new roots in the earth;
wives send their prayers up: O, save us, dear Jesus!
Children keep striking new roots in the earth.

Sacks in their arms, and exhausted thighs gartered,
garments uncared for—all tattered and torn!
Year in, year out, you go on, seldom happy—
feet caked in mud, faces dirty and worn.

Melech Ravitch (1893–1976)

MELECH RAVITCH was born Zachariah Berger in 1893 in Radimno, Eastern Galicia. His early volumes include *At the Threshold* (1912) and *Spinoza* (1918). He lived in Vienna after World War I; then, along with Peretz Markish, he led Warsaw's rambunctious "gang" of Khaliastre poets in the mid-1920s. Among his books of that time are *The Kernel of My Songs* and *Prehistoric Landscapes,* both published in 1922, and *Blood on the Flag,* issued in 1929. Later he became a world traveler—his *Continents and Oceans* was published in 1937—and in 1941 he settled in Canada. *The Songs of My Songs,* a selected edition, appeared in 1954. The same year he moved to Israel but in 1958 returned to Montreal, where he completed an

163

ambitious biographical encyclopedia of Yiddish writers and a major autobiography, *The Story of My Life*. He died in Montreal in 1976.

INSIDE NEW YORK'S STATUE OF LIBERTY

I am a man of blood and flesh and bones;
my soul is love and laughter, tears and groans.
And you—a hollow iron giant—stand
holding the torch aloft in your right hand,
a golem-woman, one whose metal skin
conceals the skeleton of steel within.
No bread was ever kissed by your cold lips;
no man's been cradled in your iron ribs.
And—with a youngling's passion I adore you;
these thirty years I've hungered for you,
for my first sight of you.

I am a poet and a wanderer and a Jew.
The stairways to *my* soul are the unsteady stanzas of my song;
to *yours*—unique amid the billion-headed throng—
to your head and your thought—hundreds of iron stairs.
Your soul is hollow: cold in winter, hot in summer's glare.

And yet how great it is, how wondrous, to be leagued
with others in your soul, to wander up the stairs and grow
    fatigued,
to carry a warm song in me about the love I feel
for you!—through whose thick veins of wire and steel
electric power instead of blood is sent
because you're only golem, symbol—Freedom's monument.

Because you're golem, symbol, monument of Liberty,
I write this song with love, my hand with young excitement
    shakes,
my eyes glow, my blood wakes.
Believe me, woman, when I press my lips to your cold walls of
    metal,
the walls of your proud throat (and kiss them secretly
so none can say: maybe a poet . . . maybe his wits have come
    unsettled),

164

the love I feel is pure and strong,
and like a love song is this song,
because I've never felt such love
for any woman as I have
for Liberty—whose beacon-star
you are.

Although your bright torch seems to face
New York, in fact it sends its rays
across the universe.
One blesses you, another flings his curse;
one honors you, and one detests;
one's serious, another jests;
and I—I offer you my love and perfect trust,
for curse and hate are wind, are dust.

Woman of Freedom, you're a fallen woman, true,
and maybe—maybe that explains my tenderness toward you.
Within your womb, you metal Type, lies curled
the new emancipator of the world.
Though some defame you, make of you their mirth,
alone, in faith and radiance, you'll give birth.
You'll hold your son aloft with his Redeemer-face:
torchlike over the whole human race.

And he who weeps today will rock with laughter,
and he by whom you're now reviled
will weep hereafter.
Fused as one,
led by a child!
Freedom, belovèd, only through your son
will mankind's glory be recovered—
son of the spirit of all your lovers.
O may this song, conceived in love for you, become
part of the spirit whose seed awakes your womb!

HORSES

They lived their lives for eighteen years
and heavy were the loads they drew

and they were a poor twosome—two
forgotten horses, lorn and lone.

And thus for eighteen years that pair
stood in the stall with its floor of stone,
and dust kept falling on their hair
until it lost its radiant hue.

And eighteen years these horses knew
the whip that twists a creature's hide,
and faithfully they earned the straw
of midday and of eventide.

And as they stood one night in the shed
drenched by rain and gnawed by frost,
the elder huddled close in trust,
and, coughing, this is what he said:

I'm weary, brother; without a word
we've toiled together all our days.
Our hide has sores, our vision's blurred,
our knees tremble. It's time to graze.

And as they stood there once at night,
that sad and solitary pair,
their master met a horsemeat-man
in a saloon somewhere.

And with a handshake came to terms
and estimated the market worth
of a sad and lonesome horse
over all the earth.

And it was agreed that one day more
he'd drive his horses into the wood,
one final ride, and part with them
as coldly as one could.

They plodded along like eighteen years.
Into their bodies bit the whip.
A wagon piled with winter logs
they fetched home on this final trip.

And this time, when they came from the woods,
their midday portion was denied—
and sorrowfully to the slaughterhouse
they dragged their own worn hide.

And as they sniffed the blood, this pair
of horses trembled where they stood
and leaned together their long heads
and listened to the blood.

And as their neck-yokes were removed
after full eighteen years of wear
a band of black hide was revealed
where there had once been hair.

And soon, as they rolled about in blood
on the stone floor of the slaughterhouse,
wildly thundered the iron thud
of horseshoes on the slaughterhouse floor.

And this recalled their hoofbeats, year
by year, along hard streets of stone,
that, breathing heavily, had gone
over the wide earth, a poor pair
of horses, lorn and lone.

Meyer-Zimmel Tkatch (1894–1986)

MEYER-ZIMMEL TKATCH was born in 1894 in Priborsk, a Ukrainian village near Kiev. At nineteen he emigrated to the United States, where he became a house painter. His first poems, in Russian, were published in 1914. Afterward he turned to Yiddish, and his work—fables as well as poems—appeared in many journals, including those of the Left. His first collection, *At God's Behest* (1927), was followed by several more in the 1930s, all published in Chicago. A volume of Holocaust poems, *Blood Shrieks From the*

167

Ground, was issued in 1946. Then came *From Generation to Generation* (1947), *Thirst For the Source* (1952), *Fall of Leaves* (1960), and *Mein Hob un Gob* (My Treasures and My Gifts), a 1962 two-volume collected edition. These were followed by *Fruits of Age From the Blossoms of Youth* (1971), *My Anthology of Russian Poetry* (1973), and *One's Own and Another's* (1977). His home was New York, and it was there that he died in 1986.

CALIFORNIA LAND

On the peaks of the land
there descended a snow,
and a battlement rose
as if built by a foe.

And the region around,
unconcerned to the core—
and the region around
greens and blooms as before. . . .

Like a child free of cares
with his mother close by,
California lies calm
in the sun's watchful eye.

IN THE LURAY CAVERNS

"You're in the cave," declares the guide,
and lights a lamp for me.
I look around: it's not a cave—
a temple's what I see.

On sturdy pillars nimbly carved
are hanging mystic drapes,
and altars stand, erected for
the praise of godly shapes.

Nor into sinful human hands
has their command been given—

with holy fear the earth itself
makes real the wraiths of heaven.

And birds, wild creatures, fish and all
can be beheld in stone,
as if Earth brought her family
to worship at God's throne.

And from the ceiling organs hang,
set all aglow, a-trembling.
The guide performs as organist;
one feels a priest is mumbling.

The place is holy. Here was sung
Shekinah's lullaby.
I hear a silken rush, as soft
cherubic wings go by.

I want to fall upon my knees
and offer God my prayers;
and what the guide is chattering
must not now vex my ears.

Kadia Molodowsky (1894–1975)

Born in 1894 in Bereza Kartuska, Lithuania, KADIA MOLODOWSKY
first taught and published in Odessa and Kiev, then became an
extraordinary Yiddish schoolteacher in Warsaw, where she was
persecuted by the police for her anti-Fascist activities. Her early
volumes include *Autumn Nights* (1928), *Dzika Street* (1930), and
Small Shoes Go Away (1933). In 1935 she emigrated to New York,
where she produced *Young Jews* (1945) and *King David Remained
Alone* (1946). Except for a two-year sojourn in Israel (1950–52),
she lived in New York until her death in 1975. Distinguished for
her work in drama and fiction, she is best-known for several
volumes of luminous prophetic poetry, notably *Angels Come to
Jerusalem* (1952), *A Room With Seven Windows* (1957), and *Light of a*

Thorn-Tree (1965), and for her children's verse, collected in *Marzipans* (1970).

JONAH

Though seven times you may transform your form,
disguise the bonework underneath your skin,
yet God will sign and call you through the storm:
To Nineveh!
and cleanse her of her sin.

With covered eyes, obliterated name,
you'll run away to quietude and rest.
God, from the deep, will call you all the same:
To Nineveh!
and do as I request.

You'll give up your old language for the new,
and on your tongue another will be born.
Yet God will call, with genius sprinkle you:
To Nineveh!
and what I ask—perform!

You'll hide in holes, a fugitive cast out with stones,
your body torn with brand and scourge.
Yet God will start a fever in your bones:
To Nineveh!
And as I bid you—urge!

Then you will turn to God with a lament:
Why pick on me to voice your sternest thought?
There is an apple tree I'd like to plant,
or is that not enough for Jonah?
It is enough for all else you have wrought!

Out of the storm a mighty voice replies:
Forget your apple tree, your house and kine.
You've been picked out to care and agonize—
To Nineveh!
and cleanse her of her crime.

170

STAINED LEAVES

Before me an old *siddur** lies
with yellow leaves turned in at certain corners:
at *tkhines*† begging dew and rain,
at Isaac's sacrifice,
and at the blazing lime ovens of Nimrod.
Silent tears have fallen there
and made those pages soft,
as hearts are softened by a prayer,
and all the *yehi ratsons*‡ followed by a finger
and turning black from being seven times said.
Who now, under her arm, will bear
the siddur of God's dread?
And who will turn its yellow pages over?
Perhaps I ought to place it on my table, at the center
of my green cover,
and when a dryness grips
my heart, I'll lift the siddur to my lips.

LIGHT YOUR LAMP

Perhaps I am the last one of my age.
That's no concern of mine.
Not I prepare the seeds of Time.
My day, my only day, was granted
on loan to me.
And I don't know
when its return will be demanded:
at sixty years, or seventy. . . .
I was informed:
You are not waste.
Your day, your only day, must not be harmed.
It's your today, your yesterday, your always, yours alone.
No matter at what table you'll be placed,
there light your lamp, and set your lectern there.

---

*A *Siddur* is a daily prayer book.
†*Tkhines* are women's prayers.
‡A *yehi ratson* is a segment of prayer beginning with "May Your will be
realized!"

Your lamp, too, was bequeathed to you on loan.
You're neither its extinguisher nor lighter.
Whether the day be brighter
than bright, or a hell-blackness blinds the air,
whether it's tranquil or a thunderstorm,
is not for you to care—
just light your lamp and keep it from all harm.
Your flame is in the orb of lights. Where it
was lighted, and by whose hand it was lit,
you do not know. And when it blazes, you
must bear the brilliance, and the burn marks too.

And maybe there's no age that is the last.
I'm not a goldsmith bent upon his task,
forging a chain.
Already he has made the final link,
already he goes home, is at his door,
already eats his bread and drinks his drink.
His chain's complete, and so it shall remain
now and forevermore.

An age of chaos.
An age that saw the heavens fall.
The sun sipped gloom.
On Sinai's slopes were set the stalls of shame.
Here at this table: wrecked, lopsided, lame,
renew your flame.
Set up your lectern on the quaking earth where you encamp,
and light your lamp.
Bone to bone and vein to vein,
tear after tear and splinter on splinter—
that isn't your concern.
Light your lamp and make sure that it burns.

MY LANGUAGE

It does no good
forever grieving
a word that's spoken
or been stilled.
In me

172

there's a white language living,
a word that I
have not unsealed.
And though my language white
is mute,
composed of words as yet unformed,
she strikes my deepest, truest note;
by her my very soul is stormed.

My language white
is letterless
and has no tongue
for her expression.
Deep down in a white silentness
she's marking time for her Creation.

When I myself at last lie mute,
and wonder
at my being dead,
my language white
will tinder
and unseal the words I never said.

I often hear them, when I'm soiled
by nasty jibe
and saucy hoot.
My language white—
she answers back,
she speaks, although my lips are mute.

Rachel Veprinski (1895–1981)

Born near Kiev in 1895, RACHEL VEPRINSKI arrived in the United
States at twelve and became a factory worker a year later. Especially influenced by Morris Rosenfeld, she began writing at
fifteen. Her first book, *Birdcall*, appeared in 1926. For a time she

was an executive board member of the ILGWU. Beginning in 1954, many of her biographical essays were published in the *Forward*. The wife of Mani-Leib, she assembled his scattered writings for the two-volume posthumous *Songs and Ballads* (1955). A 1971 autobiographical novel, *The Crossing of the Hands*, was followed by *Night-Fires* in 1976 and *Poems* in 1979. She died two years later in New York.

AT DUSK

He came home worn by the workaday dust;
the workaday worry was grayed by his suit.
Thus, gaily she set the table with bread
and meat and not a syllable said,
nourishing him like something mute.
As soon as he'd eaten, he went to bed
with a friendly roof over his head.

Softly, softly the evening sang—
and into a sweet repose he sank. . . .
Somewhere out in the field warm sheep
huddled, warmed themselves in their sleep.
Sleep-wings flutter singingly sweet.
She takes a cushion, covers his feet,
and her heart is complete, more than complete.

Jacob I. Segal (1896–1954)

JACOB I. SEGAL was born in 1896 in Solovkovitch, a Ukrainian village. At fifteen he settled in Montreal, where he worked first as a tailor and then as a Yiddish teacher. His early poems were in Russian and Hebrew, but from 1916 on he chose Yiddish, and in 1918 his first collection, *From My World*, appeared. In 1921 he edited *Nuances*, and in 1922, *Epochs*. A second volume, *Poems*, was published in 1926, and a third, *My Melody,* in 1934. For many years he led the Canadian Jewish Writers Association. After the Holocaust he produced *Songs and Praises* (1945) and *A Jewish Book* (1950). Following his death in Montreal in 1954, two more collections—*Last Poems* (1955) and *Poems For Jewish Children* (1961)—were issued.

ABLOOM

Up here at my window,
up in my soundless rooms,
I look for the warm affection
of my neighbor's pretty wife—
each day her face emerges
with soft, kissing eyes
at the opposite horizon
of her window.
And I turn into a thornbush
when the branches of the evening sun
shower it with blood
like a girl's cut fingers.

AUTUMN

The park warden
has let the little fires
out of his green house.
They stand under trees
and eat their leaf-dinner.
With hot lips they kiss
and lick the tasty leaves.
With golden teeth
they crack a twig.
And when they've had their fill,
and when they've stuffed themselves,
onto soft beds of ash
they sink exhausted,
and, thin and soft,

175

blue puffs of sleep come from them,
blue puffs of sleep.

Jacob Glatstein (1896–1971)

Born in 1896 in Lublin, Poland, JACOB GLATSTEIN was first published at seventeen. A year later he settled in New York and, in
1919, turned to Yiddish. The same year he joined N. B. Minkoff
and A. Glanz-Leyeles in founding the introspectivist group and
their controversial publication, *In Zich*. His early volumes include
Poetry (1921), *Free Verse* (1926), and *Credo* (1929); transformed by
the Holocaust, as were most Yiddish poets, his voice deepened in
such works as *Songs From Memory* (1943), *My Father's Shadow*
(1953), *The Joy of the Yiddish Verb* (1961), and *A Jew from Lublin*
(1967). For years he contributed a twice-weekly column, "Plain
and Simple," to the *Day-Morning-Journal*, and a book of his essays
appeared in 1956. Ruth Whitman's translations of his *Selected
Poems* were issued in 1966. Two years later he co-edited, in English, an *Anthology of Holocaust Literature*. He died in 1971.

SMOKE

Through the stack of a crematory
a puff of Jew goes up to glory;
and just as the smoke thins out of view,
his wife and children go up too.

And in those heavenly upper regions
smoke wisps yearn and weep in legions.
God, where you are thought to dwell,
all of us are not there as well.

PRE-SUMMER

On the island
wild thickets thicken.
Wells awake.
Rivers warble.
When spring arrives,
summerkin
bites like a snake.
Youngsummer darts about like a matchmaker.
Newsummer overflows the river.
On the eve of summer, songs multiply in the woods.
Little Summer bites everybody
like a snake—
everybody, everybody,
on the island where the wells awake.

MEMORIAL POEM

Eyes of strangers do not see
how I unlock the door in my small room
and my nocturnal walk begins from tomb to tomb.
(How much soil do puffs of smoke require?)
There one passes peaks and vales,
and meandering, hidden trails
enough to last a walker all night long.
In the darkness grave-marks shine
before me with a mournful song.
Graves of the entire
annihilated Jewish world
bloom in this wretched tent of mine.
And I implore:
Be my father, my mother,
my sister, my brother,
the children I've cherished—
be real as a moan,
my own blood and bone;
become my own perished;
let me know the full pain
of six million slain.

At dawn I lock the door
to the graveyard of my people.
I sit at the table
and set myself a-dreaming with a tune.
The enemy did not master them.
Fathers, mothers, babes out of the cradle,
surrounded Death and conquered him.
Astounded, all the little children
ran toward the Death that sought to kill them,
without crying, like lullabied little Jewish tales.
And soon each blazed forth into flame
like little carriers of God's name.

Who else has such a private
garden of death at night
as I?
Who else will share my fate?
Whom else does so much charnel-ground await?
When I die,
who will inherit my small cemetery
and the radiant grace
of a memorial candle, bright
with everlasting praise?

WATCHMAN OF THE DARK

Day returns, day is fled.
Night returns, night is fled.
In the flux lie joy and dread.

Watchman, watchman of the dark:
Has it wakened yet, your heart?
My heart is forged of steel and flint.
From the valley—a lament.

Here I'll sit and here I'll stay
a million nights, till Judgment Day.

Naftali Gross (1896–1956)

NAFTALI GROSS was born in Kolomai, eastern Galicia, in 1896, to a rabbinical family. He became an apprentice printer in 1910, in 1913 he migrated to Italy, then Canada, and finally settled in New York. There he worked in a print shop until 1917, when he became a Yiddish teacher. Reuben Brainin published his first poems in the *Canadian Eagle*. In 1917 he was a major contributor to the Yiddish edition of Heine. Later he translated the German poets Dehmel, Hofmannstal, and Goethe; the Americans Edgar Lee Masters and Edwin A. Robinson; and, in collaboration with Avrom Reisen, the Spanish Hebrew poet Gabirol. In the 1930s he edited the children's section of the *Day*. In 1943 he became a regular contributor to the *Forward*. Among his volumes are *Psalms* (1919), *Poems* (1920), *The White Knight* (1925), and *Jews* (Volume 1, 1929; Volume 2, 1938). His prose works include a 1933 biography of Eugene V. Debs and *Pictures of the Life of Jewish Workers in America* (1935). His brother, the great artist Chaim Gross, illustrated his selected stories. He died in 1956.

THE OPERATOR

He's as absorbed in what he sews as though
this work is all he was created for.
Beyond the pane he sees no pigeons soar,
nor on the sunlit roofs the melting snow.

At the machines around him, row on row,
bent at their work like him sit many more.
As if under a heavy film they are.
His ear is shattered by a cry of woe.

To slaves of distant times he's brother sworn:
of Egypt, Babylon, Jerusalem
and Rome—an endless chain uniting him
with all the slaves that ever have been born.

And deep within his low and narrow brow
a fire darts about and shoots up strong;

179

as if the battle's being born inside his brain right now,
out of the uproar leaps a liberation song!

Malke Heifetz-Tussman (1896– 1987)

Ranked by Avrom Sutzkever "among the most original of modern Yiddish poets," MALKE HEIFETZ-TUSSMAN was born in 1896 on a Volhynian estate managed by her grandfather, under whose strict guidance she and her many siblings and cousins studied with private tutors. At nine she won her astonishing battle to attend a Russian school in nearby Narinsk, and very early began writing poetry in Russian. Arriving in the United States in 1912, she mastered English quickly and in 1914 wrote for Chicago's anarchist *Alarm.* Four years later her first Yiddish work appeared in New York journals. In 1924, while attending the University of Wisconsin, she began teaching in a Milwaukee Yiddish school. Settling in Los Angeles, she became a public school teacher and in 1949 joined the University of Judaism's faculty. That year her first collection, *Poems,* appeared in Los Angeles, followed nine years later by *Mild My Wild.* Other volumes, issued in Tel Aviv, include *Shadows of Memory* (1965), *Leaves Do Not Fall* (1972), *Under Your Sign* (1974), and *Today is Forever* (1977). Four years later she won Israel's coveted Itzik Manger Prize. It was in Berkeley, California, where her son is a professor of philosophy, that she died in 1987.

FORGIVE

I set foot on your earth adorned in light
and my five senses instantly came open:
I had a "seeing" before I had sight;
a "hearing," but did not hear what was spoken;

180

a "knowing," but knew not one blessed thing.
Thus, haughty as a king,
I strode along your lanes and terraces;
my ears did not accept the chattering
among your children on the streets;
in alien languages
I led discussions at your sabbath feasts;
declaiming in a strident voice, I strolled
along your ways.
I drank your waters, ate your bread,
and gave no thanks before or after.
In short—sweet was the life I led,
and wantonly I laughed un-Jewish laughter.

And woe unto my hurried pace,
woe the bold gait at which I strutted on:
amid your hills I lay and saw my face
reflected in the eye
of your most lovely swan.

Forgive.

Hinde Zaretsky (1899–)

HINDE ZARETSKY was born in 1899 near Minsk. She came to the United States in 1914 and attended Barnard College from 1928 to 1930. Among her books are *The Fourth Melody* (1960), *And He Sang* (1968), *Dream Melody* (1973), and *To the Shores of Tel-Aviv* (1979). She is a longtime resident of The Bronx, New York.

OUR TROUBADOURS

Not from Parnassus did they thunder
praise to a Maker of gray sorrows.

Our troubadours discovered wonders:
their eagle-stare found bright tomorrows.

At the machine they wove their vision.
Greeting the dawn that was to be,
they bathed in joys not yet arisen;
dreaming, our bards set themselves free.

Brotherly love lit up their verses—
not of some distant star they sang.
They saw at odds two mighty forces—
in the front ranks their voices rang!

Joseph Papiernikoff (1899–)

JOSEPH PAPIERNIKOFF was born in Warsaw in 1899. He studied with the cantor Gershon Sirota. During World War I he was held in a German forced-labor camp; afterward he returned to Warsaw, and in 1924 joined the young Zionist Socialist pioneers in Palestine, where he worked in construction and farming for five years. He went back to Poland, but in 1933 he settled permanently in Palestine, where he fought for recognition of the Yiddish language and became known as the poet of labor. His career as a revolutionary and lyric poet began in 1918, and he has been extraordinarily prolific ever since. The three earliest collections of his own work and his 1933 Essenin translations appeared in Warsaw; from 1934, his books have been published in Tel Aviv. Among them are *For Me and Everyone* (1936), *Under Fire* (1939), *My Burning Source* (1945), *The Land of the Second Genesis* (1954), *The Sun Behind Me* (1961), and *Over the Ruins* (1967). In 1973 he produced an anthology, *Jerusalem in Yiddish Verse*. His latest collection is *Renewal* (1985).

MY SPEECH

My speech is the speech of my mother;
whether my love of it pleases the world does not matter;
my lungs thrive on Yiddish no less than on air, though it carry
the odor of leaves on the ground that October has scattered. . . .

I can't change my speech for another
like some kind of shirt; it lies deep in my blood, in my tears;
I sing and will still sing in Yiddish—as long as there's someone
who leans toward my Yiddish and wants it to ring in his ears.

ME

Me, me, me, the same incessant me—
as long as we remain a mystery
to our own selves, we'll never leave ourselves,
and never reach toward anybody else;
as long as we don't search the cave inside
our skeletons, arrive at where we hide,
and that great miracle is ours to see—
it's me, me, me, the same incessant me.

Esther Schumiatcher (1899–1985)

Born in 1899 in the Byelorussian city of Gomel, ESTHER
SCHUMIATCHER moved with her family to Calgary, Canada, in
1911 and studied in the local schools, composing her first poems
in English. She married the great Yiddish novelist Peretz Hirsh-
bein and a worldwide period of traveling began in 1918. Her first
Yiddish book, *In the Valley* (1920), was followed by *Streaks of Light*
five years later and *Hours of Love* in 1930. During that decade she
published both in such nonpolitical journals as *In Zich* and in the
left-wing *Hammer, Freiheit,* and *Red World,* among others. She also

wrote critical essays on such figures as Mani-Leib and Yehoash. She moved from New York to Los Angeles and back; it was in Los Angeles that her *Poems* (1956) appeared. From that time until her death in 1985, her poetry frequently graced the pages of Sutzkever's *Golden Chain* and other journals.

TOM MOONEY

How can I bear the festival of such real, such rooted days,
while for you each sunset yellows to a blazing gallows
and every rush of blood behind the leaden face of you
kindles the anguish of a class in hunger?

The sand here blooms.
Rocks pulse with power.
This soil's been bred to yield up bounties rich and true.
So much room!
a desert so despondent . . .
and one's own blood behind the lock runs true!

I walk here amid dirt roads—
I scarce believe that I am free today.
The sea pours out to the horizon its great heart of blue.
And all at once I sense—the smell of May. . . .
Your barred heart rises like a dawn before me;
the wine is bloody that wells up across the desert sand:
Tom Mooney,
there pushes forward, push by push, a hungry power!
The heart craves open grazing, the heart of this rich land!

From the woe of bread, the woe of deep-cut wounds, the dead,
tidings break forth spectacularly bright:
a crimson rain is falling—
and on the desert's heart
our generation wells up bloodily
and, rooted, row by row the lines ignite.
Over the head of hungry Sorrow
the First of May falls like the rain's sweet dew. . . .

The sand here blooms.
Rocks pulse with power.

This soil's been bred to yield up bounties rich and true.
So much room!
a desert so despondent . . .
and one's own blood behind the lock runs true.

Avrom-Ber Tabachnik (1901–1967)

AVROM-BER TABACHNIK was born in 1901 in Nizhni Altchedaiev, a Ukrainian village, and grew up in nearby Konotkovitch. He emigrated to Waterbury, Connecticut, in 1921 and taught Yiddish for the Workmen's Circle throughout the northeast from 1925 to 1936. His first verse was in Russian, but from 1923 he contributed Yiddish poems to the full spectrum of journals, including those of the Left (*Proletarian Thought, Signal,* and the like). From 1928 to 1931, with Stoltzenberg and Shtiker, he produced *Feiln* (Arrows), an annual collection. His own first volume of poems, *In the Scabbard,* appeared in 1936. From 1938 to 1940 he was on the staff of Philadelphia's *Yiddish World,* and the following year he produced *The Man of Song,* a monograph on Zische Landau. *Poets and Poetry,* his second book of verse, was issued in 1949, followed two years later by a monograph on Stoltzenberg. In 1959 he again joined Shtiker, this time in editing the short-lived *Vogshol* (Scale). A major compilation of his essays, *Poets and Poetry,* appeared in 1965. Perhaps his most extraordinary achievement was a series of recorded interviews with more than twenty Yiddish-American poets. He died in 1967.

YOUR WORD IS FIRE

Your word on my lips is fire,
and I'm drawn to you with my blood;
I will go with you through fire,
I will go with you through blood.

On all sides a desert—and you are the thirsting
of stones, of bones, of sand;
there flamed and flamed in the midst of the prickles
a hawthorn in that land.

Your word is the word of a prophet:
all fire and hardihood;
I will go with you through fire,
I will go with you through blood.

You are a cloud and I your shadow;
you are the fire and I the coal.
I will soar with you to the heavens,
like the dust that sticks to your sole.

THE YOUNG POET
(for Avrom Reisen)

A frost sits in the house;
ice-cold hands and feet;
in the corner scrambles a mouse;
a smoky lamp burns weak.

On the table papers are strewn
with writing scribbled and fine:
"As if it were precious stone,
he chose his every rhyme."

Cold. On the windows form
flowers frosty and fair;
young songs hum like a storm
of silver doves in the air.

Inside his brow, like lightning,
a vein begins to shoot.
The moon climbs slowly, brightening
heaven, a silver hoop—

climbs, and her smile is gracious
as over his roof she swims—

the moon, bright and vivacious
and free, as are his dreams.

MORRIS ROSENFELD ON THE DAY OF HIS 60TH JUBILEE

He lays the pen down; to the windowpane he goes
and looks out:—There's the old street, for whose sake
I put aside a life of exquisite repose
and plunged into the pot of gall and hate.

I was the beggar here, and here I was the prince;
on eagle wings I raised their spirits from the sod;
they paid me back with lies and curses more than once,
and with a cold, a patronizing, nod.

Awake, O Muse, and take a look
at what have been your poet's gains!
I've groaned away my wretched bit of luck:
the rose is withering; the thorn remains.

And do they know? It wasn't this I wanted.
The birds invited me to try the woods.
Before me gleamed the blissful vision I'd been granted
of summer fields that golden sunlight floods.

But in me cried a voice: Yours be the song
of slaves—such groans, such griefs as none but they know!
At that the heart tore loose in me, a flaming seized my tongue—
the song burst forth as if from a volcano,

and streamed out as hot waves of lava pour,
ignited hearts, woke yearnings long kept down;
but . . . my foot sticks to the icy floor,
my stormiest songs are falling to the ground.

You see how I am ranked and prized, how lone I am and ill,
the eyes worn out, the heart half worn away.
And he, the pale one, sits there sweating still;
Motke still lurks to pounce upon his prey.

Boss Motke won—he mocked my roar, outscreamed my song of
    fire;
the lion's old now, all its teeth knocked out;
a heap of ash remains to mark each failed desire;
he has the meat; the bones stick in my throat.

Is it the start or finish? is it nothing
but fools' play, or an evil dream at best?
As if before deep sleep, my lids are shutting;
is that where I at last will win my rest?

But it's my jubilee today; today I'm throned:
a Lear whose realm they take before his final breath,
a Purim-king, imperially crowned,
an ailing Jew, who's ready for his death.

Itzik Manger (1910–1969)

ITZIK MANGER was born in Czernowicz, Rumania, in 1901. He
began writing Yiddish verse at seventeen and was published for
the first time in 1921 in Eliezer Steinbarg's journal. In 1929 he
edited a journal of his own, *With Measured Words,* and saw the
publication of his first collection, *Stars on the Roof.* This was followed by *Songs of the Pentateuch* (1935), among other volumes.
When Hitler took Poland, Manger escaped—first to Paris, then to
London, where he lived from 1940 to 1951. There, in 1949, he
issued a memorial volume for his brother Noteh, who had perished in Uzbekistan during the war. *Midrach Itzik* appeared in
Paris in 1951. The same year Manger settled in New York, where
Songs and Ballads was published in 1952. He made Israel his final
home in 1967, and died there two years later.

EVENSONG

Quiet evening. Dusky gold.
A chair, a glass of wine.
What has happened to my day?
A shadow and a shine—
may something dusky gold at least
reach this song of mine.

Quiet evening. Dusky gold.
An old Jew with gray hair
devoutly prays away the dust
of the thoroughfare—
may there at least enrich my song
a murmur of his prayer.

Quiet evening. Dusky gold.
Wind—world out, world in—
sleeps like a pup. Within
my song may at least a breath of the grief
that was awake but is now asleep
brush through the lines again.

Quiet evening. Dusky gold.
With feathers gold and gray
a summer bird in "God's own keep"
goes fluttering away.
May a tremor of his flight, at least,
enter my song today.

Quiet evening. Dusky gold.
Wind and way and wine.
What has happened to my day?
A shadow and a shine—
may something dusky gold at least
reach this song of mine.

EPITAPH

Here lies the sad, exhausted nightingale
for the first time in a bed that's all his own.

189

The journeyman tailor, plodder, and bard whose well
of song shall henceforth be as still as stone.

Don't tear the nettles from his narrow house,
and in the winter don't brush off the snow.
Nothing can hurt him now, who sleeps below.
He lives in harmony with worm and mouse.

Don't scatter blossoms on the little mound;
don't straighten what the storm wind batters down;
don't chase the owl that makes the grave its throne.

Let flies around him buzz, and bumblebees;
let the gravedigger's goat graze near in peace;
and as for him who sleeps, leave him alone.

THE BALLAD OF WHITE BREAD

Mothers in their tattered shawls
stand at their doors when evening falls.

Extinguished fingers, faces gray,
thirteen apostles of hunger are they.

Evening lights up overhead
the moon like a white loaf of bread.

Sorrowfully their patched hands reach
up toward the loaf that shines on each.

"Save us, holy wheat bread; drop,
holy loaf, into our lap.

"Hunger kneads our daughters and sons
into a city of skeletons."

Past all windows the bright moon floats,
past children-heads, past night-ghosts.

The children smile in the white bread's light
and die an easy death tonight.

In the river the moon burns up her rays,
moon, who cannot fall from her place.

Mothers at their doors stand bent
in tattered shawls, with eyes half-spent.

and soon sit *shiveh** for their dead,
and soon sit shiveh for the white bread.

THE BALLAD OF THE WHITE GLOW

—Enough of crying, daughter mine,
and sobbing forth your woe!
—See, mother, on the flag of night
there is a cool white glow.

—An ignis fatuus, no more,
an ignis fatuus.
To houseless forests let it go,
and not come back to us!

—You tell me that the flame is false,
but how can it be so?
I feel my own heart quivering
within the cool white glow.

—Say quickly, child, your evening prayer.
God knows what may befall!
—It's coming from the other side,
and, mother, it's a call.

And if somebody calls, how can,
how dare I linger here?
Or can I send my heart alone
to answer for me there?

Outdoors a storm wind's started up;
outdoors there falls a snow.

---

*Shiveh comprises seven days of mourning.

191

One moment more, you streaming flakes,
one moment and I go.

She wraps the shawl around herself:
a red one, scarlet-bright;
and her own blood is redder still;
and death? its glow is white.

The mother peers and peers outside;
she sees her daughter yet.
But in the white glow disappears
the slender silhouette.

THE SACRIFICE OF ISAAC

-—What do you see, my sacrifice and son?
—I see a heavy, gloomy hour spread
its wings across the bright blue overhead
and on a cross there hangs a lifeless one.

Why do you stand there, bloodless and stone-dumb,
and from your hand why does the knife slip, father?
—Your handsome death is granted to another;
so put your sorrow on, my child, and come.

—Who is he, who? I want to see his face.
He must be blest and rare and full of grace
who stole my sacrifice!—Come, child, the night

already darkens on the field. We are
a long way from our tent, the road runs far,
and he, the lucky one, not yet in sight.

QUEEN JEZEBEL

Hush. She's lulled her gods, and see how each one sleeps.
(Her gods are marble, gopherwood, and elephant bone.)

Now she stands proud on the veranda—quite alone.
Secretly, coolly through her hair the dusk wind creeps.

Night falls. The old play starts. A firefly cluster leaps
up from the grass with a sad beauty: turn themselves on,
then off, without design, soon kindled, and soon gone,
and deep within her heart at last a small voice speaks,

saying she's one with this, that flares and disappears;
but what does the strange vineyard want of her young years,
trembling in her imagination so—so fresh and good?

The strange-tongued prophet warns. Oh, well, her gods sleep.
    No one knows.
Before her the strange vineyard blazes red. She goes
and does not hear the sorrowing of her own blood.

CAIN

Abel is dead. His death rattle slinks
behind me. A thin wisp of moan
quivers in my wake. I stand alone
back of the hills where the sun sinks.

There, where midnight spreads her wings,
I'll stand on the riverside, head down,
gritting my teeth, awaiting the frown
of Judgment, ready for what it brings.

The first priest, as a sacrifice to you,
offered his firstborn lamb, Jehovah, hear!
Punish me, Father, if punishment be due.

But from the face of heaven falls a tear:
Cain, my child, go cultivate the land;
go forth and multiply like the stars, the sand.

REBECCA

—Why, mother, do you weep when evening blooms?
—In one hour, of two babes I was delivered;
and in one hour I'll lose them both forever.
Then who can lift away a mother's gloom?

Snuff out the sorrow in your eye, and hear:
Upon their lives a star of malice burns,
and from one child the other one will turn.
What binds them now is your maternal tear.

But someday, in the desert, when the sun descends,
one of them suddenly will cross the other's path
and, trembling, understand the perishing red flame.

And one of them will take his brother by the hand
and murmur something sad, and sadly blush with shame—
Life sundered us; now we are twinned again by death.

JOSEPH

How many brothers are you?—Ten, oh lord!
And see the youngest, still a stripling, here.
Spring's earliest wind is playing in his hair.
Our father pines for him, his most adored.

And Joseph looks a long time at the lad;
a smile, as in remembrance, lights his face;
he sees himself, a child in that far place,
and something stirs him: lonely, sweet, and sad.

A look at all the group: his face grows grim.
Then at the boy: a glow wells up in him
and his eyes turn more tranquil, weary, mild.

"I'm Joseph," he blurts out; "you saw not who I am!"
and joyfully he stretches forth his hands to them—
"I grant you pardon, brothers—for the child!"

194

JEPHTHAH'S DAUGHTER

Barefoot in plain smock, a sunflower in her hair,
long on her doorstep she stands burning, eyes
riveted on the road. Was it a pack of lies,
the dream that showed her everything so clear?

What dust clouds-forth on the horizon there?
A host of knights. A shofar blares. Leading the charge
Israel's Judge. Beard growing wild, eyes large,
he lifts the booty on his spear: a head with flowing hair.

Breathless she lets her feet fly on. All ways
blend unto her and colorfully blaze.
It's dusk. The riders' blades flash red as wrath.

"Away!" the Judge waves; but she keeps her course,
seizes the bridle of the foremost rider's horse:
it is her father's—on his face a stern mask: Death.

Ricudah Potash (1903–1965)

RICUDAH POTASH was born in 1903 in the Polish town of Chen-
stohov. At twenty-one she moved to Lodz and joined its group of
young poets. When she was sixteen her first verse was published
in Polish, but she turned to Yiddish following the 1922 pogrom in
Lemberg. Her first collection, *Wind on Keys,* appeared in Lodz in
1934. The same year she settled in Palestine, where she served as
librarian of Jerusalem's Jewish Art Museum until her death. Her
second volume, *From the Vale of Kedron,* published in London in
1952, won high praise from Sholem Asch and other critics. Eight
years later her final book, *New Moon Over Timnah,* was issued in
Jerusalem. A dramatic mystery, *Cliffs,* was staged, and parts of it
were published, as were many short stories and prose portraits.
Two additional volumes, *Jerusalem* and *Seven Graces,* were on the

verge of publication at the time of her death in 1965. Those books have not appeared.

SAFAD

In the flood of all I remember
you lie with windows of amber
and on a fiddle phrase your prayer.

So with seven swallows I sit
and with them warble the morrow;
Lord of Creation, what
can swallows know about sorrow?

Safad is the home we share;
with me on the mountains they slumber;
they cover themselves with sky
while under the leaves I lie,
the same sweet golden leaves
that once were Adam's and Eve's;
from the blue that flames from the mountains
menorah stars are lit.

In the flood of all I remember
you lie with windows of amber
and on a fiddle phrase your prayer.

Abba Stoltzenberg (1905–1941)

ABBA STOLTZENBERG was born in Galina, Galicia, in 1905. Settling in New York at eighteen, he earned a meager living as a garment worker. Turning from Polish to Yiddish poetry, he allied himself

with Di Yunge, collaborating with Meyer Shtiker on one of their
first published poems. From 1928 to 1931, with Shtiker and A.
Tabachnik, he edited the journal *Arrows*. In 1941, just before the
publication of his first book, *Poems,* he died of cancer.

ASHES

The table splashed with tea gone stale and cold;
ashes and ashes and cigarettes half-smoked;
things scattered everywhere, threadbare and old.
The doorknob's disappeared—one day it broke.
The winds, as through an empty house, career.
By now my cloak looks like a beggar's cloak.
What nails me to the naked floor? Why am I here?
Hands freeze upon an hour that long since struck.

POOR WOMEN

The women of the poor are serflike;
in heavy toil they're harnessed up;
they move obediently and sadly
as if beneath a master's whip.

The lovely hands grow rough and bony;
the slender fingers soon grow red
from scrubbing clothes, from lugging water,
from kneading clay, from kneading bread.

From plucking sacks on sacks of feathers
their shoulders gradually cave in;
the blooming years stand still, like water
in stagnant pools, like days of rain.

Their speech is soft, with words of weeping,
a sick blue lip that scarcely stirs—
but at the holy place, where women sob who're wealthy,
a poor one pulls down sepulchers.

Meyer Shtiker (1905–1983)

Born in Boiberik, Galicia, in 1905, MEYER SHTIKER studied Hebrew and German. During World War I he moved with his family to Vienna, then returned to his birthplace, where he became a member of the Hashomer Hatzair (Young Guard). Settling in New York early in 1920, he became a hatter and simultaneously attended evening classes. He was first published at nineteen; one of his early poems was written in collaboration with Abba Stolzenberg, and his first prose pieces appeared in the left-wing *Young Smithy*. His eclectic aestheticism manifested itself in translations from T. S. Eliot, Rilke, Rimbaud, Julian Tuwim, and Osip Mandelstam, among others. In 1928, with Tabachnik and Stolzenberg, he edited the journal *Arrows*. His first collection, *Poems*, was issued in 1945. From that year through 1979 he served as news editor, first on the *Morning-Journal*, then on the *Day-Morning-Journal*, and finally on the *Forward*. In 1958 another collection, *Jewish Landscape*, was published, as was a translation of Hemingway's *The Old Man and the Sea*. A year later, again with A. Tabachnik, he edited a journal, *The Scale*. *The Dream is My Witness* (1965), was followed two years later by a translation of another Nobel laureate, this time the German-Jewish Holocaust poet Nelly Sachs. Shtiker died in New York in 1983.

KARL MARX VISITS HEINRICH HEINE
(excerpt)

A pot of water's boiling on the fire
and singing into the attentive ear.
The long face—yellowed into wax, and tired—
and from the eyes a sad, unearthly stare.

Half opening his lips, he sobs: "My friend. . . .
A chair, Mathild!" Although he feels each throe
down to the seventh rib, throes without end,
suddenly soft, mild words begin to flow:

"My friend . . . I have become a burned-out bush,
a ladder's sawed-off, last rung. . . . Pardon us
a moment. . . . Come here, my La Mouche,
and wipe away the miserable pus.

"I am . . . I am . . . I am . . . Well, what am I
today? Take off my chains, Mathild!" And while
the woman buzzes round him like a fly,
he and his friend exchange a bitter smile.

ROME, OCTOBER 7

There was a pair of shoes I chanced to find
in Rome—some sidestreet onto which I'd strayed.
Near Via Labicana—it comes to mind.
The spot: a withered tree, under its shade.

The laces had been filched; the soles were hollow,
like mouths wide open in a silent scream;
the toes—bashed in, as if in rage; a yellow
glow came from the heels, an eerie sheen.

The midnight hour was close; I did not want
to miss the trolley; still, unthinkingly,
halting a moment in my tracks, I bent
into the shadow of the withered tree.

I stretched my curious fingers toward the ground;
but fire and ice at once ran through my bones:
instead of two cadaver shoes I found
myself alone upon the paving stones.

BALLAD ITZIK MANGER

—Where, Itzik, so late, so late? The way
is frightful. The way could not be longer.
Why spread your shadow over the gray

of cities, mouth open as if to pray—
whither so late, so late away?
Whither away, Itzik Manger?

—For me the way is not frightful, not long.
I go with the stars, I go with the wind.
I breathe as they breathe, sing their song.
And if the moon pales as she goes along,
I'll go on just as long, as long,
till *my* light too is dimmed.

—Why, Itzik, has your road no end?
Rest up, and give your throat a treat.
Others before your time have spanned
from city to city, from land to land,
and with an embarrassed beggar's hand
returned to their own street.

—Some feel lost on one acre of ground;
on hundreds, some feel penned and punished.
I love my destiny, duty-bound
to grieve like the stars, who sob without sound,
and fall as they fall to the ground, to the ground,
cold and mute and astonished.

MAKE MY WORDS SIMPLE, GOD

Make simple, God, the words I make,
like dusky water in a dale
that hears an echo fade and fail
in the abyss of summer's night,
and like a starbeam stirred awake
that long had been a dreaming light.

Out of my eye extract the dew.
I'm patient as an asphalt mass
within whose veins a tongue of grass
lies cold, when autumn's hour is late.
Make my words gray, and lowly too,
but give them their full scope and weight.

A last star quivers its blue ray.
The earth dreams: heavily it breathes.
A wind arrives on storm-cloud steeds
with frost-decked limb, with frost-decked mane,
and now at last my words grow gray,
and now at last my words grow plain.

WHEN I DIE

The stars will all accompany me when I die.
Amid their neat, well-tended gardens in the sky
they'll lay me out to my entire length and breadth.
Their thronging grief won't cause me a constricted death,
and their rich burial gift will be a rush of singing—
with fiddles, flutes, drums rolling, trumpets ringing.
The stars will follow me in all their mournful ranks—
I send them in advance: My warmest thanks!

Menke Katz (1906–)

MENKE KATZ was born in 1906 in Sventsian, near Vilna, into a family of woodcutters and millers. He spent part of his boyhood in the nearby town of Michalishek. With his parents, he emigrated to Passaic, New Jersey, at the age of fourteen and became a clockmaker. He studied at Brooklyn College, Columbia University, and the New York Jewish Theological Seminary. For thirty years he taught in the Yiddish schools. His poems were first published in 1925 in such left-wing journals as *Spartacus, Signal, Hammer,* and *Freiheit.* His early volumes include *Three Sisters* (1932), *Man at Dawn* (1935), and *Burning Village* (1938). With Jacob Stodolsky he edited the journal *We* in 1944. In midcareer he turned from the Proletpen circle and afterward chose English as the major language of his poetry. He has edited the English quarterly *Bitterroot* for a quarter of a century. *Safad,* a collection of

Yiddish poems written during a two-year sojourn in that village from 1954 to 1956, was published in Tel Aviv in 1979. He lives in an upstate New York town.

THE POMEGRANATE TREE IN OUR YARD

Of what does it remind us, our yard's pomegranate tree,
if not that my people will be millenniaful,
full of man's blessings and earth's, toilful and harvestful;
as full of ripe kernels, our pomegranate tree.

If Abraham rested now at the pomegranate tree,
he might see the Jews not as stars but as kernels,
uncounted kernels of the pomegranate tree.
Each of them can teach us the eternal.

Oh how many times has my people, in death and woe,
a mourner with ash on its head, been doubled over
as if God had created my people of tears alone—
now only our pomegranate tree is doubled over.

See how in joy the ripest pomegranate bends its branch.
Each bright pomegranate a childlike tomorrow on every branch!

JOY

And as for him whose step my people's soil has never known,
never has his step been blessed with the joy of coming and going.
What joy is there in the simple wonder of coming and going?
O ask a ray how often over the eastern rim the sun has gone,
ask a leaf how many Mays have come and gone;
for those who tread this soil the Burning Bush burns on.
No, he whose step my people's soil has never known,
never has his step been blessed with the joy of coming and going.

A step on my people's soil is a step through everywhere;
all the afars of time are near as one's own step.
Fair as the lily of the valley let my song be fair.

Where, if not in the Song of Songs, are flowers that live forever?
Blown by the wind, a speck of the valley seeks the hill, its father.
In the most workaday week God holds his festivals here.
A step on my people's soil is a step through everywhere;
all the afars of time are near as one's own step.

AN ORANGE

Today, for the first time in Israel,
I saw a simple orange on a tree.
The first orange I beheld in Israel
seemed like God's first gem, like the light of Genesis, to me.

Just so tremulous, in New York, I received
my first kiss on the stones of Delancey Street.
Just so curious, Adam heard the call of Eve,
bartered Eden for the taste of a fruit, earth-sweet.

As if with immortal fingers, I tore the orange free,
as if, all of a sudden, this had become
God's Tree; as if its orange was the sun's round key
for opening all the blessed years to come.

Before us the light of the End of Days will shine;
Jerusalem will yet drive Sodom from the earth;
Isaiah will yet break the sword for all time;
Eden will yet leave us a bright earthly path.

L'Chaim, Jews! Yesterday's gloom won't block the dawn that is
    ours—
Jews with the scent of fresh-ploughed desert earth—
Jews with the radiance of all Abraham's stars. . . .
Like the orange, my people is destined for sap, and feast, and
    mirth.

Today, in an orchard, for the first time, Israel
gave me a simple orange as a gift.
Today, for the first time, in Israel
I thanked God for having lived.

Nahum Bomze (1906–1954)

NAHUM BOMZE (family name Frischwasser) was born in Sasov, Galicia, in 1906, the youngest of ten children. At the outset of World War I the family fled to Nicolsberg, Moravia, returning home in 1918. Bomze studied in German and Polish-Yiddish schools in Lemberg and also learned prayer-shawl weaving, a major Sasov craft. His first book, *In the Days of the Week,* appeared in 1929. He soon moved to Warsaw, where *Barefoot Steps* appeared in 1936 and *A Guest at Twilight* in 1939. He fled east before the Nazis. His collection *Passage* appeared in Soviet-occupied Lemberg in 1941. He served in the Red Army, but was later evacuated—first to Kharkov, then to Kazakstan, where he worked in a Tashkent kindergarten. Returning to Poland in late 1945, he became editorial secretary of the Lodz journal *Yiddish Writings,* but he left for New York in 1948. There, a year later, his *Autumn Wedding* was issued. He died in 1954, while preparing Mani-Leib's posthumous volumes for the press.

ALONE

Alone at midnight lying
I whispered into my ear:
"You have done so much dying;
let Death once more appear.

"You'll wait; you'll shrug, unshaken,
and take the saber's blow.
And when the grasses waken,
up from the ground you'll grow."

Brache Kopstein (1909–)

Born in Priluki, near Kiev, in 1909, BRACHE KOPSTEIN lived with her grandfather in Kishinev after being orphaned at eleven. Migrating to Winnipeg, Canada, in 1924, she worked by day and went to night school. She moved to New York in 1933. Her poetry began appearing two years later in *Literary Leaves* (Warsaw). Her collections include *I Am Strong* (1939), *Sing My Heart* (1945), *The People Are Here* (1951), and *Selected Poems* (1968). With her husband Benjamin Katz she settled in Tel Aviv in 1949. Her brother is the distinguished Soviet choral director Moishe Kopstein.

WAITING

Two A.M. Late and drear.
And the clock strikes: Not yet here.

Night crawls on. Drear and late.
And the clock strikes: Wait up, wait!

Creak! a cricket holds its breath.
Pitch-black hush—a game of death.

Ears prick up at every tread.
Hot as live wire grows the bed.

Heartbeats tick away each minute;
bosom nests a shade within it.

Bosom cold, pale with fear:
off to look for work somewhere. . . .

Wait! a rustle—wait! one more!
Here he comes, he's at the door.

Two—the hour hand moves—then four—
knob unturned, and footless floor.

A. Lurie (dates unknown)

A. LURIE (pseudonym for Jacob Birnbaum) was born in Chernobyl, the Ukraine. In 1951, while in a displaced persons camp in Germany, he prepared a volume of his poems entitled "Almási Tér" for publication, but it did not appear in print. The collection, named for a square in Budapest, recorded his wartime experiences. The same year he emigrated to the United States. Since then he has contributed many poems and stories to such journals as *Di Goldene Keit, Bai Zich, Tsukunft, Unzer Tsait,* and *Yiddishe Kultur.* He lives in New York.

THE BIRD

You bird that are nestless, you warbler of winging,
I am your Creator, the Lord of your singing;
I breathed down your throat every sound, every tone,
so that you would not be as still as a stone.

I ripped up the clay in whose clutch you were muted,
and frolicsome notes in your palate I rooted,
that singing might sweeten your wandering ways
and that you might choke your dejection with praise.

And now you have turned into song altogether:
a flute in the blueness, on wide-floating feather;
and all that I ask is to earn what I'm due—
in radiant songs to accompany you.

Soviet Poets

David Hofstein (1889–ca. 1952)

Born in Karostichev, near Kiev, in 1889, the son of a farmer, DAVID HOFSTEIN wrote his first poem in Hebrew at nine. Later he wrote in Russian and Ukrainian as well. At seventeen he taught in a nearby village. Later he took courses in Kiev. After army service he attended Kiev's Commercial Institute and studied philology at the University of Kiev. It was not until 1917 that he wrote and published in Yiddish. Two years later his first collection, *Along the Roads,* was issued. Under attack for signing a protest against the suppression of Hebrew, he went to Berlin in 1923, leaving behind his motherless sons. His collection, *Wall Panels,* appeared there. Two years later he moved to Palestine, but he returned home in 1926 and was "rehabilitated." Many books followed, including *Selected Poems* (1931), *Orchestra* (1933), and *In Our Days* (1939). The same year, with Itzik Feffer, he edited *Nations Sing,* and in 1940 he co-edited Mayakovsky's *Poems.* In the decades from 1919 to 1939 he also translated major works by Andreyev, Upton Sinclair, Henri Barbusse, Pushkin, Schiller, and Shevchenko. In honor of his fiftieth birthday his poems were issued in Russian translation. A war volume, *I Believe,* appeared in 1944, and two years later the government gave him a medal for heroism during the war. His *Selected Works* were published in 1948. The same year he was arrested, but—according to Broderson's widow—went insane and could therefore not be shot with the others. He died later in the prison's mental ward. A volume of his poems in Russian translation was issued in 1958.

I KNOW THAT ALL
(To Russia)

I know that all things come from deepness,
I know that all things come from breadth,

and yet I love the tower of steel that mocks at weakness,
I love the flag that waves and shows the wind a path!

And I can bear my crimson sorrow lightly,
and am prepared to crave a new delight,
when I behold your sword-sharp look: how brightly
it flashes, putting multitudes to flight.

The teardrops in your eyes, that have been flowing
so bitterly for years, no longer fall.
And now, instead of tears, two drops are glowing:
two bright green drops of gall.

And I have long provided blood and marrow
to set new flags ablaze.
I'm certain that to wager on Tomorrow
                              pays!

A GREETING

From Moscow, the center of bold conflagrations,
I send you, dear mother, my warm salutations.

The fronts are all bloody; like serpents they ring us—
and ever more wide the horizons between us.

To what a wild beat must your heart now be driven,
your heart, under which you have carried eleven!

Or did your wise heart from the very first know it:
your boy had been born to the Jews as a poet?

And just as my spirit took strength from your breasts,
today it is nourished by worldwide repasts.

From Moscow, the center of bold conflagrations,
I send you, dear mother, my warm salutations.

IN EACH YIDDISH WORD

In each Yiddish word—be it wild, be it mild, be it dear—
such radiant flame, such a call to renewal rings clear,
that winds rushing off on their missions of life and of death
cannot blow away its bright breath,
and ashes of ages cannot cause its tinder to die,
its boisterous tinder that startles the hush of the sky.

In each Yiddish word, that a moment ago broke its chains,
that restlessly roves toward the steppes and the plains,
a confident peace in the breadth of an epic is heard.
And not in the speech of the holiest sentries alone—in the word
of herdsmen the songs of proud reapers begin to appear,
an omen arises of garners resounding with cheer
in each Yiddish word—be it wild, be it mild, be it dear.

Leib Kvitko (1890–1952)

LEIB KVITKO was born in Oleskovo, the Ukraine, in 1890, the son
of a teacher. Orphaned while very young, he was brought up by
his grandmother and had to earn his living at the age of ten. Two
years later he began writing verse, but it was not until 1918 that his
work saw print. In 1919 his first book, *Step*, was published. From
1922 to 1925 he worked at his government's Hamburg mission.
He lived in Kharkov from 1926 to 1936, active in the revival of
Yiddish theater and on the staff of the journal *Red World*. In 1929,
after the publication of *Struggles, 1917–1929*, he came under
attack by the Proletarian Writers' Group, Russia's equivalent of the
Proletpen. Stripped of his editorial post, he became a tractor
worker. In 1936 he moved to Moscow, and three years later he
was awarded the Red Worker's Banner. The same year his book
New Poems was issued. His works achieved immense popularity
and were published in huge editions in many Soviet languages.
Prior to his arrest in 1948 he produced two more volumes: *Songs
That Suit My Mood* (1947) and *Selected Works* (1948). He was among

those murdered in prison in August 1952. *Early Years,* about to be issued in 1941 but destroyed by Nazi bombs, was finally published in Moscow in 1984.

DAY AND NIGHT

Day and night—
frozen we wait through the fierceness of day
for moonlit night,
for the tender moon.

In terror we wait through the fierceness of night—
for sunlit day,
for the merciful sun.

Day and night—
we loom large in their eyes,
they spend themselves on us.

We're small, so very small—
fear drags us to earth
as if we belong to it.

What else can we do with ourselves,
we small ones?
What can we do with our large pain,
pain?
love?
secrets?

Day and night—
we loom large in their eyes,
they spend themselves on us.

GET UP AT BREAK OF DAY

Don't laze; get up at break of day
and from the valley hear the crows.

You'll hear on high and far away
how splendidly their echo grows.
The old are outcawed by the young.
It knocks at unseen peaks and comes
back to the vales from which it sprang
and there is shattered into crumbs.

At dawn, before things stir, the voice of nature
is lifted first of all; from wood
and field and riverbank a host of creatures
hymn all at once in brotherhood.
If you would soothe your heart and give it
the nourishment it hungers for,
be at the start of the exhibit,
thrill to the music's opening bar.

CABBAGE

Only a cabbage, you judge;
and yet it has ways of its own.
Root it too close to the hedge,
and there it will spite you, ungrown.

Wrinkled and veiny the skin,
a head coarse enough to seem vicious;
but tenderness houses within,
a nature that's proud and capricious.

It can't and it won't grow concealed
by hedges or structures or stalls.
Its world is a wide-open field;
in freedom it thrives—without walls.

A THREE-PART SONG

1.

I love you more than words can say;
as if it were myself who formed you,

213

myself, out of a special clay,
and gathered such hair to adorn you
that all the world would ring with praise,
and for your eyes chose such a pair,
with brows above them so severe,
that all the world would be amazed.

So, limb by limb, I put you together—
to live forever and love forever.

2
I run to you through suns and winter gales
as surely as the train runs on its rails.
No grief, no treason, tears the eagle's breast.
He bathes in clouds, rejoices in his nest.
Beyond the clouds, beyond the rains I fly
on unfamiliar paths across the sky,
and turn back to my nest of clay and stone
because I, like the eagle, love my home.

3
Together, together we turn the wheel,
together, together unfruit the trees,
                dance a reel,
                sail the seas!
together even the pains we feel.
Together, together we go on living,
moving together from craving to giving,
                singing with one breath,
                paving our one path,
one, even in longing and grieving.

Entirely one, in flesh and bone—
but Death arrives for each alone;
by each alone his whisper is heard—
and that I regret, regret beyond words.

214

Moishe Broderson (1890–1956)

Born in Moscow in 1890, MOISHE BRODERSON was brought up by an uncle in a Byelorussian town, then joined his father, who had settled earlier in Lodz. His first collection, *Black Leaves,* appeared in 1913. Through the First World War and the revolution he lived in Moscow, then returned to Lodz for twenty years. There he authored such volumes as *Pearls in the Trough* (1920) and *Transition* (1924), along with *Much Good Will It Do You* (1922) and other children's books. In 1939 he fled east before the Nazi invaders. The same year *Fifty Poems* appeared. He became involved in experimental theater, and his play *Before the Holiday* was performed in Moscow in 1947. Unlike many of his colleagues, he survived the murders of 1952. He was banished to a Siberian slave-labor camp, from which he was freed in 1955. A year after his release he died in Warsaw. His *Selected Writings* were issued in Buenos Aires in 1959. In 1970 he was reinterred in Haifa. Four years later *The Last Song* was published in Tel Aviv.

TIME LAUGHED

Time laughed into my eyes, its head thrown back
so violently, its guffaw-attack
so long-lasting, its thrust so sharp and biting,
that through my eye there came a bolt of lightning;
and like a splinter of the ringing laughter
insanity pierced through my skull long after.
I heard in me the whining of a cur
ever more heartless, wilder, wickeder:
"Am I my brother's keeper?"—and at this
there fell a lightning-stroke from heaven's rafter:
a rope to choke my dead and buried bliss.

Aaron Kushnirov (1891–1949)

Born in 1891 in Boyarsky, near Kiev, the son of a forest worker, AARON KUSHNIROV began writing poetry in 1909. He worked for a grain dealer and served as an army conscript from 1914 to 1917, participating in a number of battles. In 1920 he joined the Red Army. His first collection, *Walls,* was issued the next year, followed by *Whirlwind* (1929), *Poems* (1938), *East and West* (1940), and *Selected Works* (1947). He also translated Lope de Vega, Lermontov, and Gorky. His last collection, *Father Commander,* was issued in 1948, the year of the purge. Leftwich calls him a "victim" of that horror, but other sources indicate that he died in 1949 shortly after a public appearance in which he was expected to denounce his imprisoned colleagues but instead broke down and was silent.

MY EARTH LIES

Feverish my earth lies, thirst unslaken
and her lips are parched, are burned with pain—
over her the blue spring has not shaken
all its blessèd sieves heaped full of rain.

Summer glows, yet earth has not been wakened
by its lightning, thundering trumpet cry—
ah, in vain, in vain the fields are aching
for a sated song of full-grown rye.

To the creviced ears of hedges making
not a sated but a hungering song;
windmills freeze—as those whose hearts are breaking
let the sky see how their hands are wrung.

DIE, DIE MY OUTCRY

Die, die my outcry! never
in heaven will you be heard.

Night wields the moon like a cleaver
over the throat of the earth.

Soon on the dogs' mad baying
stillness will choke itself.
But night will not stop slaying,
and no one will run to help.

To whom can the cry be cried now?
For mercy, to whom can we kneel—
when stars in terror hide now
in the river's wrinkled steel?

Isaac Platner (1895–1961)

Born in Sokolov-Podliask, Poland on 17 November 1895, Isaac
Platner as a boy became an active Poale-Zionist, undertaking
illegal missions. He attended the fifth World Congress of Poale-
Zion, held in Vienna in 1919. A year later he helped edit Kovno's
left-wing Poale-Zion *Workers' Press*. His poems began appearing in
Kovno, Vilna, and Bialystok in 1921, the year he left for the
United States. He remained here for a decade, first as a shop
worker, later as a teacher. A key member of the Union Square
group and of Proletpen, in whose publications his work appeared,
he emigrated to the Soviet Union in 1932. Settling in Minsk, he
enjoyed a distinguished career as editor and poet until his incar-
ceration in a Siberian labor camp during the purge of Yiddish
writers. Eight years later, in 1956, he was released and returned to
Minsk, resuming his interrupted work. Especially noteworthy
were four volumes of children's poetry, published in Russian and
Byelorussian editions from 1957 to 1962, the year after his death,
and a commemorative book on the murdered Soviet-Jewish writers, *About the Missing*.

OF MY OWN SELF

Of my own self I've made a full confession;
and, after all, what is there to confess?
since more than what's in his possession
a person can't possess. . . .

But with my own self what is to be done,
who cannot keep his mouth shut even now?
Mine is the loneness of a setting sun,
and mine the joy of April's greening bough.

The genuine poet fashions his own song.
With his own tune the true composer charms our ears.
Or else the earth would tire of having turned too long,
and Time would grow embittered, bored to tears.

Of my own self not one word have I said,
and there is more to say than can be reckoned.
I see how Time keeps galloping ahead,
nor can I overtake a single second.

I'm no more than a drop in the sea-swell,
a mote in the enormous universe;
but on life's tide my poems crest as well,
and I can craft the tones of my own verse.

And something would be lacked, were I not here;
and something, when I'm not here, will be missing
—because the wholeness and the beauty of this sphere
are in each sound, each song to which men listen.

Peretz Markish (1895–1952)

Born in 1895 in Polnoe, Volhynia, PERETZ MARKISH began writing
Russian poetry at fifteen. He joined the army in 1916, fought on
the German front, and was wounded. A year later his first Yiddish

poems were published. Kvitko, Hofstein, and Bergelson joined him in founding the Kiev School of writers in 1918; with the publication of their anthology *Eigens* (Our Own), Soviet Yiddish literature was born. From that time until his sojourn in Poland three years later, he produced five volumes of poetry, beginning with *Thresholds*. In Warsaw, with Uri-Zvi Greenberg, Ravitch, and Zeitlin, he moved Yiddish poetry into exuberant and shocking new paths; they defiantly accepted the contemptuous epithet of "Khaliastre" (The Gang) as their name. In Paris he co-edited the anthology *Khaliastre*. In 1926 he returned to his homeland. *The Brothers* appeared three years later, and *Selected Poems,* in 1933. The Spanish civil war inspired *Poems for Spain* (1938), but it was the anti-Hitler struggle that called forth his greatest responses, culminating in the epic, *War,* published in 1948, and a huge novel, *March of Generations.* Along with many other Yiddish writers he was imprisoned in 1948, and was murdered on 12 August 1952. His *Works* were issued in a two-volume Russian edition in 1960.

IN THE LAST GLIMMER

In the last glimmer of the sun,
    alone
on roads that darken fast—
    what can I ask?

In the black ashes of the night that falls,
    played false,
swinging from peak to dizzying peak—
    what goal is mine to seek?

In the black woods of rest
    where branches darkly, densely throng—
who will draw close to me at last?
    to whom at last can I belong?

NIGHTCRY

From back of the mountains a sorrow comes creeping:
so hunted a howling, so haunted a cry!

219

What is it? the darkness, that's set itself weeping?
or do the hills moan at the darkening sky?

What makes the hills cry? Have they also been frightened
by heaven's weird stillness, the sunsetting frost?
The wind and the saplings are certainly fighting
because in their lonely ascent they've got lost. . . .

And maybe a man too is lost there and lonesome
and night falls there too and the wind hounds him there. . . .
From back of the hills the mysterious moan comes,
and sneaks away into the darkness somewhere.

SPLINTERS

Unblinded, recognizing once again the me I've known,
it wounds me to awake and with my eyes torn open
see that my heart's dropped like a mirror on a stone
and with a loud crash into pieces it has broken.

Indeed, not every smithereen has been flung free
to witness all my being, all I was allotted.
O Time, my judge, I beg you not to trample me
till I have sought out all the splinters that lie scattered. . . .

I'll try to gather them together—one by one—
unite them, side by side, till every finger's bloody
—and yet, for all my cunning, when the job is done
I'll still see in the glass a warped, fragmented body.

In sorrow the solution comes to me at last—
now, in the pain of fracture, in a flash I see
the grief of wishing one's self in the looking glass
whole, who lies splintered over all the seven seas.

IN AND OUT

The day diminishes. The sky falls, bleak and chill.
The sunset warns how little time we're to be granted.

220

As in a wood, I go around within you still,
where—in and out—everything's tangled and enchanted.

Your heart is close. I hear its music like a well
of my own self, but don't know how to reach its rim.
As in a wood, I go around within you still,
a wood where I've not ever been.

The shadows greet each other. Each confounds my will.
They streak the trail—bewilderment instead of trail.
As in a wood, I go around within you still;
the more I go, the more I fail.

Within my heart, from every eye I hide you well;
but also hide the path to you from my own eye.
As in a wood, I go around within you still,
and every moment I go faster, till I fly.

The day fades. Soon it will sink behind a hill.
What if it's gone? if night falls, night with not one star?
As in a wood, I go around within you still,
and, like the first time, blaze a path to where you are!

Moishe Kulbak (1896–1940)

MOISHE KULBAK was born in Smorgon, Lithuania, in 1896, the son of a forester and a farm girl. Like many others, he began as a writer of Hebrew poetry, but soon turned to Yiddish. His first volume, *Songs*, appeared in 1920. That year he left to study in Berlin, where he completed a second book, *New Songs* (1922). Returning to Vilna in 1923, he became a professor of literature and wrote two prose works, *Messiah, Son of Ephraim* (1924) and *Monday* (1926). Two years later he moved to Byelorussia and joined the Minsk group of Yiddish poets, equivalent to the Proletpen. In 1929 a three-volume edition of his *Works* was issued, followed by a novel, *Zelmenianer* (1931) and a Byronic mock epic,

221

Childe Harold of Dissen (1933). He also translated Gogol's *Inspector-General* for the Yiddish Theatre of Minsk. *Selected Poems*, 1934, marked the zenith of his career. Three years later he was arrested, along with Izzy Charik, charged with "nationalism." Both were sentenced to deportation. He died in an internment camp in 1940.

ROUND AND ROUND AND ROUND I GO

Round and round and round—that's how I go—
a year, two, three, and more—for all I know.
So there I come, unasked for, everywhere;
and everywhere it's bleak and bare. . . .

It's bleak and bare
and lonely there,
and dull and drear,
brr! . . .

RECOGNITION

Pressed full length upon the ground
and looking round—
I strained to hear
once more the raw peaks' and the flatlands' sound.
The soul, that has already wandered
here and there,
has tranquil dreams;
but like the field, the body ponders—
as the gnarled willows leaning over streams
ponder on things.

Thou whom, housed behind all gates,
I fail to see—
Thou, with bright curtains hung about Thy dwelling place,
art veiled from me—
I've dragged Thy toilsome weights,
astounded
each time Thy step has sounded.

TWO . . .

Two people, whose homes are as close as can be;
two neighbors, two tall fellows.
One of them girlish and one of them sallow
(in me, in me, in me).
Two people, whose homes are as close as can be.

I sleep. All at once someone's hand starts to pulse
(one wakes up as soon as the other is sleeping).
Unfurling a ladder of shade, he goes creeping;
he creeps on the walls, on the walls, on the walls.
I sleep. All at once someone's hand starts to pulse.

At times, when one sits with a wineglass someplace
(it happens, if only it never would happen),
the person then pushes a little door open
and spits into somebody's face,
at times, when one sits with a wineglass someplace.

Two people, whose homes are as close as can be;
two neighbors, two tall fellows.
One of them girlish and one of them sallow
(in me, in me, in me).
Two people, whose homes are as close as can be.

THE YOUNG WHITE GOAT

I chase the young white goat into the pastureland
that it may learn to graze alone—
the young white goat that, for two silver coins,
two silver coins,
I've bought and own.

But as the meadows go, so goes the little goat,
and I go too;
in age-old woods, in barren fields, we blunder on
the whole week through,
the whole week through.

Friday, at noon, my goat stops suddenly,
my goat of white,

223

and I can see: far off there lies a land outspread
in the blue light,
in the blue light.

A land—a land
where hinds are hovering on every little hill,
weasel and buffalo sleep free of fear;
a land—a land,
a tremulous, a dream-enveloped land
that at the slightest touch may disappear.

The day is gone. The young white goat is lying next to me,
and the white goat himself will soon be gone,
the young white goat that for two silver coins,
two silver coins,
I've bought and own.

Izzy Charik (1898–1937)

Son of a cobbler and grandson of a famous *bodchn* (wedding
minstrel), IZZY CHARIK was born in Zembin, Byelorussia, in 1898,
and began his own working life in a bakery, then as a druggist's
assistant. In 1917 he ran a school; in 1919 he was a librarian in
Minsk. *Quake* (1922) was the first of his nine collections, culminating with *Our Courage* (1935), *Five Poems* (1936), and *At a Stranger's
Wedding* (1936). He also translated from Russian, Byelorussian,
and Ukrainian poetry, contributed to the Proletpen's journals
(*Morning Freiheit, Hammer, Signal, Young Smithy,* among others),
and co-edited four Minsk anthologies in 1934 and 1935. His
adaptation of Sholom Aleichem's *A Holiday in Kazrilovke*, with
lyrics, was performed at the Moscow Yiddish Theatre. In 1936 a
schriftfest volume, *Izzy Charik: Fifteen Years of Poetic Achievement,*
appeared in Minsk. He had sat as a deputy in the Byelorussian
parliament from 1928 and had served on the presidium of the
Union of Soviet Writers. Nevertheless, in June 1937 he was falsely
accused, along with Moishe Kulbak, of "deviations"; months of

unspeakable torture in a series of prisons drove him mad, and he perished in a northern detention camp that October.

AND BLUE BURSTS JUST THE SAME FROM HEAVEN

Not because it's crowded here
have I a notion of returning
for one more look at how you're yearning
with a transparent, lonely air.

What did I want from you, my town?
What was the flaw with which I quarreled?
I wanted you to be appareled
in a great steel and granite gown.

I wished your every hut would grow
into a haughty high-rise dwelling,
not humbly stoop without once telling
your history of weal and woe. . . .

Not because it's mild of late
and May explodes here, bright and breezy,
do I feel tranquil now and easy
and can't remember you with hate.

For you too it's the time of May,
though you still speak of it as Sivan;*
and blue bursts just the same from heaven
on all that's not yet gone away.

Sivan is the ninth month in the Jewish calendar (May/June).

Samuel Halkin (1899–1960)

Born in 1899 in Rogatchev, Byelorussia, SAMUEL HALKIN became an apprentice painter in Kiev. He began his writing career in Hebrew but turned to Yiddish, and in 1922 his first collection, *Poems,* was published. This was followed by *Suffering and Courage* (1929), *Contact* (1936), *Bar Kochba* (1939), and *Earthways* (1945). He also wrote plays and translated Shakespeare, Pushkin, and Gorky. Arrested in 1948 shortly after the publication of *The Tree of Life* and *Selected Works,* he was incarcerated for a few years, then moved to a prison hospital due to a severe heart condition and eventually freed. In 1958 a massive volume, *Halkin's Poetry in Russian Translation,* was issued in Moscow. He died two years later.

THE GLASS

Transparent is the glass, and clear—
it gives the whole world to your eyes.
You see who laughs, you see who cries.
But just block off one of its sides
with silver foil—a penny's worth,
on sale at the first store you pass—
vanished from sight is all the earth;
the glass becomes a looking glass,
and though it be more clear than clear,
only your features will appear.

PRECIOUS IS THIS STAR TO ME

Precious is this star to me
for its flame's integrity,
coming among swarms of brothers
self-sparked and unlike the others,
and because it treasures up
all its radiance in one drop.

226

Dear this star, whose flame will never
split, but holds its glow forever.
When it grants the tide its light,
it does not become less bright
on its long and golden round
from the heavens to the ground.

This star is the one I prize,
awed by its enormous size—
for its measurement I've won
and in me its light I've spun
and it is beyond all worth
being both of sky and earth.

POETS

Homer was blind, or so at least we've heard.
But a great wonder seems to have occurred.
With each new age, from Homer's time to ours,
he's multiplied his visionary powers.

But miracles are all too rare on earth.
If such a marvel's more than we are worth,
at least let no report be left behind
that during our own life span we were blind.

Itzik Feffer (1900–1952)

Born in 1900 in Spole, near Kiev, ITZIK FEFFER started work at the
age of twelve as a compositor. He became a Communist during
the revolution, joined the Red Army, and participated in a
number of battles. He saw the publication of his first poem at
nineteen and soon plunged into literary activity, editing the journals *Prolit* and *Challenge*, equivalents of the Proletpen publica-

tions, and eventually becoming a member of the presidium of the Union of Soviet Writers. He authored many collections, from *Shavings* in 1922 through *Of the Red Army,* issued in 1943 by the Proletpen's successor, YKUF, in New York. The same year, with the great actor Solomon Mikhoels, he toured England and the United States, drawing huge anti-Hitler audiences. His final book, *Once More,* appeared in 1948 shortly before his imprisonment. With Markish, Bergelson, Kvitko, Mikhoels, and many others, he was shot on 12 August 1952. Fifteen years later, a large selected edition of his work, *Songs, Ballads, Poems,* was issued in Moscow.

MY CURSE

My curse—may it fall like a fiery hail in your way.
Your luck—may it smash into bits like a vessel of clay.
And may my curse rankle and roast you wherever you range,
until your vile gullet is choked by my grip of revenge.

Accurst be the mother who thrust you alive from her womb.
The grain in your field—may it wilt and forget how to bloom.
Before the red hand of your reaper can sickle it down,
may nothing but dry, naked sticks be the yield of your ground.

And if you attempt to replenish your acres once more,
then once again let this my curse, that explodes through the roar
of children, through shrieks of the ravaged, through wild
    conflagration,
besiege you and carry your shame to the tenth generation!

May heaven grant you and your deathmates no merciful rains;
your swastika, may it be rinsed by the mud from your veins.
Wherever you go, may you trip on an ambushing stone;
may hooves trample *you* and whatever you thievishly own. . . .

May street curs assemble to shit upon you and your shrine.
Henceforth upon you may the smile of a child never shine.
Across your whole earth, row on row, may the mounds fester
    high.
And may, like your country, the tree at your window soon die.

Wherever your foot tries to go, where it stops, where it veers,
your murderous flesh—may it sink in the rivers of tears
that drop from the eyes of the mothers, from children's sad eyes,
and shroud the whole world like a smothering cloud in the skies.

The hate for your crimes in the ghettos, no more may it snivel,
but be a great sword, crushing you and your hideouts of evil.
On meadows, on cobbles, on streets, may the blood of the Jew
rise up and turn into the flame that annihilates you.

Accurst be your name, and erased may it be from now on
here under the snows of the stars and the stalks of the sun.
Your crew, may they vanish like dust, and your funeral hearse—
may no one and nothing accompany it but my curse!

THE VOW

I swear by the horrified stars, by the sun and its rays,
I swear by whatever a plain man can swear by these days.
I swear by the hearts that are seething where battles rage on;
I swear by the sources of joy that the foe has undone;
I swear by the willows that grieve where the Dnieper is flowing;
I swear by my blood, the unrest in my eyes that keeps growing;
—my hate will not slacken, my wrath will not cool in the storm,
until I can feel it—the enemy's blood on my arm.

Should one of my hands be plucked off by the whirlwind of
    death,
my second has power to throttle the enemy's breath;
and if, in the path of a bullet, my second goes lame,
my great, holy hate has the power to muffle the pain.

As long as my loyal feet go where I tell them to go—
in fire, in water—I'll find him, the murderous foe.

And if the night blows out my eyes, then in blindness my hate
—my sister in battle—will not let me bow to my fate.
The eyes of my heart will, I swear, hunt you down like a beast
till every last vestige of you is forever erased!

This, then, is my oath, which I swear to my fatherland now,
my tribe, my old mother and father; and this is my vow;
and if I prove false to the pledge that so solemnly binds me,
that day let my people's contempt be the swordpoint that finds
    me!

And if I don't beat back the foe from my sweet, sacred ground
so that not a shred of his ugliness ever is found,
then fixed be my name to the pillory—shame without end,
the ash of my body refused by the planet. Amen!

Ziame Talessin (1907–)

Born in Kalinkovitch, Byelorussia, in 1907, ZIAME TALESSIN lived
in Moscow for many years and was a regular contributor to
Sovietish Heimland, an influential literary journal. His Soviet collections of verse include *On My Own Ground, In the Bright World, Songs
and Poems,* and *On My Responsibility,* along with several books in
Russian. With his wife, the great lyric poet Rochel Boimvoll, he
later emigrated to Israel, where he published first the collection
Memorial Lament, followed in 1980 by *Kometz Alef - O.*

"GEH ICH MIR AROIS OIFN GANIKL"

The porch—the "ganikl"—is gone;
nor is the village here.
The song's sweet words are dying out
and soon may disappear.

And its heart-stirring melody
evaporates as well—
the melody that I have heard
as long as I can tell.

But one thing you should not forget—
cry or refuse to cry—
more than the song, the little bird
is destined not to die.

Nor is it so much to the bird
I bend the knee, as knowing
that she can fly, and soon into
a new song she'll be going.

THIRST

Sand, harsh as salt, on the palate;
ahead of you, fire and smoke.
Where's one to search out some water?
Drier than dust is your throat.

Across there, behind the barbed wire,
back there, where the foe lies entrenched—
the well of sweet coolness is ours,
but they alone drink and are quenched.

I can't say for certain what drove us
to fight—whether hatred or thirst.
We crept toward the well and, exhausted,
against its sweet coolness we burst.

And then! a weird moving asunder
came down like a rock on my brain:
the well of sweet coolness before me
was clogged to the brim with our slain.

Hirsh Osherowitz (1908–)

Born in Poniewicz, Lithuania, in 1908, Hirsh Osherowitz studied at the University of Kovno. He was first published in 1934. During the war he found refuge in Kazakstan. Afterward he settled in Vilna. His first volume, *Dawn,* appeared in 1941. His second, *Freed From Shackles* (1947), contains many poems about the Kovno ghetto, in which his mother and other family members perished. In 1949 he was accused of Zionist activity and sentenced to ten years in exile. Freed in 1956, he returned to Vilna. His 1962 volume, *My Good Maple,* was translated into Russian. *The Honey of Recognition* (1964) was translated into Lithuanian. *The Course of the Sun* appeared in 1969. Two years later he emigrated to Israel, where he has received major awards and seen the publication of numerous volumes, from *Amid Lightning and Thunder* (1973) to *At the Tree of Knowledge* (1981).

DUSK

I know the little white cloud
I now see
is the hide of a kid
that, on his first day of life,
lost his mother
and—orphaned already—
was butchered.

And there in the distance—
where the field ends,
right at the very, very heaven—
I actually see blood.
Is it the kid's
or his ill-fated mother's?

It's springtime.
The day—filled to the brim
with fresh young green.
But whatever spills over
turns red at once.

Who's the magician here?
Is it really the sun?

No, someone has butchered a kid
and having just
shed blood upon earth
has hung up the hide
to dry in heaven. . . .

Shike Driz (1908–1971)

SHIKE DRIZ was born in Krasna, the Ukraine, in 1908. He was
widely known for his children's poems; his *Bright Reality* appeared
in 1930 and *Steel Might* in 1934. A Red Army volunteer, he served
in Galician border towns from 1939 to 1941, aiding many refugees from the Nazis as well as local Jewish villagers. Afterward
he lived in Moscow. His final collection, *The Fourth Rail,* appeared
two years before his death in 1971.

THE SOUL OF THE FIDDLE

I had a fiddle; now it hangs
yearning for my touch.
I'd like to play a *viva,* but
my fingers shake too much.
I've thought of giving it away
(Please take it, show some pity!)
but one by one they've torn the strings
that used to sound so pretty.

So I seek a master,
beg him for a favor:
My fiddle's soul—is there perhaps
a chance that you can save her?

My mother's own melodious voice
rang in the first sweet string.
The second had the very sound
of a small valley-spring.
The third one, like a tiny child
that asks in pantomime,
was able both to weep and laugh
at one and the same time.

So I seek a master,
beg him for a favor:
My fiddle's soul—is there perhaps
a chance that you can save her?

My mother's voice—no longer heard—
weaned me and drifted by.
The little spring—an eye wept out,
tear-spent and all wrung dry.
The child turned gray one gruesome night
that was not meant for sleep,
and something happened to him: now
he'll neither laugh nor weep.

So I seek a master,
beg him for a favor:
My fiddle's soul—is there perhaps
a chance that you can save her?

The fourth string is so stretched, it has
a sad, exhausted twang. . . .
I'd like to stroke it fondly with
the songs my mother sang,
revive it with the valley-spring
that sparkles in the sun,
and bring back to the little child
the laughter that is gone. . . .

So I seek a master,
beg him for a favor:
My fiddle's soul—is there perhaps
a chance that you can save her?

Meyer Charatz (1912–)

MEYER CHARATZ was born in Shuri in 1912, grew up in Markulesh, a Jewish colony near Beltz, Bessarabia, and moved to Czernowicz, Bukovina, in 1934. He began writing poems as a boy but was not published until 1934, making a great public impression with his "Don Quixote." After serving in the Rumanian army, he was among thousands of Jews stripped of their citizenship. At the outset of the Nazi invasion in 1941, he fled to Central Asia, returning in 1945. Early in 1949 he was imprisoned; granted amnesty seven years later, he contributed hundreds of poems to *Sovietish Heimland,* Warsaw's *Folks-Shtimme,* and various left-wing journals abroad. But in 1960 he was the target of attacks by several Jewish colleagues, charged with "bourgeois nationalist tendencies." In 1972 he left for Israel, where his work finally achieved book form with such volumes as *In an Alien Paradise* and *Heaven and Earth* (both 1974), *The Fifth Wheel* (1978), and *Green Winter* (1982). *Selected Poems* appeared in Jerusalem in 1983. The most recent of his many honors is the Itzik Manger Award for 1986.

TO THE SKIES OF ISRAEL

Give me, O skies, a bit of space;
I want to sepulcher my mother.
And let the stone that marks her place
flame where the clouds of Israel gather.

"Braine Charatz"—I don't know where
she breathed her last, on what grim path.
I beg a wisp of upper air
from you, from you, on her behalf.

I beg a little soft white cloud
to fashion her a fitting shroud;
and, one by one, let silent stars
stand at her grave like honor guards.

235

Give me, O skies, a bit of space;
I want to sepulcher my mother.
And let the stone that marks her place
flame where the clouds of Israel gather.

Rochel Boimvoll (1914–)

Rochel Boimvoll, daughter of a theater family, was born in 1914 in Odessa. Her first book, *Children's Poems* (1930), was followed in 1934 by *Pioneers* and *Poems*. Two years later she graduated from Moscow University. *Cherry Trees Are Blooming* appeared in 1939, followed by *Poems* in 1940. During World War II she was evacuated to Tashkent, where the first of her many Russian volumes, *The Heart on Guard*, was issued in 1943. *Love*, a new Yiddish collection, was published in 1947. *A Small Comb* (1959) was written in collaboration with her husband, Ziame Talessin. Several of her poems were translated into Russian by Anna Akhmatova. According to the *Soviet Encyclopedia of Literature* her *Stories for Adults* is among the most significant Yiddish works of the 1960s. With her husband she later emigrated to Israel, settling in Jerusalem in 1971. New books of her Yiddish poetry appeared in 1972, 1977, and 1979. *There Once Was an Elephant: Stories for Young and Old* was issued in 1973, and *Poems of Many Years,* a compilation of her Russian verse, in 1976.

A LANGUAGE

To speak a language till one's dying day
is of great consequence, you'll surely say.
For long years in that tongue I did no speaking,
although within my blood it went on shrieking.

And now I know: it's of great consequence
for long years not to speak a language once.

236

A tongue in which you're bidden to be dumb
is one that never will succumb!

A SMILE

Trust me, we ought to marvel at the fact
that smiling's a uniquely human act.
He curls the corners of his mouth, and see:
the world improves at once, and so does he.

Even a beaver weeps; a popinjay
can imitate whatever people say;
owls laugh; we hear the teeth gnashed by a wolf;
and smiling—none can smile but man himself.

That smile is his as long as he keeps living.
Thanks to a smile may be forgiven
the fool his foolishness, the wise his wile;
and till our death, our youth lives in a smile.

A CONVERSATION WITH THE READER

It's been so long since we spoke,
and you've patiently marked time.
Don't aim at me with a rock—
believe me, the fault was not mine.

I didn't hush, like a snake;
I didn't turn mute, like a fish;
the flow of my song didn't break,
like a hill-brook once friskily fresh.

But a stone stood in my way,
nor did it stand alone.
You will understand what I say,
I trust, and drop *your* stone.

I'm chatting with you again.
For a poet, what could be dearer?

I have no closer friend;
I have no judge who's severer.

You're a genuine expert, able
to find each merit and fault.
We've finished off, at our table,
more than one *pood** of salt.

Who made us unable to talk
the way we used to do?
Who made us as gray as chalk,
I and you?

Dovid Bromberg (1915–)

Born in Haisin, the Ukraine, in 1915, Dovid Bromberg was
seventeen when his poetry was first published. Three years later
he was represented in the Kharkov anthology, *Children's Writings.*
For a score of years he has contributed frequently to the journal
Soviet Homeland, and a volume of his poems, *A Year Older,* was
issued in Moscow in 1977.

IN THE BASEMENT OF MY MEMORY

I often go down memory's basement stairs
where reminiscences are kept from many years,
from birth—my earliest smiles and tears.
Up from the gloom I drag into the shine
remembrances like flasks of old flat wine;

---

*A *pood* is approximately thirty-six pounds (Russian).

from them, as from a drink, I suddenly grow overheated—
a moment more, and I'll become inebriated.
I often go down memory's basement steps
where recollections of so many years are kept.
Up from the gloom I drag them into day, and before long
like wine they turn gall-bitter on the tongue,
those episodes of old
which burn forever, burn like coal,
and do not burn away these many years
I often go down memory's basement stairs.

Yosl Kerler (1918–)

YOSL KERLER was born in Haisin, the Ukraine, in 1918. In 1930
his family settled in a new Jewish colony in North Crimea. Here
he worked on a kolkhoz. From 1934 to 1937 he attended the
Odessa Jewish Institute for Machinery Production; his first poem
was published in Odessa in 1935. Later he trained at the Moscow
Yiddish Folk Theatre School but left for the front in 1941 and was
wounded three times. *For My Soil,* his first book, appeared in
1944. Six years later he was arrested and sentenced to a decade of
imprisonment in the Vortuka camp. Rehabilitated in 1955, he
wrote for the little theater. Two books of his poetry were published in Russian (1957, 1965). After a six-year struggle to emi-
grate, he settled in Jerusalem in 1971. Here he produced such
volumes as *Singing Through One's Teeth* (1971), *You See, However*
(1972) *August 12, 1952* (1978), and *The First Seven Years* (1979).

TIMBER

I love timber—
beams, girders, and boards
from which the breath of the live forest
issues forth.

239

Through branches' shady foliage
the sifted radiance of rays
has settled thick
as aging mead
into intoxicating resin scents.

I even hear the twittering of birds
when wood is sawed and hewn;
and chips go hopping
like vivacious hares
when wood is planed
and shavings fly out gaily.

In brown, bronze rings
on sawed-off oak stems I behold
the eternal cycles in the fate
of the tribe from which I stem.

Wooden
the masts of wandering vessels;
and, alas, the ancient wanderstaff
is made of plain wood too.

The cabins that first sprouted
in Galilee
were made of wood
and also the first
little trees that fluttered in the wind,
harbingers of a freely thickening forest
here on my homey-old
millennially ravaged
sand and stone. . . .

I love timber!

MY RIB

What does it mean,
I love you?—Now
I know it: you're my rib; somehow

I overslept the fact for ages;
then, ever hopeful, I would go
through barren lands on pilgrimages
alone in yearning and in woe,
and when I reached the precipice
and stood right over the abyss
and stretched my hands forth in despair—
I suddenly beheld you there:
a private, secret, cosy sight
and fresher than the day's first light
upon God's wild, sweet earth, that He
—bless Him—bestows on you and me.

What does it mean,
I love you?—You're
my rib, mine to the very core.

AUGUST 12, 1952

On this day of wrong,
on this infamous day,
our grief and our moan
we shut tighter away.
The grief—in our hearts;
between teeth—the moan.
Markish, Kvitko, Hofstein, Bergelson.

In the middle of night
they took their last breath
and no one consoled them
before their death.

And the only glow
allowed them that night
was the flash of the volley
butchering-bright.

On this infamous day,
on this day of wrong,
I lift up and carry

241

my bloodied song;
my song—a tombstone;
a candle—my heart;
but it seems I won't be
playing my part:
there's nowhere to place
a candle and stone—
Markish, Kvitko, Hofstein, Bergelson.

Poets of the Left

Abraham Victor (1871–1954)

ABRAHAM VICTOR (born Vigdorovitch) moved to Odessa at twenty from his birthplace, Kartuz-Bereza, Byelorussia. Here he worked as teacher, bookkeeper, and manager of a drugstore. He left for the United States in 1904. For three years he worked in cigar factories in New York and Detroit as well as in Chicago, where he later became a pharmacist. His earliest poems appeared in 1906, and his first collection was *Sheaves of Grain* (1920). Moving to the Left, he contributed mainly to the *Freiheit, Hammer, Zamlungen,* and the like. From 1937 until his death in 1954 at the age of eighty-three, he lived in Los Angeles. Here he produced the collection *I See a Land* (1942).

DENVER

The city—a whirlpool
that does not either seethe or boil,
but holds on to the mountain range;
that moss and rust already spoil;
that carries still the marks of ruinous fires,
ash heaps, ghost towns half-decayed;
the Golden City of the past
has left its cost of heavy toil unpaid.

But in the ring of mountainhood
the style of Denver still is grand;
all round, the titans wigged in snow
before her throne like pages stand;
and from the Capitol, her golden crown,
her cupola looks down,
and through its oval glass—
her monocle—a watchfulness

which seems as quiet as a dove, but which
could pounce like an infuriated bitch.

Below—Cathedral, Mint, invite the eye;
temples of Greek and modern art are there;
over one's head—a pure blue sky,
and thin and clean the air—
and sharply, piercingly, in dawn's gray time
the whistle wakes and calls men to the mine.

And an incessant cough is wrung
from each half-rotted chest and lung;
behind it comes a tramp of toiling feet
in which all races mix and meet;
and near the road, behind a grated fence,
in dawn's red glow, in dusk's magnificence,
on a bronze leaf, in blazing print,
Edelshtat lifts aloft his Testament.

Simeon Nepom (1882–1939)

SIMEON NEPOM was born in 1882 in Yelisavetgrad, near Cherson, the Ukraine. He left for Paris in 1904 and four years later settled in Canada, first in Montreal, finally in Toronto, where he worked for decades as a trolley conductor. His poems, many on social themes, were first published in 1910 in such militant journals as Montreal's *Canadian Eagle* and Toronto's *Worker's Newspaper*. Among his books, all issued in Toronto, are *In the Struggle* (1926), *Fetters* (1928), and *Of My Days*, a collection of selected poems with a foreword by the Marxist critic Kalman Marmor, published in 1940, a year after the poet's death.

IN THE TROLLEY

The wheels clatter loudly by night and by day
on glittering rails, on a pathway of steel.
The cars packed with riders go rushing away
on streets, squares, and bridges across to the vale.

I stand at my post, automatically sad—
the windowpanes rattling, the bell like a gong.
The lights glimmer down on each passenger's head.
I call out the stations like lines in a song.

I call out the stops, but am haunted by moans—
here sit fellow creatures absorbed in their cares.
Like me they have bartered their brains and their bones
and buried their days and surrendered their years.

A sound trembles up and the air rocks with wings;
there suddenly wakens a tempest of woe;
the trolley car gasps; and the motorman rings,
as if we were battling some powerful foe:

some powerful foe who has locked us away,
away in a cage on a pathway of night.
We'll shatter the yoke!—and I secretly say:
The bell . . . it announces a dawn of delight!

Moishe Nadir (1885–1943)

Moishe Nadir (pen name of Isaac Reis) was born in 1885 in
Narayev, Galicia. He emigrated to New York in 1898; his first
poem was published four years later. In 1910–11, with Jacob
Adler, he edited a journal of humor, *The Yiddish Bandit*. His first
collection, *The Wild Roses*, appeared in 1915. From 1920 until
shortly before his death he worked as a journalist, satiric essayist,
and translator of such works as Anatol France's *Red Lily*. His

complete works, in five volumes, were issued in 1931–32; a selected edition, *Nadirgang*, followed in 1937. He contributed prolifically to the *Morning Freiheit* and other left-wing publications, but made a sensational public renunciation in protest of Soviet policies and died in embittered isolation in 1943. The following year *I Confess* was published.

FINALLY

By the sea. In grayness. Gray, gray, gray.
Fog on my soul.
Fog on my eyes.
Fog on my lips.

Joys sink at the rim of things,
weep and sink,
like silent ships
on the waters.

By the sea. In grayness. My pencil writes
gray words, carefully.
A flask of poison and a faithful wife
at home, awaiting me.

IT'S GAY OUT

It's gay out. I stroll in the city,
whistling and twirling my stick.
In people—a heart ripe with sorrow;
on branches—fruit ready to pick.

It's gay out. I stroll in the city,
and play with my cane and sing.
It's hard to feel gay, however,
and sorrow's so easy a thing! . . .

MONUMENT TO THE UNKNOWN SOLDIER

I was the earth's defender once
against its enemy;
I ride now on a horse of bronze
with seven more like me. . . .

Now side by side we eight men ride
through distance and through dark;
the jaws of Death long since gaped wide
with teeth that grin and mock.

We eight men ride; "Hop! hop!" go all
our medals and our spurs;
and on each rider's brainless skull
a shower of laughing stars. . . .

Against earth's enemy I once
arose with sword and shield.
I ride now on a horse of bronze
in heaven's battlefield.

I'm stuffed with praise now, glorified
in marble with my armor.
But from the low dust as I ride
I hear a laughing murmur.

SPAIN

I talk about literature and think: Spain.
I laugh, bathe, read, telephone, always thinking: Spain—
Each night there marches before me, covered in mealy
    Andalusian dust,
the People's Front of Spain.
Like a bullet shot into my body is your struggle,
Spain—
No matter what I do or where I am, you're in me;
you're my exhausting conscience.
Days open over me and close,
but you stay at the center,

Spain—
Till your struggle is won
against the tigers of darkness,
you'll drill yourself into me, sinking deeper and deeper in my
    flesh,
holding on tighter and tighter to the threads of my marrow,
Spain.

MOTHER TONGUE

No, I do not claim as kin
the prophets and the priests:
my language toiled aplenty in
Vienna's fish-store streets.

No bells accompany my song,
collars nor epaulets.
I take my heritage along
in ordinary packs.

I write on day with bits of air
—as clear as a good morrow—
and all who need, and all who care,
are welcome to come borrow.

HEINRICH HEINE

Like the scent of hops from Narayev, my town,
your dear name follows across years and miles.
Day after day I lovingly lift down
Heine—the book of gold and bile.

I see you altogether drenched in pain
and altogether luminous in dreaming.
Your temples shoot off sparks of bitter flame,
and through the fumes your bloodied eyes are gleaming.

250

We speak, like closest neighbors, heart to heart:
I cry to you, as you in love have cried.
In halves the world has since been split apart—
your songs sob equally on either side.

Tormented now as you were, hounded now
in freedom's cause, my brows singed in the fight,
I send a line of greetings, like a plough
across a field, nor ask to whom I write. . . .

Like you, I don't know where my grave shall be:
in Brooklyn, or the desert, or the sea?
I follow in a manner true to me,
dandling fiery puppets on my knee.

Like yours, my foot has trod the rainbow-road,
the desert-road, where red-hot stars explode.
Like you, I know the mattress-grave, the hours
that sucked the marrow of your mental powers.

Like you, I've taken fat Mathilds to wife,
succumbed each time a hangman's daughter smiled.
Like you, I've shunned the bright broadway of life
in favor of the backroads: narrow, wild.

Your song is snow, is milk and grapes! I hear
its growling, too—its blood and fire and gold.
O Heine, my belovèd, Heinrich, my most dear,
your song-doves are a-warbling in my soul.

The time is ten years younger: she and I
stand in Montmartre, where you have slept so long.
New generations come to birth and die;
but each in turn embraces Heine's song.

COW

My clever cow at the barn door
is standing still.
On wind and hay and rays of sun
she feasts her fill.

251

My clever cow is not stuck up—
makes no great fuss—
but quietly gives milk and cheese
to nourish us.

My meek cow stands bemused against
the sky. She closes
her velvet eyes, and into blessèd
dreams she dozes.

1928

Suddenly summer:
bluebells and female
blouses returning—
and in me un-Jewish lusts
are burning.

My fresh bride, earth;
on fresh earth, my bride;
and near us grazes
the blue horse, whom everything
amazes.

BACCHANAL

In storm it is their left side
leaves display;
leaves can sense a storm
far away.

We, leaves in the storm,
on the great world-tree,
sense the lightning's
electricity.

Stubborn we'll cling to
the branch; who foretell

storms, insist on
rainbows as well.

Sara Barkan (ca. 1888–1957)

Sara Barkan was born about 1888 in Dvinsk, Latvia. Her father
was a Yiddish teacher and writer. She married a tailor, Morris
Silverman, and in 1907 followed him to America with their first
child. In 1922 she made her debut as a writer of verse for children. *Good Springtime,* her first volume, was published in 1936,
followed by *Gifts* a decade later. *About You and Me,* a book of
stories, appeared in 1949. *Stories and Songs of Every Day for Big and
Small,* her fourth collection, was issued by the YKUF in 1956. A
year later she died in her hometown of many years, Maplewood,
New Jersey.

THE LITTLE BREADWINNER AND HER
FATHER

Dawn knocks at every house. In one
a man, ashamed, lies still as stone.
Early or late, why should he care?
His work's not wanted anywhere.

The house, with all its people, lies
asleep. His daughter rubs her eyes.
The soft white pillow pleads with her:
It's early yet . . . no need to stir.

Ignoring what the pillow said,
she hastily hops out of bed.
She lifts the coffee off the shelf
and boils a cupful for herself.

With bundle snug inside one arm,
she leaves her bed, that still is warm.
She says good morning on her way:
"Don't worry, mom, I'll be okay!"

He feigns sleep, like a naughty son
punished for something bad he's done.

A WAR MOTHER

A mother lives
across the way,
not very old,
but very gray.

She's at the window
all day long
like a gray dove
who mourns her young.

Blinder and blinder
her gray eyes grow
because of the many
tears that flow.

Outdoors it's spring;
the sunbeams dance;
but she sits holding
her head in her hands.

Her white drape nightens
all at once;
softly she murmurs:
My sons, my sons.

FROM THE SICKBED

No, the summer's not yet at an end,
though green boughs quiver at the frost that rages;

I hear a singing in the fiercest wind,
and birds are tearing wires from their cages.

No, my summertime has not yet ended,
though leaves begin to turn, and branches shed;
the hues of heaven still are rich and splendid;
and through the trees the sky laughs tinder-red.

No, the birds won't flee to where it's warm—
my garret will not cease to give them shelter.
I'll beg a special favor of the storm:
to pity them, not drive them helter-skelter.

No, my fate, you shall not overwhelm me.
Keep your seven good-fortunes, keep them all,
as long as I can sing the songs that fill me,
songs with a power to quicken and console.

Shifre Weiss (1889–1955)

Born near Kovno, Lithuania, in 1889, SHIFRE WEISS was orphaned
at twelve when her father, on his way to America, was murdered
in a neighboring village. Three years later she joined the Bund
and became a skilled orator. Hunted by the police, she escaped to
America in 1905. She lived first in Pittsburgh, then in Chicago,
and finally settled in California in 1917. A founder of the Hollywood Workmen's Circle, she later moved to the far Left. Her
poems and articles appeared in *Die Freie Arbeiter-Shtimme, Freiheit,
Yiddishe Kultur,* and others. Among her books are *On the Way*
(1932), *To the World* (1943), and *To the Dawning Day* (1953). She
died in 1955, while traveling from Los Angeles to Florida.

DREAMS

I am the tablets
of all the dreams I've dreamt.
Wild storms have torn up
my Testament.

My fathers wrote a Torah
that I was proud to shield
as the sun tends May buds
for ripe October's yield.

The hailstones of life
hammered at my panes—
tore up my holy pages,
swept them away in the rains.

I live now to assemble
the alphabet of the ages—
to rescue the dreams I dreamt,
rewrite the holy pages.

L. Gorelik (1889–1941)

L. GORELIK was born in 1889 in Zhlobin, Byelorussia. Migrating to the United States at seventeen, he toiled at various trades all his life. His early work was published in the *Freie Arbeiter-Shtimme, Tsukunft,* and Mani-Leib's anthology *New York,* among others. Active in the Chicago Poets' Group, he contributed verse cycles to *Young Chicago* and *Together* that linked him with the Inzichists. His first collection, *Poems,* was issued in Cleveland in 1919. As the theme of oppressed labor deepened in his work, he began publishing in the *Freiheit* and various Proletpen journals. The Chicago YKUF issued his second collection, *Among Ourselves,* in 1941, the year of his death.

TO THE ENEMY

We know that you will not be silent;
you'll order the knaves in your hire
to rout us with sabers and bullets,
and smother our militant fire.

We know you have stationed your bloodhounds
astride every sea, every nation.
Wherever a spark is ignited,
they stamp out each young conflagration.

But not for all time can they stamp out,
nor smother forever the humming
that floats through the air with its message:
the real conflagration is coming!

Louis Miller (1889–1968)

Louis Miller (pen name of Eliezer Meler) was born in Lonowitz, Volhynia, in 1889 and emigrated to New York in 1906. For some years he was connected with Di Yunge, and his first volume, *In God's World,* appeared in 1919. From 1922, when the *Morning Freiheit* began publication, he was among the most active of the left-wing poets. Whitman had always influenced his style and vision, and he devoted many years to a translation of *Leaves of Grass,* which appeared in 1941. *Storms and Rainbows* was issued in 1948. The McCarthy repression drove him, along with others, into self-exile. In France he produced his final collections, *Life Forever* (1959) and *All of Us* (1965). He died in Paris in 1968.

IN THE SHOP

There was a young girl crying in our shop today.
She huddled at her work: so lost, so far away.
Noontime, when the hushed machines rang in our ears,
she read a letter—on the pages fell her tears.

Without a sound we worked—pale, and without a sound.
The hands upon the clock seemed scarcely to go round.
And when at night we left the shop and came outside,
it seemed to us somehow that everyone had cried.

SUNDAY ON 14TH STREET

Bellowing of billboard, flood of neon glare,
alluring posters with their siren limbs,
flash dreams of happiness
at famished eyes, at him who seeks his share
of pleasure on the day of rest.

Onto 14th Street they come—in twos, in ones;
couples stroll quietly and at a Sunday pace.
More come. More parched eyes seek
the seamy phantom of delight, the drink of fun
that is their due after a long, hard week.

Two young women exit from a movie house,
their lips blue-green in the electric spray,
a disappointed pair
with empty look, whose hoodwinked faces seem to say:
"We did not find our yearned-for joy in there."

One lets out a lazy, weary sound,
and—fingers on a yawning mouth—looks round:
"Where to? where next?" "Let's try
another show, the one across the way,"
her friend, as if ashamed, says with a sigh.

PEACE—PEACE!—
—"Peace broke out"—

The longed-for word, the precious word of peace
exploded skyward
with atomic violence.
At which the earth,
in a drunken rondo, reeled around.
Under a rainbow-tinted whirlwind
day confused itself with night
and night with day—
amid its revels Joy broke down and cried,
and Sorrow suddenly was gay. . . .

All the hidden wells burst open:
from every cranny Hope came gushing, streaming forth;
swept onward with the might of waterfalls,
washed clean and dressed the gaping wounds of earth—
washed clean and dressed and fitted festive gowns
upon the devastated towns.

In one split second of one hour
the grief, the joy
of a millennium flashed by—
the vision and the real were one
to the astounded eye. . . .
Hate wore a lying smile upon his face;
Love forgave everything and everyone. . . .
Misfortune grabbed Good Luck, and round they spun,
dancing a dance of peace
right in the marketplace. . . .

From mighty trumpets, a rejoicing roar
rang out, and yet it had a hollow sound;
and mingling multitudes went round
in a bewildered gaiety,
like bad-off relatives on the wedding day
who can't quite smile at what they see. . . .

Late at night.
The cataracting roar had disappeared somewhere—
run out—

and Joy, exhausted,
leaned against a stranger's stair
and fell asleep;
a hem of the city's festive gown
was slightly raised,
and bared an ugly speck of blood—
a wound. . . .
A dissolute fellow, a drunken bully,
suddenly appears,
ready to bend the whole world to his will,
ready to rape and kill.

Somewhere in a house
a mother sits
and reads with quivering lips
a faded letter
from a son cut down in battle. . . .
She weeps with covered mouth, so that
her husband will not hear. . . .
He sits at the table with closed eyes
so that he will not see the way she cries
—and swallows his own tears. . . .
His heart aches, and within him sounds
a pain-filled prayer:
O God, may it at least not be in vain!
He gets up sharply from the chair
and goes with soft steps toward the window's light—

* * *

There is a new day rising in the east. . . .

Aaron Maisel (1890–1936)

AARON MAISEL was born in Berezin, Byelorussia, in 1890. At twelve he became a worker. In 1911 he settled in America. From 1919 he taught Yiddish in the Workmen's Circle schools, first in New Haven, then, from 1927, in The Bronx. His poems, stories, and critical essays appeared regularly in such left-wing publications as *Union Square, Morning Freiheit, Hammer,* and the like. His books include *The White Bear and Other Stories* (1927), *History of the Jews in the United States* (1929), and two volumes of *Stories* published posthumously. He died in 1936.

THE SONG OF THE UNEMPLOYED

Giant city, pulsing city,
you have burgeoned far and wide:
up into the clouds, your towers;
deep within the earth, your roots;
brightly painted, all your temples;
smoothly paved, your meanest street;
and of stones the firmest, hardest,
has your every limb been hewn;
and your breath—that boils and sizzles—
beats like waves against a rock.

Giant city, pulsing city,
arms I lift defiantly!
First I bugle, first I bellow
pleadings—thunderclaps will follow.
Answer me! answer me!
I want work! to build, to make things,
build the bricks, and mix the mortar,
break the stones, and dam the rivers,
empty, empty all my bubbling
energies into your breast!

You have thrust me from my nature;
to the lowest depths you've sunk me;
from the mires that drag me under
unto you I lift my hand.
I want work! to build, to make things,
let my hammer once more echo,
let my arm once more come crashing,
let my wrath cool off a little.

I your maker, I your builder,
deeply bent and deeply bowed,

call you, beg you: Answer me!
Open wide your arms of welcome;
let me live within your glory.
If my wrath churns up much longer,
from my hand will fall the hammer,
and my fist will be uplifted,
and I'll smash you into bits.

Louis Dinsky (1890–1976)

LOUIS DINSKY was born in Suwalki, Poland, in 1890. He migrated to Paris at fifteen, and worked there at various trades, leaving for the United States in 1913. He helped organize the Chicago Poets' Group, whose work was featured in *Together*. Later, in New York, he joined the Proletpen and published in its journals. His early free-verse lyrics were collected in *Meanwhile* (1922). *Days in the Factory*, a revolutionary volume, was issued by the Proletpen in 1936. His later years were spent in Rochdale Village, Queens, New York, where he remained active in Yiddish cultural groups until his death in 1976.

THE FACE OF ANGUISH

First off, they threw us out of factory and workshop;
as if lopped by a knife, our livelihood was ours no longer.
Now they evict us from our melancholy dwellings
in which the last thin twig is gnawed upon by Hunger. . . .

Like bloodhounds on the hunt, the "Guardians of the Law" are
    foaming;
the scene's a feast for every newsman sniffing in the jungle:
our poor scraps, all our worldly goods, lie helpless on the
    sidewalk—
the bloody total of a life of toil heaped in a jumble. . . .

You wealthy "Law and Order" folk, come see the face of
    Anguish;
but also see the fury that ignites among the masses.
Beware the day such fury breaks its bounds; for like a forest
our vengeance will engulf the streets the day our patience passes.

Arn Kurtz (1891–1964)

ARN KURTZ was born in 1891 in Asve, near Vitebsk, Byelorussia.
At thirteen he began wandering through the big cities of Russia,
working in theaters and circuses as a barber, his lifelong trade. At
eighteen he returned to his father's home in the village of Old-
Sloboda. Two years later he migrated to Philadelphia, where his
first poems, under the pseudonym of "Azrael," appeared in 1916
in the *Jewish World* and in Z. Weinper's *At the Fire* four years later.
He also published several journals of his own before moving to
New York, where his work appeared in *In Zich*. His first collection,
Chaos, appeared in Philadelphia in 1920. By 1926 he had joined
the Communist Party and from then on he contributed exclusively to left-wing publications: *Morning Freiheit, Hammer, Signal, Zamlungen, Yiddishe Kultur, Sovietish Heimland.* Among his
works are *Placards* (1927), *The City of Gold* (1935), *No Pasaran*
(1938), and *Marc Chagall* (1946). From 1957 until his death seven
years later, he published his own quarterly, *Poems of Today.* His
selected poems, utterly omitting his pre-Communist work, were
seen through the press in 1966 by his widow, the poet Olga
Cabral.

THE PRISONER

I sit behind bars in the gloom of a cell.
A newly fledged eagle alights on my sill.
My friend, free as air, folds his wings on the stone,
and watching him feast I become less alone.

263

He gulps and discards and looks in through the pane
as if what we're thinking is one and the same.
He calls me with bright eagle-voice, eagle-stare;
I feel like replying: "Go, brother, fly there!
go quickly, escape, not a minute to lose!
out there where through cloud banks the mountaintop glows;
out there where the sea rocks its blueness asleep;
where no one but I and the wind dare to leap!"

HUNGER IN GOLDEN VATS

In the country of golden vats there's a hunger—
not that the earth has not yielded wheat,
not that the sun has not made the fruit juicy,
but that there's more than enough to eat.

Frigid corridors serve as bedrooms—
not that beds are scarce in this realm—
O gold mine, O flophouse, America,
dress-coated swine in the swankest hotel!

Behold, in all the wide squares of the towns
bejeweled manikins wallow in light,
and in all the wide squares of New York
toilets provide lodgings for the night.

A winter-long snowstorm
riots over New York;
each day more starving-frozen
are moved into the morgue.

Huddled with mice in cellars,
in hallways that freeze tears,
like garbage bags, like refuse,
they crumple up their years;

crumple up the bygone
with a now of wandering and hunger;
hide the head inside the collar
to escape from what they remember.

Four hundred thousand
broken spirits and cots.
Chimneys and hats
blizzarded white;
and a white wind knocks
with the metal tops
of empty breadboxes
into the night.

Lone
on all the sidewalks
lone
in forty million steps.
He
who still has a home
can't much longer lull himself with hopes:
Laws come,
thugs come,
and soon, down squalid stairs,
Home, with its bitter life, escapes.

Winter has no walls—
and through the land such "home" we now behold.
Feet in frost-manacles
trudge—and gulp, gulp down the cold.

Itzik Efros (1892–ca. 1960)

ITZIK EFROS, born in 1892, arrived in the United States in 1912.
He settled in Los Angeles and was associated with the Proletpen
group. *Restless Years,* a collection of his poems, was published by
the Los Angeles Book Committee in 1951. His death was noted in
the 1961 issue of *Kalifornier Shriftn.*

THE JEWISH FLAG

From the logs a spark leaped high,
and a wind blew it wondrously far.
And now there grows in the sky
a newborn star—
and human hands spin silken threads
of the light it sheds.

Open your folds like wings!
Your cloth—let it be unfurled!
And your free voice, let it ring
to the very ends of the world!
O, Israel, for your gallantry—
live, and be free!

Zische Weinper (1893–1957)

ZISCHE WEINPER (originally Zisse Weinperlich) was born in 1893 in
Trisk, Volhynia province, the Ukraine. At sixteen he began working as a teacher and at times as a bookkeeper in various Ukrainian
and Polish towns. A year later he was living and publishing poems
in Warsaw. At twenty he emigrated to New York, finding employ-
ment first as a house painter, then as a Yiddish teacher. His poems
and articles appeared in *Tsukunft, Warheit,* and the like. In 1918 he
joined the Jewish Legion of the British army and for two years
fought at the Palestinian border. Afterward he edited *At the Fire*
(1920), *Breath* (1922, with co-editor M. L. Halpern), *The Quill*
(beginning in 1924), and *Upsurge* (1932, again with Halpern). His
books include *Of Our Country* (1920), *Golden Cock* (1925), *Possessions*
(1929), *Selected Poems,* 1932, *On the Way,* 1935, *Song of the Believer,*
1943, *At the Grand Canyon,* 1947, and *Poems About the Prophets,*
1951. A volume of English translations appeared in 1936. After
the World Congress of Jewish Culture in 1937, he moved from
Zionist radicalism to the left-wing circles around the *Morning*

266

Freiheit and remained a leader of the YKUF (founded that year) until his death in 1957.

THE OLD INDIAN

Silent stony giants
puncture the air and in defiance
pierce to the sky.
Sunk in a dream nearby
there sits upon a stone
all alone
the primally American
old Indian.

Has something taken place?
Has something been erased?
Of course!
Roads don't take an even course:
they meander, circle, wind.
What delight can he now find,
since the arrow left his bow
long ago
and it failed to hit the mark?
What remains for him is sleep, by day or dark!

Silent stony giants—
all their thrustings of defiance
ended without triumphs:
no, they did not puncture through to reach the sky.
Therefore, dreaming on a stone nearby,
the primally American
old Indian
snuggles in his woolly shawls.
As the storm of winter falls,
so the enemy swooped down
on his brown
ancestors; and what today is such a one
as he? Amid the stones, a stone,
a giant amid giants, mute as they,

who's found a way
to last: an echo of an anger
that was, and was and is no longer.

AT THE GRANITE

What am I doing here? What drove me to this spot?
Is nothing else left for my restless foot
on all the planet
except this silent granite?
Behold! palaces labyrinthinely erected,
without one door, one threshold architected.
So many windowless and paneless walls.
A forest of tall towers and above them sprawls
a cool, hushed heaven radiantly gleaming
as if beyond it someone's dozed off and is dreaming
after a hard day's toil with chisel and with hammer.
A world's asleep in stone's mute clamor
enchanted by a nightmarish not-to-be-spokenness.
A flung-wide-openness and a forever-unopenedness
of iron locks and bolts that will not give or rust.
Only on empty streets, on the wind's back, a light dust
seeks mutely to escape, to reach the world of earth and sky.
What is it? what do its seeking and its craving signify?
The same desire, I guess, that's in me, bursting to break out!
So powerful a craving, I would shout
if in my throat the cry were not struck dumb.
For what? to what then have I come?
Was my route fixed? my destination mapped?
Here lies my luggage still unpacked
and ready for new roadways wheresoever they may wind.
Who knows what else there is for me to find!
I spur on, drive on without end,
just like the restless dust that rides upon the wind,
forever on the trail of something not yet found.
Often I feel it is a spider's web in which I'm bound,
and have no choice but to devour
web, life—with my last power.
And my eyes look, and look, and won't give up;
my shoulders twitch, and twitch, and will not stop.

OUR TREASURE

The Yiddish language—our accumulated treasure—is a gleam
  forever blazing, brightening.
In mankind's granary what would we be without that treasure-
  trove?
We'd be a wasteland without plowers, sowers, reapers, singing as
  they gather in what's ripening—
we'd be a ruin buried under dust—we'd be a fireless stove.

Who'd show us grandma's naiveté and grandpa's stately features
  full of serious opinions
and father's kindly countenance and the concern in mother's
  lovely eyes?
Blest be the Yiddish language, whether in the privacy of prayer,
  or in the noisy minyans *
reaping our grain, then binding them in sheaves, the sheaves
  then stacked beneath the sunlit skies!

Blest be America, that has contributed new colors to our golden
  Yiddish language!
Hear, hear—a multinational fraternity sings through our tongue.
There's not a storm wind that can cause such rootedness to rot
  and languish;
a glow so charged can be extinguished by no wind, despite how
  strong.

When Man became no more here than the five rushed fingers of
  a needle stitcher
for parasites that fatten on the sweat and blood of others,
the Yiddish word took fire at the machine, grew mightier and
  richer,
and turned dejection into fury with a cry: "Awake, and break
  your bonds, O brothers!"

The song of Rosenfeld, Winchevsky, Edelshtat, and Bovshover,
  born in that hour,
inspired by Whitman's largeness, Lincoln's grace, and the clear
  logic of Karl Marx,

---

*A *minyan* refers to the minimum number of ten adult males required for
religious services.

expelled dejection, stirred awake a Maccabean bravery and
   power,
and like a sunrise bright and large, the Jewish heart arose from
   meekness, from the dark.

Nahum Weissman (1894–1944)

NAHUM WEISSMAN, born in 1894 in a Rumanian village near
Foltitschen, attended normal school and began publishing Rumanian poems in the Bucharest weekly *Equality*. He turned to Yiddish in 1917. After serving in his country's army, he taught Rumanian language, literature, and history in Kishenev. He arrived in
New York in 1920 and taught first in the Workmen's Circle
schools, later in the schools of the International Workers Order
(I.W.O.). Active in the Proletpen, he published his poems and
stories, many of them for children, in the *Freiheit*. His books are
The Ballad of a "Children's Camp" (1926), *Little Songs of Mine* (1940),
The Little Lass in the Scarlet Dress (1940), and *Selected Poems,* published in 1950, six years after his death.

DAWN AT GRAND CENTRAL

Restlessly on New York roofs the night still turns and tosses;
quivering on swordpoints the new day ascends;
shuffling, half-asleep, like shadows dancing on the walls,
the window washers come with boxes and long brushes in their
   hands.

Somewhere each has left behind her sleeping children;
maybe they are dreaming about shoes and bread.
It was her children's hunger drove her to Grand Central,
drove her out of bed.

Even now, on golden cupolas, the night is dreaming;
on my city's streets the neon lights are bright as fire.
Footsteps sing on stairs that lead up from the subways,
a song of hunger dancing on the red-hot wire! . . .

Just awhile ago some Pullmans pulled into the station;
even now, where the warm engine rests, the smoke is thick;
great long dancing brushes sing on all the windows;
hands are also dancing, powerful and quick.

And if little children left at home should chance to waken
and, in daybreak's blueness, weep with none to hear,
who shall pay for them—those pure and precious teardrops—
in the sunrise of an ever-turning year?

Sarah Fell-Yellin (1895–1968)

Born in Krynki, near Grodno, in 1895, SARAH FELL-YELLIN inherited a history of revolutionary struggle. Her mother had been active in organizing the cigarette workers. Her father, a tinsmith, had been imprisoned by the tsarist police. She herself helped organize schools and shelters for refugee children during the First World War. Teaching in German schools during the occupation, she fought for the right to have Yiddish taught in a Jewish school. At the end of 1920 she arrived in Boston, where she produced *Step by Step* (1937), *Closer* (1941), and *Bright Beacons* (1946). Migrating west in 1952, she became president of the Los Angeles Writers Group of YKUF and wrote *Toward Sun and Joy* (1957), *On the Wings of a Dream* (1961), and *Songs of Man and Time* (1965). In 1969, a year after her death, her husband issued a collection of her poems in English translation, *Songs of Days and Years*.

"DEMOCRACY"

"Democracy!"
An ancient, threadbare
curtain
over the rotted conscience
of a thieving world!
a firmly rooted tree
whose innards worms
have eaten up entirely
and left it hollow
at the very heart.
When nights are dark,
ghosts come forth
wrapped in the curtain
and praise with hymns of wonder
their god of thunder—
seductively they lure
the wanderer from his path
to murky corners on dead-end back roads.
And night fowls,
that make themselves a house
inside the hollowed tree,
laugh and hoot
when from the loftiest boughs
they look at us
and wildly pray unto their god—
the god of darkness—
to block the break of day!

Yosl Kotler (1896–1935)

YOSL KOTLER, born in Troianetz, Volhynia, in 1896, was orphaned very early and at eleven began working in a tavern. He taught himself the art of portraiture and in 1911 left for the United States, where he took art lessons. In 1922, with the encouragement of Moishe Nadir, he began writing poetry, and prose tales as well; some of them were published in journals for children and in Avrom Reisen's *New Yiddish*, but his work appeared most frequently in the Proletpen's *Hammer* and in the *Freiheit*, to which he contributed a daily column. In 1925, with Zuni Maud and Jack Charkoff, he created Modikot, a Yiddish marionette theater that was popular on both sides of the Atlantic, as were his hilarious chalk talks. *Muntergang,* his only book, appeared in 1934, one year before his fatal road accident in Memphis, while on tour.

OVER THE SEA WITHOUT A VISA

In the sleep-garden
your eyes stuff themselves
on black
velvet flowers
and go to sleep.
With a dream at the head of the bed
and a cat at the foot
you dream back
the young goat
of your old home
as you rode her
when little, when young.
And the lips of sleep
babble
little talk,
young talk,
out of the dream.
And in this way
(or slightly different)
without a ticket
you sail yourself over
to there,
far over the wet sea
on a dry bed
(probably)
and recognize your goat
by the black spot
on her tail.

AT THE WINDOW

My shoes have more holes
than are good for one's feet,
so I watch at the window
the roofs on my street.

I envy my birds
that fly without care
barefoot, on strong
young wings through the air.

Outdoors the flakes
are beginning to drop;
indoors some coal
might help us warm up.

My father sits idle;
his job's at an end.
"Rent!" howls the landlord
as if he's been skinned.

I'm eleven; I've almost
outgrown my father.
The holes in my shoes
outgrow one another.

I envy my birds
that fly without care
barefoot, on strong
young wings through the air.

They fly and they sing,
they laugh and trade news;
but out of a bird
you cannot make shoes.

Well, what won't you do
when times are bad?
To hell with the landlord—
you've got to have bread!

Some rags round the shoes,
and ready to go!
A quarter an hour—
I'm shoveling snow.

All shoveled . . . my shoes
are no use to my feet;
so I watch at the window
the roofs on my street.

Yosl Cohen (1897–1977)

YOSL COHEN was born in Krynki, near Grodno, in 1897. At twelve
he emigrated to America and here attended a left-wing secondary
school. His earliest work was published in *The Voice of the Industrial
Worker* (IWW) in 1920. He helped found the Proletpen and contributed to its publications, *Signal, Union Square,* and *Hammer. City,*
his first collection, appeared in 1926. From 1931 to 1933 he lived
in the Soviet Union, and his second book, *From the Other Side of the
Ocean,* was issued in Moscow in 1932. Returning to New York, he
saw the publication of *Crooked Ways* in 1936. His political views
shifted, and from 1944 to 1952 he served as editor of labor news
for the *Morning Journal.* During that time *Tomorrow is Forever*
(1948) was published. *A Spark in the Dark* appeared when he was
seventy. He died ten years later.

1905

So many thousands
of shattered, disheveled days before us,
separated by such dizzying distances!
Yet even now I am blazing
wild trails here

with the enduring freshness
of 1905.
Oh, what a fortified faith
you paved under my feet!
I have not, to this day,
allowed myself to be devoured
by the rotted gold-mouth.
Over the cackle of laughter
I carry my faith entire
from shore to shore.
Such radiant sun rays
you rooted in our blood!
Such dancing joy
you poured into our spirits!
Not by miracle
did this brightness reach to all horizons:
from our own exploded fury,
with a roar of ripped limbs,
and from our own blood
on fertile fields, faith blossomed.
And along with myself I brought to the earth a ripened fury
bred by the tanneries of Krynki.
To this day I carry on my shoulders
the blooming life
that readied your October.

Shmuel Don (1897–1972)

Born in Pultusk, Poland, in 1897, SHMUEL DON emigrated to the
United States at seventeen. He wandered about the country in
extreme poverty, working briefly at various trades, then joined the
Jewish Legion and fought in Palestine. After his return, he published a few poems in *Di Feder* (The Pen), then apparently wrote
nothing for more than twenty years. During the 1950s he began
contributing to all the journals of the Left, and in 1959 the YKUF

issued *Under the Burden of Days,* a collection of his poems. He died in 1972.

SNOW ON THE MOUNTAINS

Not holy temples, hewn of clear-white marble,
with sculpted cornices, with notched adornments,
with domes and towers that press and poke toward heaven;
with burnished, polished windows of clear crystal
that flash a blue-white shimmer—
but snow on the mountains.

Not white sailboats on gigantic, foaming billows,
that stormily, in a cosmic cataclysm,
have pitched from deep abysses toward the heavens,
and halfway up stood frozen.
These are mountains,
and snow on the mountains.

Not a city, royally white, undone by epic battles,
that blazes afar like a bronze conflagration
under the flaming clouds of a fiery winter sun
on white, demolished palaces,
blood-blotched monuments,
spattered brass of crumbled crosses,
cold copper cupolas,
broken, marble-sculpted turrets.
Oh, no! these are mountains,
welded together, risen together,
mountain on mountain, row on row,
altogether;
and a sun above the world,
brightening, lightening, aglow,
and in the midst I go.
And snow on the mountains,
oh, snow on the mountains!

FROM MY DEPTHS

A tortured man, a killer in his cell,
even he's allowed some rest.
The rapid whistling of the whip
slows when a slave is on the verge of falling.
Sometimes the death moan of a tortured man
awakes his torturer at night.

And you, merciless one, brute lord of me,
no matter who you are,
I beg you, from my depths, on bended knee.

Moishe Shifris (1897–1977)

Born in Kisnitsa, Podolia province, in 1897, MOISHE SHIFRIS
grew up in Beltz, Bessarabia, where he was orphaned young. At
seventeen he migrated to the United States. Four years later he
enlisted in the Jewish Legion in Palestine and returned to New
York in 1919. There he worked first as a milliner, then as a
teacher in the Yiddish schools. His first poems appeared in 1917
in the Brooklyn weekly *Progress*. He also wrote for many other
publications, including Weinper's *Upsurge* and the *Vegetarian
World,* which carried weekly stories by him for several years. In
1922 he edited *Mountain Voice*. Eventually he contributed almost
exclusively to such Proletpen and YKUF organs as *Hammer, Signal, Morning Freiheit, Yiddishe Kultur,* and *Zamlungen.* Toward the
end of his life the *Morning Freiheit* featured two autobiographical
prose series, *From Beltz to New York* and *Long Ago in New York.* His
collections include *Poems* (1922), *Rachama and Other Poems* (1925),
War Days (1937), and *Under One Roof* (1971). Shifris wrote many
stories and plays, especially for children, and translated historical
prose works by John L. Spivak, Anna L. Strong, and others. He
died in New Jersey in 1977.

SONG OF THE SHOESHINE BOY

My skin is dark as coal,
darker the grief in my soul.
No joy—no hope.
My home a gloomy hole.
And cut into the bark of every tree—
"Beware the rope!"
   Shine them, black boy, shine them quick!
   Make them nice and slick!
   —Yes, sir.
   Not a word more.
   —Yes, sir.

At rich folk's feasts my father stands
with lowered head,
while all day, for a crust of bread,
my mother's wilted hands
revive a stranger's floors.
Master struts by with smirking face,
and we—who "live but by his grace"—
must do the filthy chores.

   Hey, black boy! I haven't all night;
   make them nice and bright!
   —Yes, sir.
   Not a word more.
   —Yes, sir.

On cotton fields beneath the Southern sky,
in Africa, where swampland trees grow high—
work, black boy!
White lords gather barrelfuls of glee
and string a black man up on every tree—
hang, hang, black boy!

   Shine them, black boy, shine them quick!
   Make them nice and slick!
   —Yes, sir.
   Not a word more.
   —Yes, sir.

In our own neighborhoods
fiery crosses and white hoods—
quake, quake, black boy.
Here's fire and rope, and a ball of lead;
in heaven you'll find your joy. . . .
Work, work, black boy!

Hey, black boy, haven't all night!
Make them nice and bright!
—Yes, sir.
Not a word more.
—Yes, sir.

EMPTY CHIMNEYS

Chimneys pointing skyward
with hollow throats
crave smoke—as wind
is craved by boats.

Machines gnaw at the deadness
with teeth of steel;
extinguished ovens gag
on their embers' chill.

Windows blind with dust
look out of the wall.
Dawns strain their ears
for the factory's call.

Idleness turns on conveyors
standing numb,
as the mouse turns in a barn
that hasn't a crumb.

Yudica (1898–?)

YUDICA, born Judith Tsik in 1898 in Gorshd, Lithuania, was taken to London by her family; they returned when she was six. She was "farmed out" first to an aunt in Prussia, then to a brother in Frankfurt, where she had her first job. At the outset of World War I she was interned as a Russian national, but in 1915 she managed to reach Kharkov. For five years she worked in various cities as a seamstress and a nursemaid. In 1920 she left for Stockholm, returning to her birthplace two years later. Her first books—*New Youth* (1923) and *Person and Time* (1926)—appeared in Kovno. Arriving in Canada in 1929, she was published widely but leaned toward such left-wing journals as the *Morning Freiheit, Zamlungen*, and *Yiddishe Kultur*. Two more volumes—*Splinters* and *Wander-way*—were issued in 1934. Her major collection, *Grief and Joy*, appeared fifteen years later in Toronto.

I WAIT FOR WORK

How often at night's edge I stand, as now,
and wait for morning,
and look up at the great grim wall
to the sixth story—
the street, through all its length and breadth,
still lies bound up in night,
and I am standing bound up too
like a bespidered fly.

And as I wait, it seems the world
waits lonely, just like me,
for panes to come alive with light
in every factory.
Through me the chill November wind
shudderingly blows;
yet even now I've not replaced
my scanty summer clothes.

I'm gnawed at by a silent grief
that goes to where I dwell:

a dark room on the second floor,
a small and icy cell.
Alone, my child must guard himself
as many nights before.
Is he in tears? or still asleep?
—I guard this grim sixth floor.

Isaac Elchonen Ronch (1899–1985)

Born in Konin, Poland, in 1899, ISAAC ELCHONEN RONCH lived in
Lodz from 1906 to 1913, when he emigrated to the United States.
He was sixteen when his first poem was published. In Chicago he
attended Northwestern University, taught in the Yiddish schools,
saw the publication of *Winds* in 1923, and co-edited *Young Chicago*.
In 1924 he settled in New York, where he became a leader in the
Proletpen movement, co-editing *Signal*. During the 1930s he edited *Proletarian Upbringing*, coordinated a Yiddish Writers Project
for the W.P.A., and wrote several volumes of poetry, including
Indian Summer (1930) and *Hungry Hands* (1936). Later he produced such prose works as *Our Folks* (1939), *America in Yiddish
Literature* (1945), and the novel *Motek*, a trilogy, the first part of
which appeared in English translation in 1953. His *Selected Poems*
were also issued in English translation, in 1961, as was *In the Desert*
a decade later. By then he had made Los Angeles his home,
writing prolifically until his death in 1985, contributing essays,
fiction, and poetry almost daily to the *Morning Freiheit*. Among his
later works are such volumes as *The World of Marc Chagall* (1968)
and a bilingual collection, *Praise and Thanks* (1981).

HANDS

What are the trees, turned always to the sky?
They're outstretched hands, that never cease to cry:
Keep us alive!

What are the mountains, rising through the mists?
They're hands of giants, clenched colossal fists,
that strain and strive.

What are the billows, crests of foam and spray?
They're trembling magic-hands, that seem to play
upon the river.

What is that miracle upon which stands
the world? A pair of tender human hands
that give forever.

THE SONG OF THE KITCHEN

Now is the time I miss you: in the deep
of night. I gaze far past the windowpane,
and listen to the message of the rain,
and think: you must have rocked the house asleep.

Now, scene by scene, I live it all again.
When were you closer? When were you more precious?
—You're in the kitchen, rubbing bright the dishes,
your voice as gentle now as it was then.

That spotless room! That dream I treasure so!
Has any sight more fair been granted me?
The old tree knows: the old and silent tree;
the table knows—and you and I, we know.

At that white table, oh what hours we spent!
How many things our eyes expressed and guessed!
The clothes you wore were always freshly pressed.
I filled my lungs with their delicious scent
and took it with me—like the loveliest
of perfumes—everywhere I went.

To me your apron was the prettiest dress;
your ornaments—the sparkling kitchenware.
In that room lived my greatest happiness,
because your smile made every corner fair.

283

At evening, after work, you're sitting, too,
and thinking about me—I know you are.
It's late. I miss you now. My gaze goes far.
The rain drums loud, but what I hear is you.

MOSES' KISS

When the lines across the brow are multiplying,
and the end is drawing near, the time of dying—

let the waterfalls then altogether stop;
let us have what Moses had: a summing up;

let the soul, so long at war with life, surrender
after she receives a kiss that's soft and tender.

Though the granaries have all the yield we nourished,
must we perish now, before desire has perished?

Thus did Moses plead unto the dale, the mountain,
to uphold him when he came to his accounting.

Years—six score; for Moses they were minutes merely!
bushels heaped with truth his life had yielded yearly;

and he ached to set his foot on virgin land,
hold a humble shoot of grass within his hand.

But, since Adam, there has been no other way:
all his caring, prizing, reaches its last day.

He would like to look around a little longer,
but the Mighty Mother summons him to slumber.

Moses scaled the mountain to its utmost peak,
but no thunders, lightnings, hushed to hear him speak;

neither hill nor dale gave help at his behest
and the sunset went on crimsoning the west.

Through the dusk he saw the country of his hope,
and with that he stretched out on the rocky slope.

And he there received a kiss from his Creator;
only the name Moses was remembered later.

To expire with a silent kiss has merit;
every heir should have such kisses to inherit.

Since it was awarded the redeemer Moses,
dear to all should be the kiss with which life closes.

To assuage our burning bush, life's fiery burden,
comes the kiss of death, our everlasting guerdon.

Death is sundown, red as tinder in the west;
on the peak one silent kiss, and all is rest.

Moishe Kish (1899–?)

Born in 1899 in Dvinsk, Latvia, MOISHE KISH arrived in the
United States at thirteen. He earned his reputation first as a
painter, but in 1920 began contributing poetry to a wide range of
periodicals, mostly those of the Left, including *Hammer, Yiddishe
Kultur, Zamlungen,* and the *Morning Freiheit.* In 1969 the YKUF
published his collected poems, *The World is My Home.* His paintings are housed in several major museums.

IN THE TOWN OF THE PERISHING LORD

Like a Gulliver towering over the pygmies of Lilliput,
the Empire State Building dazzles our sight

in its breadth and its height
—in the town of the lord,
the perishing lord.

Like a huge carousel runs the el round the Empire State
round and around through the day and the night
round its breadth and its height
—in the town of the lord,
the perishing lord.

Like the tightrope dancer we gasp at from below,
on a girder of steel the worker to and fro
strides without worry
near the hundredth story
—in the town of the lord,
the perishing lord.

He thinks of the might
that reigns uncontrolled
and the spider that spreads
its gossamer threads
round the idol of gold
—in the town of the lord,
the perishing lord.

And like a Gulliver the workingman would like
to seize the Chrysler with its silver spike
and pierce through the heart, the half-eaten heart
of the Clown King of Old, with his idol of gold
—in the town of the lord,
the perishing lord.

Shaye Budin (1899–)

SHAYE BUDIN was born in 1899 in the Ukrainian village of
Korostichev. He emigrated to New York in 1915 and has lived
there ever since. For several years he worked for HIAS. Among

his works are *Days and Life* (1955), *May My Poems Live* (1969), and *Songs of My Days* (1983).

AT JEFFERSON'S GRAVE IN MONTICELLO

It is good
that I carry light in my eyes,
and it is good
to hold you by the hand.
My love,
what I wish to tell you now
you must keep secret
as a precious necklace of pearls.

The nation that did not give birth to me,
the ground that did not see me
take my first steps,
has bound me to itself as strongly
as the placenta in my mother's belly.

Gettysburg and Yorktown,
Harper's Ferry and Bunker Hill,
Washington and Jefferson,
Garrison and Franklin,
Virginia's Blue Mountains
and Carolina's singing valleys,
Madison and Lincoln,
Patrick Henry and John Brown—
their every step and stir
is part of me—
they'll live within my heart
until my final day and night.

Ber Green (1901–)

Born in Yaruga, Podolia, in 1901, BER GREEN (pseudonym of Itzik Greenberg) was orphaned in infancy. His first poems were in Hebrew and Russian; at thirteen he achieved publication. After experiencing the pogroms and the civil war in the Ukraine, he taught in Rumania (1921–23). Settling in New York in 1923, he became a shop worker, then a Yiddish schoolteacher. He turned to Yiddish poetry in 1924; from that time he was an indispensable participant in every left-wing Yiddish publication and literary group, a tireless creative force as organizer, editor, lecturer, critic, poet and translator. For half a century (1931–81) he co-edited the *Morning Freiheit. Flowers Under Snow,* his first collection, was issued in 1939. A compilation of critical essays, *Yiddish Poets in America,* appeared in 1963. *Forever Green,* his second volume of poems, was published in Warsaw three years later. A second collection of literary essays, *From Generation to Generation,* followed in 1971. In recent years his memoirs have been serialized in the *Morning Freiheit.* One section, "Sholom Aleichem in My Life," was issued in English translation in 1985.

I SHALL NOT DISAPPEAR WITHOUT A TRACE

I shall not disappear without a trace;
within your hearts my flame shall find a place.
I'll carry this great truth across the earth:
that Man is holy, yes, beyond all worth.

From land to land I'll seek my radiant goal
till Man shall reach the heights of his own soul,
till every demon shall be overthrown,
and freedom come at last into its own.

The path I choose leads on from heart to heart—
no, not without a trace shall I depart:
the treasures of my life are yours to keep—
the harvest of my days is your to reap.

For it was you unfathomed life to me,
showed what a giant this poor dwarf might be.
Not every thing I reach for can be mine,
yet this I know: at least I'll leave a sign.

In every miracle of my refrain
I see your footprints; all your ageless pain
is mine now; all your laughter I've embraced.
I know: my life shall never be erased.

HUNGRY

Hungry I wander
in a sated land.
My hunger shrieks at the world
like a pack of wolves.
I live on the last of my juices
as the bear on his fat in the winter.
My face grows pale and ascetic.
Hunger by now has lapped up
its last drop of blood.
Around me: faces of hunger. Half-moons.
Everywhere I look: Loaves. Loaves.
The hungry pry open grain bins.
I whisper the cry of someone hungry,
hot as fresh-baked corn bread:
after all, hungry brothers, it's yours—
the bread of earth.

The hungry pry open grain bins.
Sated I wander
in a hungry land.

GASTONIA

Gastonia ignites the South with a red flame.
Gastonia glows with fiery print in our book *America*.
The pages, "Haymarket Tragedy," flutter like holy banners.

The ghosts—Sacco, Vanzetti—still hang over Boston.
Our land breathes hot with blood and war,
and in the South, the Stately, a red blaze has bloomed: Gastonia!
Then judges muffled themselves in robes of black;
they armed themselves with Death in each black fold.
Black robes dream: Inquisition. Bonfire-kindling. Fifteen lives
    are burning.
The South sits on the Judgment Seat,
but a thundering voice, from Boston to Gastonia,
shakes the Seat:
"Sacco and Vanzetti live.
Sacco and Vanzetti storm the South.
Beware, Judge, of our fiery judgment!"

Alexander Pomerantz (1901–1965)

Born in Grodno in 1901, ALEXANDER POMERANTZ published his
first poem, a tribute to Leib Neidus, in 1919, on the first anniver-
sary of his townsman's death. Two years later he moved to New
York. In 1924–1925 he edited *Young Smithy* and *Spartacus*, issued
by the Young Worker-Writers' League, predecessor of the Proletpen, and served on the staffs of *Hammer, Signal,* and *Youth.*
From 1933 to 1935 he studied in Kiev, earned the title Master of
Yiddish Literature, and wrote *Proletpen,* a historical account. From
1935 to 1950 he worked for the *Morning Freiheit. A Girl From Minsk*
was published in 1942; *The Caucasus, Torn Chains,* and *Engineers of
Souls* appeared a year later; and *Voyage Into the Future* was issued in
1944. He left the Communist movement in 1950 and was a librarian at the New York Jewish Theological Seminary from 1955
until his death. In 1962 the YIVO published his massive *Soviet
Kingdom of Slaughter.* He died three years later.

BALLAD OF AN ITALIAN GYPSY GIRL

Though I wish that I could wander
free and happy—by God's grace—
I knit stockings, tell your fortune,
stray alone from place to place.

I knit stockings, tell your fortune. . . .
Sometimes I begrudge the dead.
Let the Devil take such winters:
cold, without a crust of bread!

I knit stockings, tell your fortune,
look for bargains on the street;
add a penny to a penny
till I've saved enough to eat.

Sometimes I get sick of living:
stockings, fortunes, all the day.
How I wish that I could take my
tambourine, and run away!

I would dance in far-off cities—
full of gusto, full of joy;
and I'd find myself a partner
in a handsome, slender boy.

Then I'd be forever singing:
Tra-la-la-la, tra-la-la. . . .
And I'd hear the echoes ringing
through the whole world: Ha-ha-ha!

Nathan D. Korman (1901–1981)

NATHAN D. KORMAN was born in Rodem, Poland, in 1901. At
twenty-five he migrated to Havana, where his slender volume, *On
Island Earth,* appeared. It was the first Yiddish book of verse ever
produced in Cuba. A year later he settled in Philadelphia and

worked for decades at the milliner's trade. At first a Poale-Zionist, he moved further left, contributing regularly to all the Proletpen and YKUF publications. His works include *Uphill* (1943) and *Days and Years* (1970). He died in 1981.

I'M ARRESTED

Midnight; policemen hammer at the door.
I open; back against the wall I'm pressed.
A secret agent, an inquisitor,
shows me a paper: warrant for arrest;
my face, he says, was known to him before.

They search the drawers, the cabinets; they kick
the table over with its four legs up;
my mother cowers, tremulous and sick,
as if her life were draining, drop by drop.

It's hard for me to look her in the eye,
and doubly hard to hear her trembling moan.
I whisper: Ma, don't be afraid, don't cry;
perhaps in a few hours I'll be home.

Street after street they march me, on and on.
From house and courtyard other footsteps come;
familiar faces are led forth—and none
can guess how many years until we're home.

THE DEVILS' DANCE

Heine goes up in flame, and the Gomorrah;
Spinoza burns, the Rambam and Karl Marx;
around the bonfire Hitler's bullies roar a
devils' dance and hop around the sparks.

Scrolls go up in flame, the holiest pages;
every letter burns, and every line—

all things sacred, treasures of the ages,
are defiled, are plundered from their shrine.

Letters scream into a flaming word:
"Dance, and dance! the final devils' reel!
There'll be no Fourth Reich following the Third;
and every wounded scroll will heal . . .!"

Books laugh as the vandals romp around;
each reads aloud the text that is its own. . . .
But though the whole world hears the crackling sound,
men bury in their breasts the bitter moan. . . .

Round and round the Nazi ruffians whirl;
with drunkards' nerve they dance around the flame;
it gobbles up and guzzles down the world—
and after? Afterward let ash remain. . . .

* * *

Heine goes up in flame, and the Gomorrah;
Spinoza, Marx, the Rambam—torn from shelves;
around the bonfire Hitler's dancers roar a
devils' curse—but only curse themselves.

Chaneh Safran(1902–)

CHANEH SAFRAN's birthplace was Schedlitz, Poland. Her father ran a small butcher shop. Under the guidance of a wise and culturally oriented mother, she turned to writing at an early age, showing a special gift for the drama. In 1916, at the age of fourteen, she left Poland and settled in New York. Her first collection of poems, *Victory,* appeared in 1946. This was followed by a second volume, *Today,* and three novels—*The Dancer* (1952), *Vivian and Her Friends* (1954), and *Parents and Children* (1971–72)—all serialized in the *Morning Freiheit. Life Calls,* her third book of poems, was issued in 1968. She now resides in Florida.

293

ON THE UPHILL OF TIME

We're making our way up the high hill of Time;
its top is concealed in gloom.
Below us is Yesterday—here is Today,
Today with its rot and its bloom.

And when a great searchlight thrusts forth in the night,
illumines the hilltop and dies,
it's only revealed to the ones who look up,
in whom its bright beacons arise.

It happens, on nights that are frosty and dark,
when winds rock the air with their wrath:
a dense fog may cover the top of the hill
and blot out the upgoing path.

The climbers in panic attempt to get down
to Yesterday's "happier time";
but those who have once seen the top of the hill
will never go back—they will climb.

IN TERRIBLE DAYS

My singing was born during terrible days—
on broken, on blood-splattered ways.
Protected from flames were my home and my street then;
I therefore went marching to meet them.

I heard through the air the combined lamentation
of man and of earth in oppression;
I drank from the sea of the sorrows of others
the griefs that imprisoned my brothers.

I wrestled dejection with all my young might
—as fiercely as day wrestles night.
The faith in my heart did not wither away—
no matter how bitter the fray.

This faith was my dower; it came to me through
my father, that virtuous Jew;

294

within him the strength of his fathers ran strong;
like wine, it fermented my song.

Through me the despair of the wronged found its word,
the courage of heroes was heard;
my blood seethed with battle—revenge was its roar;
my world I created in war.

There clamored through me the afflictions of mothers,
of lost little sisters and brothers;
I cheered for the peoples who fought back and won,
who can't be and won't be undone.

Oh I am the mourner, and I am the heir:
man's holiness lies in my care!
With trembling, my song to its sources I tie
and lift the great legacy high!

Joseph Greenspan (1902–1934)

Born in Kletzk, Byelorussia, in 1902 JOSEPH GREENSPAN migrated
to Canada at sixteen, then moved to the United States. At first
employed as a cobbler, he later taught in the Yiddish schools of
the left-wing I.W.O. His poems began appearing in 1927 in the
Freiheit and *Hammer,* and he served on the editorial board of the
Proletpen's *Signal.* His first collection, *Between Walls,* was issued
jointly with Leib Sobrin's *Between People* in 1931. He died at thirty-
two. A posthumous volume, *Songs and Poems,* appeared in 1937.

THE JOBLESS BRICKLAYER

It was at the outset of autumn
that Jim the bricklayer,
on a New York pier,

295

for forty cents an hour,
dumped the last scraps of his Yankee pride
into a freight car.

Since then he's strayed
through gray, mangy dawns
and heaps of shopyard rust
and keeps his head
sunk between bony shoulders
as a broken, famished dog
hangs his tail between his hind legs;
and in empty pockets
ten fingers dangle
like ten worthless, worn-out bolts.

A LAST SOUND

Somewhere, far away, a last sound fades.
Already at the window the blue sorcery of dawn!
Why am I drawn to sunset's song, drawn to a day withdrawn?
Why does it weave a haunting mood in me with its gray shades?

Can I, too, be perhaps a late-September leaf
suspended wilting on a branch of a death-stricken tree?
and is this why I'm shaken, why I waken to the grief
that the wind wafts across the great savannas of the sea?

Far off, one last throat suspires its song somewhere.
Astride the towers the sun weaves her brave flag of purple-gold.
Why, when a last sound vanishes in air,
do I grow hushed and old?

Chaim Schwartz (1903–)

CHAIM SCHWARTZ was born in 1903 in Berezin, Byelorussia. His earliest poems were in Hebrew and Russian, but he soon turned to Yiddish. He emigrated to the United States in 1922 and settled in St. Louis, where *First Blossoms* appeared in 1928. Among the most prominent Proletpen poets outside of New York, he began contributing to the Canadian journal *Kamf* and the Proletpen's *Signal* in 1925. He moved to Los Angeles in 1937; there he soon became a central figure in left-wing cultural circles. Among his volumes of poetry are *The Great Struggle* (1943), *In the Light of Dawn* (1968), *Radiant Stairways* (1975), and *Sun Above Clouds* (1986). The last volume includes translations by Schwartz from several languages and many of his own poems in English translation.

MOSES
(excerpt)

Two roadways lie open: the first is not wide,
and darkness leans in on the path from each side;

it's chosen by wretches with eyes never lifted,
tied up in the anguish of wounds self-inflicted.

Remote and untraveled, it stretches ahead;
to life's empty outskirts the lone one is led.

The second's for people: a spacious, broad path
sown well by humanity's sweet, dewy breath.

On *that* road, like heroes, march those who behold
through night's thickest cover the bright morning gold;

they fling themselves forward with eyes full of morning,
and don't care a fig for the autumn winds' warning. . . .

IN ONE DAY

In one day the Maker created a man,
and cursed him and blessed him and thus it began:
"Your bread will be soaked in the sweat of your face
till Death in his mercy awards you release. . . ."

He carried his burden for thousands of years;
he suffered its weight with a hate that grew fierce—
his back buckling under, his footstep unfree,
restrained in the yoke of his Maker's decree.

But as he trod hard on the glorious ground,
his mind began turning these matters around . . .
and, thinking more deeply, in wonder he gaped
at all he himself had created and shaped:
his bread from the earth and his wine from the vine,
the flame that he cooked with, that made his walls shine,
the sheltering garments that covered his skin
and kept the foul weather from getting at him . . .
with singing and dancing, on stone and on scroll
with pen in his hand he unfolded his soul.

He rivaled the birds in the realms of the air,
surpassing what only in dreams he had dared—
he stood on the moon—left his print on its sand. . . .
What more? Are there distances yet to be spanned . . .?

Mankind, whom his Maker had hated and cursed,
became, through his burden, far more than at first;
earth's powers he fused, like a second Creator,
and made their old greatness ten thousand times greater;
with this in his confident grasp, he takes wing
straight into tomorrow—whatever it bring . . .
as good as his Maker, a partner at last,
God's sentence reversed—he is praised, he is blessed. . . .

Now, pondering, stunned and astounded he stands,
becrowned by the works of his brains and his hands:
the glorious earth, will he doom it to bear
an endless succession of blight and despair,
or wisely and bravely, with resolute toil,
caress it and coax into flower this soil . . .?

David Seltzer (1904–)

Born in Soroki, Bessarabia, in 1904, DAVID SELTZER became an apprentice printer at sixteen and emigrated to New York. The following year his poetry for children began to be published. He became news editor of the *Morning Freiheit* in 1932 and served as its Detroit correspondent from 1933 to 1935. A year later he edited the left-wing journal *Spark*. His first collection, *Bessarabian Poems* (1937), was followed by *Song of Brownsville* (1942), *The Hour That We Have Hungered For* (1947), and *Songs for Peace and Joy* (1964), a four-decade selection. With William Gropper he produced *Pictures and People of Soroki*, a collection of drawings and prose, in 1961.

BALLAD OF TWO SISTERS

Beside the Dniester
there stands an old mill.
The voice of its water
is never still:

"Here dwelled a miller;
lovely and slim
as pines, were the daughters
who lived with him.

"The elder one knitted
all the day long;
sorrow was in her
eyes and her song.

"The younger one scampered
to forest and sea;
over the mountains
her joy rang free.

"When evening comes
with cricket and star,

a shadow steals
toward the mill from afar:

"a lad like an oak,
with two mighty hands,
a hairy breast
that burns and commands.

"The younger one whispers
into his ears.
At a window the elder one
swallows her tears.

"They'll be weaving wreaths
on the Dniester soon,
fiddling and fluting
a wedding tune.

"They'll be clinking cups
on Dniester's shore:
old folks and young folks
drunk on the floor. . . .

"Home to her husband
was carried the bride;
the elder one drowned
her grief in the tide."

Deserted now
stands the old mill.
Only the water
is not still.

AT THE BLAZING BONFIRE

A twilight bonfire
has lit up the Square.
From circles of tinder
a song finds the air:

"Friend! to the fire,
and get your hands warm!
Backs walled together,
we're braced for a storm.

"Come to the great tongue
that licks at the dark;
we're warmer together
than freezing apart.

"Feed it your anger;
don't let it go tame;
spark touched by spark
shoots up into flame.

"Cold, are you? needy?
come, brothers, come near!
It's flame, it's storm
we are gathering here."

David Opalov (1904–1986)

DAVID OPALOV, who dropped his family name of Podoksik, was born in Riga, Latvia, in 1904. His first Russian poems appeared in local newspapers in 1918. Three years later he left for New York, where his Russian poems continued to be published. In 1933 he began writing in Yiddish as well; his work appeared in Chicago, Paris, Mexico City, London, and Buenos Aires. In 1940 his poems were collected in *Morning Red and Sunset*. Besides translating several Yiddish poets into Russian under the pseudonym of Leonid Opalov, he also wrote poems that were published in English under the name of Leonard Opalov. He was a regular contributor to Menke Katz's *Bitterroot* from its inception to his death in 1986.

THE HAYMARKET TRAGEDY (1886–1936)

Like a heart's wound deep and fresh
I am pierced by Joliet's slaying;
from the rope, as blue as wash,
Fischer, Parsons, Speiss, are swaying;

Engels too; by his own hand
Louis Lingg, a wheat stalk, fell.
Death, with sickle, takes his stand,
slashing at his own free will.

Heroes of an age in shackles,
martyrs of Haymarket Square—
now your praise is sung with Sacco's
and Vanzetti's—sainted pair!

With your blood you wrote a new
chapter in the freedom-battle
when at last the toilers grew
tired of chains, of being chattel.

You awoke them to alliance,
called them to the First of May;
now they span the streets like giants,
sing of you, who led the way.

Martin Birnbaum (1904–1986)

MARTIN BIRNBAUM (Hebrew given name, Mordecai-Ezriel) was
born in Horodenko, East Galicia, in 1904. During World War I he
lived in the Carpathian region of Bukovina, then in a Viennese
home for refugee children, and finally in Brno. He returned to
his birthplace in 1917 and planned to settle in Palestine. Instead,
he went to Vienna in 1920 and three years later emigrated to the
United States, where he became a fur worker and attended night

302

school. His first poems were in German, but he turned to Yiddish in 1929 and joined the Proletpen group, publishing in the *Freiheit*, *Hammer*, and *Signal* (which he co-edited). He also taught in the left-wing Yiddish schools for decades. Many years passed between his early collections, *The Hands of the Clock* (1934) and *The Way Up* (1939), and his next volumes, the ripe productions of a prolific old age: *Poems of Today and Yesterday* (1978) and *Poems About The Poem* (1981). He died in New York in 1986.

SONG OF AN OLD OPERATOR

Nightly like a pair of logs my hands are hanging,
and exhaustion pulls apart my knees;
all day long I drudge in the bleak factory,
and at dawn, despite a night of sleep, I feel no ease.

So many yesterdays lie heaped across my shoulder;
every one of them has left its mark.
I try to think: A better time is coming!
But now my days are burdensome and dark.

It's not my work that scares me in the morning,
the hours ahead, the speedup and the heat.
There's a dread that never fails to hound me:
tomorrow I'll be thrown out on the street.

I know too well those dreary days around the Market:
each one brings you two days closer to the last;
the weeks and months flow into one another,
and night no longer brings refreshing rest.

At dawn you break a bagel with your fingers;
some friend may buy you tea now and again;
later on, you trudge home from the Market—
after all, it's a nickel on the train.

And the apartment is so dark, so lonely;
your red-eyed wife goes round and groans her hours away;
there's dried-up bread to stuff your children's bellies;
a spoonful of hot food becomes a holiday!

303

In times like these, each day is hard and bitter.
You wish that the machine were once more breaking you!
True, you've known the bitterness of toil for ages—
but the hunger of each day is new.

So, while drudgery lies like lead on every muscle,
while I'm drained here in the speedup, in the heat—
I'd face my days at the machine with a calm spirit
but for the dread: tomorrow I'll be on the street!

THE BLIND WOMAN

With her cane a sightless woman
taps along the bustling street—
every tap a sign, that wards her
from the pitfalls she may meet.

Every tap a listening, every
tap a looking, sharp and quick.
Loaded with a thousand senses
is the old blind woman's stick.

Soundlessly she seems to murmur
words for no one else to hear,
secret whisperings, that only
to the crooked cane are clear.

Tenderly her fingers fondle
him who warns of what may be,
him who taps out on the pavement
all her hot, blind agony.

Benjamin Katz (1905–)

Born in Horodnitza, the Ukraine, in 1905, BENJAMIN KATZ left for Canada at fifteen and remained there until 1937. A printer by trade, he also taught Yiddish in the Workmen's Circle schools of Windsor, Boston, Detroit, and New York. His poems, proletarian in nature, began appearing in 1924, and he contributed to the Proletpen's journals, *Hammer* and *Signal,* as well as to the *Morning Freiheit.* Among his collections of poetry are *Dawn* (1928; with others), *Spetzaine* (1930), and *The Dream of Brothers,* (1947). With his wife, the poet Brache Kopstein, he settled in Tel Aviv in 1949. There, in 1976, they edited an anthology of Yiddish lullabies, *Under Yankele's Cradle.*

MY FATHER THE POTTER

At the wheel my father lingers,
shaping dishes, shaping plates;
"Like clay within the potter's fingers"*
—great is the prayer a potter makes.

The wheel, as in a dream, is turning;
the clay obeys the master's art;
while secretly a poison's burning
into lungs and into heart. . . .

Now a glare falls on the form
and the clay is greenly glowing;
the wheel turns round as in a storm,
turns as if a whirlwind's blowing.

On it whirl both plates and dishes
shaped of yearning, shaped of need;
this is as the potter wishes,
and his will is great indeed.

---

*Jer. 18:6.

The mute clay that his hand is molding
gnaws at his blood in a secret way—
from the clay a dream's unfolding;
and his dream is in the clay.

Sholem Shtern (1907–)

Born in Tiszewitz, near Lublin, in 1907, SHOLEM SHTERN emigrated to Canada in 1926. Here he worked first in a fruit store, then as a bookstore clerk. Later he taught in Montreal's Morris Winchevsky School and eventually became its principal. His early poems appeared in the anthology *Dawn* and such journals as A. Liesin's *Tsukunft* (Future) as well as Z. Weinper's *Upsurge,* the *Morning Freiheit, Hammer,* and *Signal.* His first collection, *It Brightens* (1941), was followed four years later by *Morning.* Then came two autobiographical masterpieces, the verse-novel *In Canada* (1960) and *The White House in the Mountains* (1963), which depicts a Jewish sanatorium where Shtern himself recuperated from tuberculosis (1927–29). *The Family in Canada* appeared in 1970. Twelve years later a valuable prose work, *Writers I Have Known,* was issued. Three brothers—Jacob Zipper, Yehiel, and Dr. Israel Stern—a sister, Shifre Krishtalka, and a nephew, Aaron Krishtalka, have also contributed to Yiddish letters. Shtern lives in Montreal.

FIGHT
(from *In Canada*)

Surprise. The street grows full
and packed with people. Rush and roar.
A hunger march of unemployed
pushes toward City Hall.
Through sunny streets there flows

306

a human tide in long, straight rows.
But officers on neighing steeds, who guard
each foot of ground in the old town,
train loaded guns on the marching ones:
"Your way to City Hall is barred!"

Ranks of jobless, close and long,
bellow forth their battle song.
Horse-mouths froth.
Police with eyes of wrath
block the hungry path.
Church bells dazzle and ring.
Marching masses hurtle
to the tower walls and sing.
Mounties circle
the Square on every side.
Thugs and officers alike
chase and beat those on strike.
People run. One horse, a-flutter,
drags a capsized cart along the gutter.
The streets resound. Hot, piercing rays
saw blue roads across the sky.
Police-hoofs leap about and keep
the sidewalks pent.
A shot rings out. The throng in terror falls
clustered against the greenly rusted walls
of the tall monument.
Trolleys gape with shattered windowpanes.
Above them, with a hue and cry,
frightened pigeons fly.
Horses grind their yellow teeth;
under the thunder of their feet
cobbles split asunder.
The air, splintered by fury, shrieks
the despair of hungry weeks.
Ambulances howl and zoom along.
The throng hurls flasks and flagons
at paddy wagons.
Broken glass is gleaming.
In the Square the birds are screaming,
plummeting to bloodied grass.
The sun saws through shattered windowpanes
and licks warm blood

307

from scattered bricks.
Woeful and wild, the whole outdoors
sobs and roars.
The church tower resonates.
And the heart, brimful of hate,
leaps with a shriek: Storm, storm the blocked-off street!
Make it yours!

Yuri Suhl (1908–1986)

YURI SUHL was born in Pedayetz, Galicia, in 1908. At fifteen he
came to the United States and settled in Brooklyn. He graduated
from the Jewish Workers University in 1932 and began teaching
in the Yiddish schools of New York. Inspired by his teacher Ber
Green, he soon developed into one of the outstanding Proletpen
poets. His first collection, *The Light on My Street* (1935), was followed three years later by *Toward the Day* and, in 1942, *Israel
Partisan,* a tribute to the anti-Hitler resistance. After serving in the
U.S. Army during World War II he turned to English prose,
producing two enormously successful autobiographical novels,
One Foot in America (1950) and *Cowboy on a Wooden Horse* (1953).
His documentary volume, *They Fought Back: The Story of Jewish
Resistance in Nazi Europe* (1967), remains a classic of Holocaust
literature, as his *Ernestine L. Rose and the Battle for Human Rights*
(1959) is a classic biography of the early feminist movement. He
also produced many prize-winning children's books. In recent
years he returned to Yiddish poetry and became a successful
driftwood sculptor as well. He died in 1986.

THE WIND

To him who rocks in a well-cushioned chair
and plucks the grapes in perfect comfort from their stem,
sometimes the wind will come to call:

whistles, laughs, seeks out
his panes and plays a tune on them.

To him who has the heavens for a roof
and not one crust of bread to comfort him,
the wind comes stealing in through patched-up shoes and pants
and pirouettes around his bony body
inside his sack of skin.

MY SONG WILL BE THAT FISTS FLING HIGH

Let bourgeois poets sing the greening season
and praise the tender little breeze of May;
while I have brothers rotting in a prison,
my song will celebrate the stubborn fray.

While millions mill about with good hands wasted,
and Hunger's maw devours the days and weeks,
my song will be that hands turn clenched and fisted,
my song will be that fists fling high and speak.

What shirtless man can wear the Maytime sun instead?
grow fat on roses' fragrance when he's breadless, meatless?
And if your body's hammered by a nail of lead,
will you appreciate the breeze's sweetness?

In the balance of a man's existence
what are spring, fall, summer, winter, worth
while an old world dies, and in the distance
there's a new world coming into birth?

Let bourgeois poets sing the greening season
and praise the tender little breeze of May;
while millions—brothers—battle for a vision,
my song will celebrate the stubborn fray.

SONG OF THE UNEMPLOYED WORKER

The bit of salt in my house
has been long unsampled by a warmed-up pot,
and futile on the shelf are the rummagings
of the hungry mouse.

My stove has forgotten the taste of coals.
The wind runs at its own free will
through the chimney, as the cold
runs through my hole-pocked soles.

My wife lies groaning in bed—
thin as a splinter and blue with cold;
but our home has forgotten even the smell
of bread.

Our son, the provider, has nothing to provide
but joining the marches to Washington.
I would gladly march myself
if only I could trust these feet of mine.

A MOTHER LAMENTS
(from *A Peace Cantata*)

Mothers of sons and of daughters—hear me!
Deep is my sorrow, and great my distress.
Gone is the laughter that used to cheer me,
and grief has moved in to be my guest.

One chair at my table's always vacant;
forever empty is one certain bed.
Only my heart is full—with mother's aching;
only my eyes are full—with tears unshed.

They tore the schoolbook from his hand, and brought him
a gun, a loaded gun, to take its place.
To crawl upon all fours—this they have taught him;
to be a people-hunter on the chase.

They tore the pencil from his hand, and gave him
a bayonet well-sharpened in its stead.
They teach him now to swoop down like a raven
on distant fields—and strike the landscape dead.

I bore a son, and brought him up, believing
he'd someday be the solace for my woes.
Now I have wept my eyes away with grieving;
who knows if he is still alive—who knows?

Chaim Plotkin (1910–)

Born in Ruzhan, Poland, in 1910, CHAIM PLOTKIN became an
apprentice tailor and a member of the left-wing Poale-Zionist
movement. Emigrating to the United States at seventeen, he
worked in various clothing factories. In 1929 he was published for
the first time. From 1930 his work appeared in all the Proletpen
and YKUF publications (*Morning Freiheit, Signal, Hammer, Yiddishe
Kultur,* and *Zamlungen,* which he helped establish). He has also
written a novel, chapters of which appeared in the *Morning
Freiheit* and *Yiddishe Kultur.* A collection of his poems, *Along My
Paths,* was issued in Tel Aviv in 1978.

I AND THE SEWING MACHINE

Just a machine—a sewing machine:
wheels and bolts, all ice, all steel.
But when I spur it, make it sing,
it's like a windsong through a field.
Sometimes the machine's a horse;
I, a galloper bent low,
although it halts, pursue my course—
on, on I go.

I have known its language long
and understand its laugh and song
and hear it as it speeds ahead:
"Quick, the cloth! Quick, the thread!
Give some oil;
give, give, give!
to the mouth that must be fed!"

The needle flies, "foot" jigs and thuds;
the "tongue" licks at the oily hook:
"Not only oil—I want some blood!
You, operator,
give me! quick!"

ASH ON THE SUN

The numbers on her arm—
nails of the beast!

She sits at *my* table
but her soul—*there*. . . .

The breath of her talk—
sparks from the smokestacks!

The flames of the ovens
split rocks

and God—
as if eyeless and earless—

her nearest and dearest—
ash on the sun

and the moon—a scythe
weary of slashing!

An hour in a day—
a mountain on her head! . . .

The hands of the ghetto clocks
circle in blood. . . .

Her tearless weeping—
a downpour from the heart

* * *

I hear and am silent:
I seek word-bandages!

She bears grudges, resents her rescuer
the miracle. . . .

Dora Teitelboim (1914–)

DORA TEITELBOIM, daughter of a house painter, was born in Brest-Litovsk, Poland, in 1914. By the age of twelve she was writing verse. She left home at eighteen for South America, where she worked several years as a milliner, going to school at night. She then came to the United States and taught briefly in the Yiddish schools. Her first volume, *In the Heart of the World,* was published by the New York YKUF in 1944. *Heaven and Earth* followed four years later. The Argentine YKUF issued *With Open Eyes* in 1955. *The Ballad of Little Rock* (1959) and *The Wind Speaks Yiddish To Me* (1963) were published in Paris, to which she had moved in 1960. *On the Way to Humanity* appeared in Warsaw two years later. For many years she has divided her residence between France and Israel, and it is in Tel Aviv that her most recent collections have appeared, including *Song of the Quicksand Generation* (1973) and *At the Gate of Day* (1979). Several of her collections have been translated into French by Charles Dobzynski and Ratimir Pavlovic.

MY LULLABIES

Mother rocked my sobs away.
Her breasts had long ago gone dry,
so I cried both night and day
until no tears were left with which to cry.

She seasoned with a moan the food,
the bits of food upon our plate;
every pot of broth she brewed
was peppered with a curse against her fate.

All the nights of childhood through
upon her breast I shut my eyes,
and my mother never knew
her curses had become my lullabies.

When mother could no longer keep
the soothing slumber from her brain,
then silently I'd beg, I'd weep:
"Wake up and lull me with your curse again!"

MY MOTHER'S HANDS

In silence we appraoched the railroad track,
as kin approach a graveyard with their dead.
In my hands—nothing but a little sack;
in hers—a good word that was never said.

Side by side, with lips shut tight, we went,
as though we'd never met before that day;
but when the train began to move, she sent
her quivering hands to help me on my way.

Ten years—ten long, hard years—have come and gone;
of my old house, only a wall still stands.
My city's nothing but a marker on
a map—yet day and night I see two hands.

Two worn old hands go with me everywhere.
Not for a moment will they let me be.

Sometimes they grow a head of golden hair:
my mother's hair. . . . Sometimes they speak to me.

Two hands, two pale hands reach toward me, and grow
out of my limbs. Awakening in wonder
I count them: count four throbbing hands, and go
to face with fists the lightning and the thunder!

SHED NO TEARS

Shed no tears for what remains
when they lay me six feet under.
I hate tears as much as chains,
like the roe that hates his hunter!

Leave no flowers for a cover;
they will do us little good.
I'll not wake; my lips will never
form the word of gratitude.

If you care about my pleasure,
if your heart still holds its vow,
send me roses now to treasure,
come with love songs to me now.

Let no tablet be assigned me;
life itself has been a stone.
Those who look for me shall find me,
hear my heartbeat in their own.

Let the breezes bear me far,
where the stream of mankind rushes;
when I am too weak for war,
let the last song be my ashes.

Poets of the Holocaust

FROM VILNA WENT FORTH STILL ANOTHER DECREE

(poet unknown)

From Vilna went forth still another decree:
to fetch in the village Jews quickly.
So all were assembled, the young and the old,
with litters to carry the sickly.

The gates of the camp were then bolted,
and each of the newcomers sorted:
the people from Ushmen remained, and to Kovno
the Sulites must now be transported.

So out of the camp the young victims
were ushered one after the other,
and into the cars they were thrust with dispatch—
like cattle, were sealed in together.

The train chugged along without hurry;
it hooted; the sirens kept screeching.
At a station called Pogar it ground to a halt,
and next came the sound of unhitching. . . .

They saw in an instant: they'd all been deceived,
it was to their death they'd been taken!
They broke down the doors of the boxcars, and tried
to snatch at some way of escaping.

They hurled themselves fiercely against the Gestapo,
and tore the brown shirt from his body.
Not far from the martyred, there also lay dead
some storm troopers, bitten and bloody.

Mordecai Gebirtig (1877–1942)

MORDECAI GEBIRTIG, whose family name was Bertig, was born in 1877 in Cracow and worked there all his life as a carpenter. Encouraged by Abraham Reisen in 1906, he became a prolific and immensely popular songwriter, composing the melodies as well as the lyrics. From 1914 until the end of the First World War, he served in the Austrian army. Two years later his first collection, *Folkstimlich* (In the Popular Tradition), was published. In 1936 *My Songs,* fifty of his poems and musical settings, was published. When a pogrom shattered Pzytyk in 1938, he responded with "Aflame!" This song, prophetic of the Holocaust about to befall them, swept the Jewish communities of Eastern Europe and is still widely known. When Hitler occupied Cracow, Gebirtig was put into the ghetto with his fellow townsmen and was killed in 1942.

AFLAME!

Aflame! Brothers! aflame!
There may come the moment of shame
when the town and you expire
together in ashes and fire.
Aside from its black, bare walls
not one trace will remain.
And you stand and look around
with hands that are tame.
And you stand and look around
while our town goes up in flame.

Aflame! Brothers! aflame!
Yours will be the praise or the blame.
If you've loved this town all your days,
take buckets and put out the blaze.
With your own blood put it out.
Show from what stock you came.
Don't stand, brothers, like this
with hands that are tame!
Don't stand and look around
while our town goes up in flame.

Aflame! Brothers! aflame!
Alas, our poor town is aflame.
The more those tongues of fire
consume, the more they desire.
And the wicked winds are droning—
everything's aflame.
Don't stand, brothers, like this
with hands that are tame!
Brothers, don't stand and look around
while our town goes up in flame.

Isaac Katzenelson (1886–1944)

Born in 1886 in Karelitz, Byelorussia, Isaac Katzenelson moved
to Warsaw as a boy. He worked for the Hebrew newspaper
Hazefirah, and was first published at sixteen. Later he wrote several well-received plays, including *The Prophet* and *The White Life.*
For some years he directed a Hebrew-Polish high school in Lodz.
He was a Hebrew writer, but when Hitler seized Poland, driving
the Jews into ghettos and death camps, he turned to Yiddish. A
false passport brought him to France in 1943, but he was interned
in the Vittel concentration camp and ultimately deported to
Auschwitz, where he perished. After the war the manuscript of
his "Song of the Slaughtered Jewish People," along with other of
his Yiddish poems in manuscript, was discovered in three her-
metically sealed bottles in the hollow of an old tree in the Vittel
camp. It aroused wide attention and was published in several
languages, including German.

THE SONG OF THE SLAUGHTERED JEWISH PEOPLE
(excerpt)

I looked out of the window and beheld the hands that struck;
observed who did the beating up, and who were beaten up;
and wrung my hands for very shame . . . oh mockery and
    shame:
It was by Jews, alas, by Jews my Jewish folk was slain!

Apostates, half-apostates, with a shiny-booted tread,
with hats whose Star of David looked like swastikas instead;
a language strange and awkward in their mouths, and mean and
    fierce,
they dragged us from our dwelling places, pitched us down the
    stairs.

They tore the doors down, tore inside with curses and
    commands;
invaded Jewish homes with clubs held ready in their hands;
found us and beat us, bullied us to where the wagons stood—
both young and old! and soiled the light of day, and spat at God.

They dragged us from beneath our beds, from closets, with a
    curse:
"The wagon's waiting! Go to hell! or death! whichever's worse!"
They dragged us out into the street and then went back to
    forage:
one final dress, one final slice of bread, one sip of porridge.

And on the street—a spectacle to drive you mad: the street
has perished, and with one tremendous clamor, one great shriek,
the street—way up and way, way down—is empty and—is
    teeming
with wagons full of Jews! just look—with wagons full of
    screaming. . . .

Wagons of Jews! some of them wring their hands, some tear
    their hair,
and some are silent—ah! that silence is too loud to bear!
They look about. . . . Is it an evil dream? Or is it true?
And round the wagons—booted, hatted—Herr Policeman Jew!

The German stands apart, as if he's laughing at the scene—
the German keeps his distance—has no need to come between;
ah, woe is me! he's managed it! by Jews my Jews are slain!
Behold the wagons! Ah, behold the agony, the shame!

(Warsaw Ghetto)

Miriam Ulinover (1890–1944)

Born in Lodz in 1890, MIRIAM ULINOVER attended a Yiddish
public school. She was orphaned at an early age. In 1916 she was
published for the first time, and a volume of her poems, *My
Grandmother's Treasure,* was issued in Warsaw in 1922 with a foreword by David Frishman. A second collection, "Sabbath," never
achieved publication, but a small segment was included in the
anthology *Yiddish Women Poets.* When the Nazis seized Lodz, she
was forced, along with all her townspeople, into the ghetto. Here,
according to a survivor, she wrote prolifically, but none of her
work has survived. She perished in the crematoria of Auschwitz in
August 1944.

MORNING

On Saturday morning it's sunny and fair.
The Pentateuch's wonders unfold everywhere,
when swiftly the tidings of grandmothers spread
of how Mother Sarah lies laughing in bed
in her prettiest kerchief, ecstatic and proud,
for all has come true that the angels vowed. . . .
From the east a delicious aroma is shed
and the orchard bathes in Barsheeba air
and the heavens look on with a wondrous blue joy
—in one's grandmother-years to bring forth a boy!

Aaron Zeitlin (1898–1973)

Eldest son of the famed Hebrew writer Hillel Zeitlin, AARON ZEITLIN was born in 1898 in Gomel, the Ukraine. His early work includes *Shadows on Snow* and *Metatron: An Apocalyptic Poem,* both issued in 1922; several plays, including *Yakov Frank* (1929); and a 1937 novel, *Earth Ablaze.* He was allied with Melech Ravitch, Uri-Zvi Greenberg, and Peretz Markish in the experimentalist Khaliastre group of the early 1920s. In 1939 he was in New York for the premiere of his play *No Man's Land* when the Nazis invaded Poland; his wife, parents, and children perished. He remained in New York, permanently scarred. *Between Fire and Deliverance* appeared in 1957. A decade later the first of a two-volume edition of his poems was published. He died in New York in 1973, as preparations were being made to celebrate his seventy-fifth birthday.

ELEGY

Unhappy chords go blundering to and fro
on streets where Jacob Gordin long ago
parodied with beard and walking stick.
On East, on Waste Broadway, no one is sick today,
and nothing will persuade a stick to wake.

And gone without a trace the gramophone
that so heart-rendingly intoned the rhyme
of "Letter to My Mother." By the time
mother came to Mr. Cohn
how old and sick she'd grown!—
and she's been lying in the graveyard long
together with her mother tongue.

I WAS NOT PRIVILEGED

I left betimes, and God protected me
from the catastrophe.
Why did I leave before what was to be?

I was not privileged to take the road of flame
on which my people came.
And it torments me like a sin beyond forgiving,
the guilt of living,
of living on and singing on in rhyme.
And I'll be poisoned by my crime
until I follow one of the three shapes
prepared to shield me from my guilt, each of which waits
and calls me with its glowing word:
Saintliness is the first, Insanity the second,
Suicide the third.

But not by suicide can one so weak as I be beckoned;
my petty nature's not ascetically inclined;
nor have I the capacity to lose my mind.

THE OLD MUSIC-MAN

Sweet little music-men,
tender and dear,
play me a bit of
"Goodbye and Good Cheer"!

Play a farewell piece,
but no tears, not one.
I too was a music-man;
time to be gone.

First it's "Hello!"
—then "Time to go"—
like an old fiddle bow
to and fro, to and fro.

325

Rochl Korn (1898–1982)

ROCHL KORN was born in 1898 in Podliski, East Galicia, and studied in Vienna. Her father, a Hebrew poet, died when she was eleven. A year later she began writing in Polish but turned to Yiddish in 1919; *Village* was published in 1928. The Polish authorities persecuted and imprisoned her for her anti-Fascist activities. Until 1939 she lived in Premisle, Galicia, then moved to Lvov, which she fled in 1941 before the Nazi troops. She lived in Kiev, Tashkent, and other Soviet cities for a number of years. Most of her family, however, had been wiped out in the Holocaust. Following the war she moved first to Sweden, then to Montreal, Canada, where she remained until her death in 1982, producing increasingly ripe collections such as *From the Other Side of a Poem* (1962), *The Grace of the Verb* (1968), *On the Edge of a Moment* (1972), and *Bitter Reality* (1977), a book dedicated to the memory of her slaughtered family.

I'D LIKE TO STOP

Someday I'd like
to stop at a house,
tiptoe close
and feel the wall—
What kind of clay was used for the bricks?
As for the door, what kind of wood?
As for destruction, what kind of god
camped there to see that none would befall?

What kind of swallow under its roof
furnished a straw and earthen nest,
and what kind of angels in human guise
entered its hall as guests?

What kind of holy men bearing water
met them as they came in from the street,
to wash the dust of earthly roadways,
the dust from off their feet?

And what kind of blessing did they leave
the children big and small,
so that Belshetz, Maidanek, Treblinka,
could not harm them at all?

From such a dwelling
with whitewashed railing
amid trees and flowerbeds
of blue and gold and flame,
there came
the killer of my brothers,
of my mother.

I'll let my anguish grow
like the hair of Samson ages back,
and turn the millstone of days
around that bloody track.

Till on some night hereafter
when I hear above me the roar
of the murderer's drunken laughter,
I'll rip the hinges from the door
and the house will be so shaken
that night itself will waken
as the tremors travel up
through every pane and brick and nail and board
from the bottom to the top.

Yet I know, I know, my Lord,
that the toppling walls will bury
only me
and my woe.

HESHVAN*

The fresh, black chunks of earth
lie ready and exhausted in the autumn sun
like childbed women in their first delivery

Heshvan is the second month in the Jewish calendar (Oct./Nov.).

who calmly smile, emerging from their labor,
prepared to become mothers once again.

Crows have gathered for the celebration;
they stroll with deliberate, dainty steps
looking with black, clever eyes for dug-up worms
and shake their heads like ancient aunties
who work at bits of cake with their blue gums:
"Not bad! let's live to celebrate again next spring."

ALL THE FORBIDDEN ROADS

All the forbidden roads are open
to the changed Real
on the far side of hoping
where Time stamps its seal
on days of shame,
and over each kicked dream
an angel stands, whose wings are drooping.

ALL THAT WITH EAGERNESS OBEYED ME

All that with eagerness obeyed me
at the least hints
of limb or sense
has now detached itself in a wild insurrection;
all that was close to me, pledged to my cause,
has now betrayed me
as if no signal merits action
but the new laws
of a reality that's changed.

Pawned to a time entirely estranged,
I try to trace
footprints to yesterdays erased.

Joseph Rubinstein (1904–1978)

Born in 1904 in Skidl, near Bialystok, JOSEPH RUBINSTEIN moved to Warsaw at fourteen. His poetry appeared for the first time in 1925. *Models,* his first book, won the Peretz Prize in 1939. Shortly afterward, the Nazis seized Warsaw and he escaped to Soviet-held Bialystok. He spent half a year in Moscow as the guest of novelist David Bergelson. When Hitler attacked the USSR, he was moved to Alma-Ata, deep in Central Asia, along with many other refugee poets. A second volume, about to be published, was destroyed when the Nazis took Minsk. After the war he moved west—first to Lodz in 1946, then to Paris a year later. As a delegate of the Paris Yiddish Writers Union, he attended the 1948 World Jewish Cultural Congress in New York and remained there. His major work is a narrative trilogy: *The Megileh of Russia* (1960), *The Destruction of Poland* (1964), and *Europe: The Exodus* (1970). He died in Tel Aviv in 1978. The same year a posthumous collection, *Visions,* was published.

THE CHIMNEY

To rest on rooftops is the clouds' delight,
to rest and dream of routes they've not yet taken.
At dusk a dream-held chimney, painted white,
awaits them with an unrequited aching.

The clouds allow themselves a bit of rest,
then climb into their carts and hurry off;

the chimney dreams: he'd like to join their quest,
escape the crumbling garret and the roof.

Long streaks of smoke pursue them down the sky:
blue smoke of evening-dreams, as if through lips.
The clouds rush past, indifferent and high,
and on his mouth the blood of sunset drips.

329

Leib Apeskin (1908–1944)

LEIB APESKIN was born in Vilna in 1908 and was trained there as a teacher of Yiddish. He was imprisoned by the Polish authorities for revolutionary activities. In the Vilna ghetto he lectured, involved himself in the school movement, and translated songs for choral use. Among his own songs were "Dawn," "Tramp, Tramp, Tramp," and "On the Death of the Teacher Gerstein." In 1939 he was published in Soviet-Yiddish journals and was afterward among the founders of the partisan organization. He is said to have assembled a collection of his songs; when Vilna was liberated, partisans found a bloody bundle of his songs beside his body. He was killed on 11 July 1944.

WHY WAS IT SO BRIGHT?

Why, yesterday, was it so bright overhead?
and why did each street look so gay?
and why should the sun that was radiant, red,
be clouded and angry today?

The heavens, the house, and the street are now crying;
the heart, in its silence, grieves on.
Can someone forget, if he tries and keeps trying,
the hours of joy that are gone?

Away with your teardrops, away with your sorrow!
To grieve cannot do any good.
Perhaps by tomorrow—yes, surely tomorrow—
the sun will burst forth as it should!

"Shmerke" Katcherginsky (1908–1955)

Born in Vilna in 1908, "SHMERKE" KATCHERGINSKY was orphaned early and brought up by his grandfather. He became a lithographer. Active in the Communist underground, he was arrested several times. Under the pseudonym of Ch. Shmerke he contributed to *Young Vilna* from 1934 to 1936. When the Soviet Union gave Vilna to Lithuania, he left with the Red Army and taught in the Bialystok area, returning when the Soviets took all of Lithuania in 1940. After the Nazi invasion he wandered about his homeland disguised as a deaf-mute, but entered the Vilna ghetto in 1942 as a cultural activist and partisan. Along with Sutzkever he rescued many priceless Jewish treasures from the Nazis, hiding them in a bunker. A year later he fled to the forests and fought as a partisan, returning to his city when the Red Army liberated it in July 1944. Disappointed in the Soviet attitude toward the revival of Jewish culture, he left for Lodz in 1946; there he served on the Central Jewish Historical Commission and completed his first anthology, *Our Songs.* After the pogrom at Keltz he moved to Paris, where in 1947 *The Songs of the Vilna Ghetto, The Destruction of Vilna,* and *Partisans on the Move* were published. These were followed by the massive anthology *Songs of the Ghettoes,* with a foreword by H. Leivick, and *Between the Hammer and Sickle,* a study of the Soviet attack on Jewish culture. He settled in Buenos Aires in 1950, and his autobiography, *I Was a Partisan,* appeared there two years later. He died in an air crash in 1955 while on a fund-raising tour for the Jewish National Fund. The same year a *Shmerke Katcherginsky Memorial Volume* was issued.

WARSAW
(written in the woods of Narotch, 18 January 1944, to commemorate the anniversary of the first Warsaw uprising)

The night does not pass and the day does not dawn.
The earth is a planet gone bloody.

A Jew flutters up like a flag in the storm,
a flag in the valley of bodies.

In ruins the ghetto; its Jews—in a fight.
Through fire he strides past his brothers.
"Take vengeance! Take vengeance!" he storms at the night—
"for children, for fathers, for mothers!"

The earth does not whiten, though snow falls and falls:
the blood goes on crimsonly writing—
it covers the whiteness—for vengeance it calls—
the blood of the Jews who died fighting.

"There won't come a day," cries the Jew, "nor a night!
The nations will not be forgiven!
Whoever among us went down in the fight,
in us will forever be living!

"Inspired, we'll think of the dangers they braved;
we'll reckon the sorrows that wrenched them.
Let three cries of blood in your heart be engraved:
Avenge them! Avenge them! Avenge them!"

BALLAD OF ITZIK WITTENBERG

The enemy hearkens: a beast in the darkness;
the Mauser—it wakes in my hand—
but wait! my heart's drumming: two sentries are coming,
and with them our first-in-command.

The ghetto is sundered by lightning and thunder;
"Beware!" shrieks a tower in fright.
Brave fighters have freed our commander and leader
and fled with him into the night.

But night soon is over—and death lies uncovered;
the flames of the city leap high.
Aroused is the ghetto—the storm troopers threaten:
"Give up your leader, or die!"

The battleground quivers as Itzik delivers
the answer—while guns hold their breath:

"Shall others be given, to pay for my living?"
And proudly he goes to his death.

Once more in the darkness the enemy hearkens;
the Mauser—it wakes in my hand.
You are now dearer—now you be my hero!
Now you be my first-in-command!

Binem Heller (1908–)

Born in Warsaw in 1908, BINEM HELLER became a glove worker at fourteen. He emerged early as a leader of Poland's proletarian poets, equivalent to the Proletpen, with his first collection, *Through the Bars,* published in Lodz in 1930. From 1937 to 1939 he lived in Belgium and Paris. He returned to Warsaw, then fled to Bialystok before the Nazi armies. After the invasion of the Soviet Union he took shelter in Alma-Ata and in 1947 returned to Poland hoping to participate in a revival of its Jewish cultural life. *Spring in Poland* appeared in 1950 and *Poems, 1932–1939,* in 1956. He then moved to Paris and Brussels, where his poem of political renunciation, "Alas, How They Shattered My Life," caused a storm of controversy. A year later he made Israel his home. His many later works include *New Poems* (1964), *It's the Month of Nissan in the Warsaw Ghetto* (1973), and *They Shall Arise* (1984).

A SONG ABOUT YIDDISH

The Jews are dead; their language is alive.
She also lives when sorrow must be spoken.
And many are her juices that revive.
And she has silences that will be broken.

All in a row some people were marched by,
and in the selfsame row they all were murdered.

They heard no other sound than the raw cry
of German jaws by which their death was ordered.

And when in thousands they stood yellow-starred
beside the graves they had been summoned for,
their mother tongue grew suddenly so hard,
and against all monstrosities—so poor.

For life, it is the living speech we speak;
for death, only the liturgy will do;
in time of death the mother tongue is weak,
and in life only, can she live anew.

The Jews are dead. With ashes and with earth
their mouths have everlastingly been shut.
But once again their mother tongue blooms forth
and does not know that she's been rooted out.

"OLD THINGS"

"Old things!"
The words sound like a foreign tongue.
A vendor in the alley sings
the phrase with an Arabian twang.

A Jew from Yemen took this pair
of Yiddish words—and gives them back.
This was my Warsaw speech—so fair!—
alas, alack!

I ask him up and show him all
the old things that belong to me.
He offers . . . well, what does one call
a good price for such "property"?

But, shall I stoop to bargaining?
Swiftly my things are in his sack;
and once again I hear him sing
the two wrecked words—
alas, alack!

Israel Emiot (1909–1978)

ISRAEL EMIOT (pen name of Israel Goldwasser) was born in 1909 in Ostrau-Mazowietsk, Poland. His father went to America in 1919 to study medicine, but instead worked as a presser and died young. The boy was brought up by his grandparents. He wrote Hebrew verse as a child; when he was seventeen his work began to be published. Among his early volumes are *Drops in the Sea* (1935) and *On the Side* (1938), both published in Warsaw, which he fled before the Nazi troops, returning to his birthplace. A week later, when the Germans shot his mother, he escaped to Bialystok. He began publishing in the Soviet Yiddish press; a new collection, *Poems,* edited by Aaron Kushnirov, appeared in Moscow in 1940. After Hitler's invasion of Russia he was among the refugees evacuated to Alma-Ata, Kazakstan. He went to Biro Bidjan in 1944 as a correspondent for the Jewish Anti-Fascist Committee and remained until 1948, when he was incarcerated for a year, then deported to an eastern Siberia camp where he met Moishe Broderson and other poets. Granted amnesty in 1953 he went to Poland, where his poems were published in Polish, and *Yearning,* a new collection, was issued in 1957. He moved to the United States, where his wife and children had found refuge in 1940, and ultimately settled in Rochester, New York, where *The Biro-Bidjan Affair,* with an introduction by Melech Ravitch, appeared in 1960, followed by *Listening to the Tune* in 1961 and *Covered Mirrors* two years later.

MENDELE

Now the Holocaust's done and there's scarcely a Jew,
I turn, Grandpa Mendele, once more to you.

You visited me as a workaday guest
to shake me, awaken some hope in my breast.

But speak to me, Mendele: do you know why
my Sender has suddenly started to cry?

—O Grandpa, it's lonely and I kiss every word
of Ben Yomen the Last, of Ben Yomen the Third,

who salutes me in Yiddish, and sets me at rest
when walls stick their ears out, as if they're nonplussed.

We heard you, dear Grandpa, and gathered your lore,
and nevertheless remained fools as before.

And I keep, as before, although years have gone past,
the old Jewish custom: hope wakes in my breast.

HAD MY MOTHER LIVED

Had my mother lived, by now she'd surely be
an old Jewish woman with hair white as snow;
even through spectacles she would not see
the difference between dream and what is so.

An old, old mother, with nothing left to do,
feet propped on a stool, a princess on her throne;
but whatever you're up to, she'd be right there with you
—and your whole life comes from her alone.

"Momma, the table waits for you," I'd say.
As portraits crown walls, she'd crown each holiday.
And if she drowsed, I'd gently take her hand
and off we'd wander to her golden land.

Chaim Grade (1910–1982)

CHAIM GRADE was born in Vilna in 1910. At twenty-two he began
contributing poems to the *Vilna Day* and became a member of the
progressive group Young Vilna. His first collection, *Yes,* appeared

in 1936. This was followed by *Musserniks* three years later. He fled
east and spent World War II in the USSR, returning in 1946 to the
city of his birth, where his wife and family had been slaughtered
with tens of thousands of others. He stayed briefly, trying to re-
establish Vilna's once-brilliant cultural life, but he left for Paris in
1947 and two years later settled in New York. From 1945 to 1950
six volumes of his poetry appeared—the first, *Epochs,* in New
York, the last, *The Radiance of Extinguished Stars,* in Buenos Aires.
A dozen years passed before his next collection, *The Man of Fire.*
In 1967 his novel, *The Well,* was published in an English translation. Two years later his last book of poems, *On My Way to You,* was
issued in Tel Aviv in a Hebrew-Yiddish edition.

A NAKED BOY

Creator of the world in all its diverse forms!
A naked boy comes with a girl-child in his arms.
He holds his sister, since she is the lastborn daughter.
He takes her from Treblinka, from the place of slaughter.
He keeps on moving in the sky above my head
on fields of ice amid the swarms of stars outspread
and in the blazing heat of sunlit mountaintops,
and never wants to get somewhere and never stops.
Around his neck the little sister's hands are clasped
as in the death march to the cell that was their last.

Creator of the tents of Heaven far away,
of our bad world, and of the good worlds in your sway!
The hissing snake that twists itself up into arcs
looks not the slightest bit like your melodious larks;
nobody can transpose the shapes of these two creatures;
but Man hides what he is by altering his features.
The hangman's fingers are as white as are his slain;
and once the hangman dies, he cannot die again.
Only the boy goes on, and carries as he goes
his sister, as the seed bag's held by one who sows.

The twelve old stars of fate have ringed me like barbed wire,
and now the star of this boy's fate. It's my desire
to find his native land, his own belovèd town

337

where he at last can lay his little sister down;
and I have found a simple hill at Galilee
where all the trees will murmur sympathetically.
But even at blue Galilee he will not trust
his sister's cold and naked body to the dust.
And still in moonlight he keeps wandering about
around Treblinka's altar, where the fire is out.

YEHUDA HALEVI

Could I sing like the great poet of Castile upon the sea,
I must be, like him, the morning star transformed and freshly
    glowing;
in my sea song, like first chapters, billows would burst free,
welling forth from the abysses with a fount of sweet tears
    flowing.

When a billow crests upon the flood, I see his graveyard stone,
how it sparkles with the fine gold of the poet's spotless name.
Ben Halevi turned his back on the good fortune he had known
for a love that led him over seething chasms like a flame.

High the Hebrew singer raised the anchor of his fate
and he flung it to the waves that pitilessly rolled.
More than by his song I am astounded by his faith
and by his ability in midlife to grow old.

All the strings that graced his lyre he tore, but kept one magic
    string
to enchant his yearning for a glimpse of that immortal shore;
I yearn also, unto swooning, for so great a song to sing
and a faith that makes all lusts turn ugly as a dried-up sore.

I'm still tortured by my youth, whose flame so hastily died down
in a fury, shedding ashes on my spirit like a shroud.
Spite of all the sorrows that have since ploughed through me,
    bone by bone,
what has come of my late autumn sowing does not make me
    proud.

338

Rajzel Zychlinsky (1910–)

Born in 1910 in Gombin, Poland, RAJZEL ZYCHLINSKY first attended a public school and later had private teachers. Her father, a leather worker, went three times to the United States, and died in Chicago in 1928. Her first volume, *Poems,* was published in Warsaw in 1936 with an introduction by Itzik Manger. Her second collection appeared shortly before the outbreak of World War II. She fled east ahead of the invaders, who slaughtered the rest of her family. Her son was born in Kazan. She returned to her native land in 1947, but a year later she left for Paris and in 1951 settled in New York, where she studied at City College and the New School for Social Research. In 1975 she received Israel's coveted Itzik Manger Prize, and in 1981 her selected poems in German translation were issued in Leipzig. Her later collections include *Silent Doors* (1962), *Autumnal Squares* (1969), and *The November Sun* (1977; Paris). In recent years she moved to Canada, but has returned to New York.

THE SILENT PARTNER

Three meters wide
six meters deep
and fifteen meters long—
these are the measurements of one of the pits
in Poland
to which the Germans drove Jews
shot them there
and buried them.
Three meters wide
six meters deep
and fifteen meters long—
the three dimensions.
And the fourth dimension,
the one in which all the slaughtered Jews
cannot die
and cannot live—
is now the silent partner
through all the days of my life.

MY MOTHER LOOKS AT ME

My mother looks at me with bloodied
eyes, out of a cloud:
Daughter, bind up my wounds.
Her gray head is bowed.

Amid the leaves of each green tree
my sister moans:
My little daughter, where is she?
Rajzel, gather her bones.

My brother swims in the waters
days, weeks, years,
dragged forward by the rivers,
flung back by the seas.

My neighbor wakes me in the night;
he makes a woeful sound:
Take me down from the gallows—
put me in the ground.

May. With my son in my arms I wander
amid shadows. I greet them all.
So many cut-down lives are clinging
to me, to my corners, to every wall.

So many cut-down lives are trembling
on the long lashes of my son.
So many cut-down lives are sobbing
in May, when the spring winds come.

A SNOW FALLS

A snow falls in the dusk
and falls.
Streetlamps stretch forth white hands.
There blunders in the snow in the dusk
a deported
alien
homeless Jew.

The snow falls and falls
not from heaven,
not to earth,
but out of some distant,
bloodless planet—
the Jew will go off
and leave no track,
and will never
again come back.

WE GO ON LIVING

We go on living on the earth
that has taken our blood to quench its thirst.
There is a green spring coming—
our bones have been ground up into ash;
we go on living, a cluster left to say Kaddish.

We eat the bread of the wheat fields,
drink from a well these days.
The sun is very kind now;
she touches us with her rays. . . .
We pass, leading our children by the hand,
wrecked homes, wrecked walls that mournfully stand.
We pass dead islands of dead childhood years.
Free as a bird the wind careers.

We go on living. The snow begins to fall.
We meet white trees, yes, we see them one and all.
Eyes dark, we drink the dusk; and without words
we speak—to little, gray birds.

WHAT HAS BECOME OF

What has become of the old gray woman
who never slept
for fear she might fall asleep forever?
Is she sleeping at last the everlasting sleep

out of which nothing in the world can wake her,
nothing horrible can shake her?
Has she re-entered the circle
of ever-wakeful stars,
white hair a-flutter
amid comets a-flutter on their white track—
the Manhattan woman—old, insomniac?

MY PRAYER TO THE CHIMNEY

Every morning I offer a prayer
to the chimney,
the godly fool on my roof:
Lessen the frosts from the north,
tame the sun in the south,
and beg the winds
not to knock you down.
For as long as you stand,
I stand too;
as long as you think,
I think too.
Don't fall,
O don't cave in,
my god!

AT NIGHT IN NEW YORK

The cry of a child
at night in New York
splits walls,
hollows houses,
sweeps away
foundations.
Stones fall:
pieces of sleep,
interrupted dreams,
head over head.
Dark walls rise up

on four feet.
They will soon deafen
with animal roar
the universe.
The mother comes.
She comes from the far, star-studded Milky Way.
She nurses the child,
calms it, stills its cries,
and once more
New York closes its eyes.

THIS IS NOT THE ROAD

> This is not the road,
> and this is not the city.
> —2 Kings

And where *is* the road?
Where *is* the city?
The sun is ready to go down,
and I have not yet found
the spot
the stone
on which to lean my head for a night's rest
and again see the ladder in my dreams
with the angels
who still deliver me
from the flames.

Jacob Friedman (1910–1973)

JACOB FRIEDMAN was born in Milnitsa, Galicia, in 1910. When he was nine, his family moved to Czernowicz. He began writing in Hebrew and Yiddish early, and was published for the first time at seventeen. From 1929 to 1933 he lived in Warsaw, then returned to Rumania. He spent the war years in the Transnistre concentration camp. From 1945 to 1947 he lived in Bucharest, where his revue *Our Way* was performed and where he co-edited a *Bucharest Anthology.* When he entered Palestine illegally in 1947 he was seized by the British and for two years was held in a displaced persons camp on Cyprus, where *Our Way* was again produced. From 1949 he lived in Israel, where his 1953 collection, *Shepherds in Israel,* and *Love* (1967) received prestigious awards. He died in 1973.

WHO BRINGS THE SONGS?

My little daughter, like a squirrel, climbs on me—
Abba, who comes carrying your songs to you?
She thinks that songs are fruit picked off a tree
by Mother in the garden in the daybreak dew.

Apricots, not songs, she sees her bring;
in astonishment her great eyes open wide.
Little daughter, it's Elijah brings the songs I sing,
from the blue woods where he and his dear children all reside.

"Take me," she says, "to the blue woods, the children blue!"
In blue woods children also must be blue, she thinks,
and in blue woods each fox is blue, each stag is, too,
that every evening comes to the blue pool and drinks.

"Abba, these songs of yours are blue as well;
Amma once said that to you, and I heard.
From the blue woods where his blue children dwell,
when will Elijah bring you your blue words?"

How can I answer? When I hear my daughter ask it,
I press her to my heart—her little body trusts me so completely.
We rock together childishly in a blue basket
filled to the brim with songs that ripen sweetly.

A SMALL DRAMA

Near the boxwood tree a donkey drinks the sun.
On the donkey, beaming, sits my little girl:
"Abba, let us play that lovely game, the one
about Messiah, who brings presents to the world."

Whereto shall we gallop, child, whereto, my crown?
And what are we to bring the world, what precious boon?
"A thousand dollies, Abba, and a tasseled clown,
and a pretty bird a-flying to the moon. . . ."

What will the world do with all those playthings, my delight?
And on the moon what pleasure is the bird to take?
"Everyone will play, Abba, they'll play from morn to night!"
She laughs, and the donkey gives himself a shake.

"Hold me, Abba! I'm afraid!" she calls.
"Take me off the donkey!" I obey.
I hold her, lift her down. The curtain falls
on our small drama, our "Redemption Play."

Avrom Sutzkever (1913–)

Born in Smorgon, near Vilna, in 1913, AVROM SUTZKEVER and his family escaped the pogroms of World War I by moving to Omsk, Siberia. At seven he witnessed his father's fatal heart attack. Two years later his mother brought her family back, first to their ruined town, then to Vilna, where her gifted five-year-old daughter died. In his early teens Sutzkever became a serious poet, especially influenced by M. L. Halpern. He joined Young Vilna, some of whose most talented members later perished in the Holocaust. *Siberia* (1937) was his first major work. During World War II his mother and his newborn baby were among the slaughtered, but he survived—first by hiding in the Vilna sewers, later as a partisan in the forests. The poems he created during those years, including the epic *Secret Town,* "succeeded," according to Jacob Glatstein, "in presenting in the purest form the greatest horror of all time." He later testified at the Nuremberg war crimes trials. Since the late 1940s he has lived in Israel, editing the quarterly *Golden Chain* and producing distinguished volumes of both poetry and prose, including *In the Fire Chariot, Ode to the Dove,* and *Songs From the Sea of Death,* a 480-page compilation of all his Holocaust poetry.

IN THE DUNGEON

As always: the gloom wants to smother me quite.
The lead-colored rodents all gnaw at my sight.
I enter the dungeon and sink underground—
if one thing that's human, one shred, could be found!

I come on a fragment of glass, in whose clutches
a moonbeam in glazen captivity twitches.
My sinking's forgot in a flame of elation:
This thing, after all, was a human creation!

Along its glass sharpness I fondle the moon:
"You want it? I'll give you my life as a boon!"
But life's very warm, and the glass very cold
to thrust at a throat less than thirty years old.

(Vilna, end of June, 1941)

MY MOTHER
(concluding sections)

I look for the precious four walls
where you drew breath;

behind me the stairs disappear
like a water hole steaming.

346

I reach for the knob, and tear
the door to your life—

it's as if a little bird weeps
in the cage of my fingers.

I enter the room in which
your dream's growing dark—

scarcely flickers the lamp
you lately lighted.

On the table a glass of tea
you did not quite sip;

fingers still quiver about
on the rims of silver. . . .

"Have mercy!" begs the tongue
of flame in the lamp—

I feed the lamp with my blood
to keep it from dying.

* * *

Not you do I find, but your smock—ripped apart.
I hold it ashamedly pressed to my heart.
The holes in your smock are the days of my life
and the seam of it runs through my heart like a knife.

I tear off my clothing and creep in your bare,
thin garment as if in myself. What I wear
no more is a smock; it's your radiant skin,
your death, left behind, I am shuddering in.

* * *

You speak to me,
and your voice rings true:
"Don't do it, my child;
it's sinful, it's wild;
accept as rightful
my parting from you.

347

"While you have breath
I too exist—
as the pit in the plum
contains what will come:
tree, nest, robin,
and all the rest."

(Vilna Ghetto, October 1942)

THE LOST ROSES
(from "The Three Roses")

I'll go off to seek you; a shovel I'll bring
to tunnel through graves, plough up meadow and farm;
I'll question the grasses and let the thorn sting;
and always your shadow will lean on my arm.

And if, after all, you are not to be found,
I'll dig into words and I'll plough every sound,
until the lost roses are freed from the ground,
that kingdom of night in whose deeps they were drowned.

(Vilna Ghetto, October 1942)

THE TEACHER MIRA

With patches of yellow to cover our bones,
past all our old streets, to the ghetto we're driven.
Each house says goodbye to its daughters, its sons,
and stone-faced we greet each command that is given.

Phylacteries crown every grandfather's head;
a calf and a cottager, paired from the start;
one drags by her nails a belovèd, half-dead,
another—a bundle of wood on a cart.

And right in the midst of them, Mira the teacher—
a child on one arm, like a bright golden zither;
and safe in her handclasp a second bright creature;
and pupils, battalions of them, always with her.

A gate's at the old Jewish quarter, its wood
as warm as a corpse that seems merely asleep;
and just like a sluice for some swift-driven flood
it opens, and swallows them into the deep.

They're chased without light, without bread, through the rubble;
a pencil's their light and a book is their bread.
She finds them a ruined apartment; with double
devotion to Mira their work moves ahead.

The children both sparkle and laugh as she reads them
a story by Sholom Aleichem; their hair
she tenderly combs, with blue ribbons she braids them,
and counts: a full hundred and thirty are there.

The teacher awakes with the sun; as it mounts,
she waits for the children, the life of her life.
They come. And she counts them. O, best not to count!
A score, overnight, were cut down by the knife.

Her face is a pane that the dusk madly streaks;
but never like this must the children behold her!
So, biting her lip with new courage, she speaks
of Leckert;* the boldness of him makes them bolder.

At midnight a grayness has quilted each yard,
and with it the hair of the teacher turns gray:
the cellar! She looks for her mother, looks hard—
with seventeen children she's vanished away.

When sun dried the blood, Mira silently hung
her orphaned apartment with green bits of spirit;
—came Gerstein the teacher: "Our song must be sung
so loudly that over the gates they can hear it!"

_____

*Hirsh Leckert, a martyred young labor leader.

It rings forth: "The spring is not far." Under ax
and sword thrust, the groundworks of tenements quiver.
They're dragged by the hair from the cellars and cracks.
"The spring is not far!" rings out louder than ever.

Now—sisterless, motherless—sixty are left.
She's mother, she's sister: My darlings, my doves—
a holiday's coming; we've got to be swift—
let's put on a program that everyone loves!

At show-time just forty remain. But each one—
with little white shirt, and with such a bright look.
The stage is transformed: there's a garden, a sun. . . .
You almost can go for a dip in the brook.

But just as the Third Gift of Peretz† was rendered,
catastrophe tore like a saw through their haven.
The enemy pounced! and by dawn, of a hundred
and thirty, there lived only Mira and seven.

And so, till her senses were split by the blade,
the children were—bees, and their teacher—a flower.
 The flower's gone gray and her limbs have decayed,
 but tall in the dew of the dawn she will tower!

(Vilna Ghetto, 10 May 1943)

A SWORD WITH WINGS

In dream and in reality you sent the Lord of Woe
unto me, and declared: Pay what you owe!
But I cried out in welcome, as is best:
O blessèd guest!

And I stripped bare my flesh and my fleshed word for him to
  see:

†Peretz's great short story, "Three Gifts."

Subdue thy passion; I am pledged to thee!
In through my limbs' coat, open to the sight,
sow thy great light!

And if I'm filled, how slight my pain beside the flood of pains!
Instead of lamentation—godly aims.
They burn away my weakness, turn me, Lord,
into a sword.

And now, when raging at the world, I am a sword with wings.
Your face, reflected in its metal, streams.
It was the Lord of Woe who made my dower
this awesome power.

(Vilna Ghetto, 20 May 1943)

SONG OF A JEWISH POET IN 1943

Am I, then, of all Europe's poets, the last?
With no one but corpses and vultures to listen?
In fire, in swamp, I am drowning—held fast
by yellow, patched hours as if in a prison.

I bite at my hours with the teeth of a beast
made strong by a tear of my mother's. I see
the million-pulsed heart of my brothers deceased
who rise from the ground and are rushing at me.

The million-pulsed heart—that am I! I'm assigned
to shelter the songs left behind when they fell.
And God, since His temples were razed by mankind,
I hide in myself, like the sun in a well.

Be open, my heart! See them burst into bloom,
those heavenly hours the future holds dear!
O strengthen their purpose, and make them come soon,
and be, in your sorrow, their trumpet, their seer!

And sing of the swamps, till a tear of your mother's
has welled once again! Give your voice to the breeze,

351

and let it be heard by the bones of your brothers,
the ghetto ablaze, and your kin overseas!

(Vilna Ghetto, 22 June 1943)

IF NO TRACE OF MY PEOPLE SHALL BE FOUND

If no trace of my people shall be found,
I pray it: From my memory disappear!
And let all graves sink deeper underground.
And let no dust remain of month or year.

And to my rifle this is what I say:
Within my hand may you become a snake,
if those unborn, those of a brighter day,
don't hear the shot I am about to take.

(The woods of Narotch, 30 January 1944)

DON'T SING THE SORROWFUL

Don't sing the sorrowful;
don't bring disgrace
upon sorrow.
Words are treacherous;
they'll about-face
tomorrow.

Look at the snow;
in its calm let your memory be
illuminated:
light is your heart's language. And you—
are re-
created.

Toward the snow, the icy fleece,
your fingers are bidden
to reach.
One touch—you release
the life that is hidden
in each.

(The woods of Narotch, 5 February 1944)

THE WORDS OF THE MASTER

A sunflower bursting-full of seeds, the concert hall
hung over the clavier, when—drowned in alcohol
that burned incessantly—my fingers ran
over the white bones of Chopin.

I'd played no nocturne such as this my whole life long—
never before was there a willing blend of notes like these.
And suddenly from the clavier a snake stuck out its tongue:
"An artist?—Play on stones, not keys!"

That night I disappeared from the hotel, the town.
That night in a bare field I bedded down.
And no one heard me play but God alone.
That night I played on stone.

A CONCERT AT NIGHT, AN INTERMENT
AT NOON

A concert at night, an interment at noon,
and coming first there and then here is our doom.

The burden I'm destined to carry is this:
two pails overflowing with anguish and bliss.

If one of the buckets hung empty, the other
might never hang full, but go dry like its brother.

The salt would no longer have taste, and would offer
for seven good grains all the gold in its coffer.

And wrinkled and sickly the sunlight would shrink
if there were no nourishing shadow to drink.

A concert at night, an interment at noon,
and coming first there and then here is our doom,

aware of the marriage of music and earth:
the pails overflowing with sorrow and mirth.

Together-together the there and the here:
a sunray makes ready to plunge without fear.

Such too is the scythe's and the cornstalk's communion;
such too is the fiddler's and melody's union;

so too are they twinned: what is now and what's done;
so too man and woman are limbed into one.

REMEMBRANCE OF THREE FLAMINGOS

At Lake Victoria were three flamingos. I remember
how they unfolded their magnificence, their splendor.
Three strings pulled taut astride a wave, and arched above them
a rainbow moved as if to pluck the inmost music of them.

Neither by violin nor lyre can such a tune be played;
such threefold instrument was never seen on sea or land.
The Master had a yen to test the marvel he had made,
to stir awake the living strings with his creator-hand.

Before me swept a wilderness of charnel nights and days;
but in my memory the stringèd three flamingos blaze.
They glitter in the same self-baring pose, astride the same
wave, as the morning sun unfolds its round and rosy flame.

And now one curious question won't stop nagging at my ears,
recalling the flamingos: Who commands that triple string?

354

We're granted one such moment, only one, in all our years—
to hear, to witness, such a thing.

PRE-DAY

It's pre-day, like pre-concert in a dark gray hall.
The morning star still shows, alone and kingly.
And somewhere trillers drowsily awake, and all
the instruments tune up, in choir or singly.

A Stradivarius in ancient garb will soon
arrive, near old as his creator, and strike up a tune
so blissfully, the heavy sun will then and there
feel all her weight give way
and become day
and will—the sun herself—attend the premiere.

REMEMBRANCE OF MARC CHAGALL

Remembrance of a walk with Marc Chagall. A summer gowned
in gaudy colors. Nature imitates Chagall's design.
The air is nothing but blue grapes. The two of us climb down
from summer's heights and crave a sampling of tomorrow's wine.

The selfsame hand that gave the earth a grace of angels, now
rests on my shoulder, and the scene grows dear at every side.
He says: From me, from praise, from envy, I can hide somehow,
but as for father, mother—from those two I cannot hide.

The air is nothing but blue grapes. And see: an agèd man
on a veranda, in an easy chair. And with his shears
in light and shade cuts out as delicately as he can
a dove of wavy paper, pure as pearl and doubly dear.

Chagall bows low: Matisse. And all at once the dove escapes,
like an affrighted creature, toward the dusk for which it
   hungers.

The old man also bends unto the crown of crimson grapes,
and from his fingers fall the shears—from his unmoving fingers.

THE THIRD HAND

The chopped-off hand that I discovered once upon a time
by the tomatoes in the garden rightfully is mine.
And since it is a man's hand with no owner of its own,
it's mine. A third hand, without which I set not one word down.

To curious readers—ten or so—I candidly admit:
it isn't I who feed them words of witchery and wit.
Into the paper's ear a stranger's recollection came:
my third hand, found by the tomatoes, is to blame.

To read that script it's not enough to know the Yiddish tongue.
I teach myself its language. Wander all alone among
its winding trailways late at night and fall on stones and thorns,
and see it in the seeds by the tomatoes when it dawns.

The hand that may have fondled a young woman at the time
they hacked its owner into bits—the chopped-off hand is mine.
I found it when he lost it, when it lay there claimed by none
by the tomatoes in September Nineteen Forty-One.

Moishe Shimmel (dates unknown)

(The poet was killed in a Jewish village in Galicia; his poem is
dated 1937.)

356

TO A LITTLE BOY

Don't cry, little boy, wipe your tears, things will yet be good.
We shall yet heal the wounds that are dripping blood.

We stand alone in the world against the sun's vanishing glow;
alone, alone with our poverty and with our woe.

We've got to find some consolation, we ourselves:
repair the doors, just you and I, put up the walls, the shelves.

Let them come to thrash us, rob us of the little that remains,
we'll patch our cushions again, install new windowpanes.

Once, and a second, a third time, until the yearned-for last;
we're patient, we can wait, until their time is passed.

Be quiet, little boy, dry your tears and weep no more;
we'll repair the chairs and table; we'll redo the floor.

We'll reconstruct the house that they set fire to;
the ruined walls will glitter in the sun anew.

Don't cry, little boy, don't spoil your eyes, bright days are at
    hand.
Spring will find its way back to us in the end.

Because the hand will be hacked down, like an old rotten stem,
the hand that seized your father and mother and slaughtered
    them.

Jacob (Jack) Gordon (ca. 1916–ca. 1943)

Jacob (Jack) Gordon was born in Bialystok; the year is uncertain. His first verses appeared in *Awakener of Youth* (1936; Warsaw). Later poems were included in Nachman Maisel's Warsaw journal *Literary Leaves*. He died as a partisan in the forests around Bialystok; after the war several of his poems were unearthed in the Bialystok ghetto.

THE BRIDGE REVERBERATES EACH STEP WE TAKE

The bridge reverberates each step we take.
We stop awhile and look below:
a train flies through, and here comes one in its wake,
and people nod at them hurtling through.
Just as they're standing now, I once stood there
spruced-up in bright new sailor-shirt and shorts.
My father with his fingers combed my hair
and promised to send chocolates and tortes.
The train's hoot mocked his hopes and plans.
You stand near me and fix your eyes
on me, and mine fix inward. I can feel your hands—
my throat senses your palm, my heart can recognize
your fingers. You're playing with me—and I'm
your child. Who told us love would be waving
more fiercely here on this bridge at this time
than the wind in the field—when the hoot of the train,
so fatefully harsh, wakes a tenfold craving
for joy? But here, where your hand slides over my skin,
tomorrow a bayonet will kiss me.
The hoot of the train, the roar of my fate,
caress, oh caress me. . . .
It's dark, it's late.

WHILE CARRYING LOADS OF TIMBER

While carrying loads of timber
we laughed at a certain grotesque;
whenever the log on his shoulders rocked
he kept his eyelids pressed;
lids pressed tight and pale lips locked,
he quietly came along
not seeing the steps he was taking.
He tripped in the grass more often than not,
log rocking and twisting, while we—
we laughed—and for what?
Now, when the darkness runs out of me
and my memories waken,
I finally see:
it was at our own selves we were making
mock, to smother
the sob within the heart,
because like that log-bent brother
our spirit had become:
ashamed, inert,
in a filthy shirt,
with burdens that spurt from clumsy hands,
with footstep weary, numb.

Leah Rudnitsky (1916–1943)

LEAH RUDNITSKY was born in 1916 in Kalvaria, a small Lithuanian town. Her talent was first recognized by the writer Yosada, who brought her to Kovno. There her work appeared in various Yiddish publications. In 1940 she joined the staff of the *Vilna Truth*. Her collection of Vilna Ghetto poems, *Mists*, reflected both the grief and the fierce spirit of that trapped population. Fighting in a partisan unit, she was captured by the Gestapo and, according to Katcherginski, perished in Treblinka.

BIRDS ARE DROWSING

Birds are drowsing on the branches;
darling, shut your eyes.
At your cradle sits a stranger
singing lullabies.
                    Liu-liu, liu-liu, liu.

Somewhere once your sleep was woven
with a skein of joy;
but your mother will not ever
come back to her boy.
                    Liu-liu, liu-liu, liu.

I have seen your father running
from a hail of stones;
over fields that did not listen
flew his orphaned moans.
                    Liu-liu, liu-liu, liu.

S. Shenker (dates uncertain)

THE GRIEF-STRICKEN HEART

Why is my heart so wrenched with grief
yet not one tear can flow?
and life is always dark for me
no matter where I go?

Why is the sun not here today
to warm me with its glare?
I have no garment, after all,
nor any shoes to wear.

And am I fatherless as well?
without a mother too?

Where are you, brothers, sisters all—
are any left of you?

O why, despite my grief, have I
not one more tear to shed?
Perhaps because the time has come
for Kaddish to be said.

(Kovno ghetto)

Lerke Rosenblum (dates unknown)

I YEARN
(the poet, a young girl, escaped from a German concentration camp.)

I yearn for the laugh, free and open,
that long ago rang through the air;
an uproar of children, unbroken
by motherless sobs of despair.

I yearn for a step to be taken
with pride and a sense of self-worth.
I yearn for the day when I'll waken
to find myself free on the earth.

(Kovno Ghetto)

361

Hirsh Glik (1922–1944)

Hirsh Glik was born in Vilna in 1922. His father dealt in scrap iron, rags, and used bottles. From early youth the poet belonged to Hashomer Hatzair (The Young Guard). He began writing Hebrew verses in 1935 but turned to Yiddish under the influence of the Young Vilna group. He formed a writers' group of his own among the neighborhood children. The poet Leizer Wolf became their mentor. Glik had left school at sixteen to work in a bookbindery and a paper factory, but a year later, under Leizer Wolf's guidance, he and his young circle managed to produce a journal of their own, *Young Forest.* When the Nazis took Vilna, he and his father were among those sent to do forced labor in the peat bogs fifteen miles from the city. He became sick there but continued inspiring the hundreds around him with his new songs, which reached Vilna and won great popularity. Among these were "The Ballad of the Brown Theater" and "Typhus Ballad." Because the peat-bog workers were in contact with the partisans, the camp was liquidated in May 1943; Glik was sent back to the ghetto, where he continued writing songs. In October the ghetto itself was liquidated; he tried to join the partisans in the forests, but the Gestapo caught him and shipped him to the concentration camp at Goldfield. He perished in 1944.

NOT A SOUND; THE NIGHT IS STARRY

Not a sound; the night is starry,
and the frost—a burning brand.
Remember: I taught you how to carry
a gun, how to grip it in your hand!

A girl, beret and fur piece matching,
crouches with pistol in her clasp.
A girl with a face of velvet, watching
the enemy's caravan go past.

Her little gun takes aim at their position
and fires once, and finds its mark.

A car full of arms and ammunition
she stops with a bullet in the dark!

Creep forth from the woods at day's beginning,
a snow-crown garlanding our hair;
one little triumph now, but sure of winning
the liberty for which we die and dare!

PARTISAN SONG

Never say that there is only death for you,
though leaden skies may be concealing days of blue,
because the hour that we have hungered for is near;
beneath our tread the earth shall tremble: "We are here!"

From land of palm tree to the far-off land of snow
we shall be coming with our torment, with our woe;
and everywhere our blood has sunk into the earth
shall our bravery, our vigor, blossom forth. . . .

We'll have the morning sun to set our day aglow,
and all our yesterdays shall vanish with the foe.
And if the time is long before the sun appears,
then let this song go like a signal through the years.

This song was written with our blood, and not with lead;
it's not a song that summer birds sing overhead;
it was a people, among toppling barricades,
that sang this song of ours with pistols and grenades.

So never say that there is only death for you.
Leaden skies may be concealing days of blue;
yet the hour that we have hungered for is near;
beneath our tread the earth shall tremble: "We are here!"

Chaneh Haitin (1925–)

Born in Shavel (Shawly), Lithuania, in 1925, CHANEH HAITIN attended a Hebrew high school, after which she worked in the brush factory in the ghetto of Shawly. From there she was moved to several German concentration camps. After liberation she went first to Lodz, then through Germany and on to Israel, where she settled. Her songs, especially "A Jewish Child," had been immensely popular in the ghettos and death camps; some are still sung. From 1945 to 1949 her poems continued to appear, first in Lodz, then in various Yiddish publications in Germany. In Israel, S. Meltzer translated her poems into Hebrew.

A JEWISH CHILD

In a Lithuanian town
there's a house that stands alone.
Through a narrow window glass
children watch the seasons pass:
Little boys with clever heads,
little girls with long blond braids,
and, amid the rest, a pair
of black eyes keeps vigil there.

Charming eyes as black as coal,
and a nose that's cute and small,
lips—created to be kissed—
black curls no one could resist.
Mother brought him wrapped from sight
in the middle of the night,
sobbed, and with a kiss half-wild,
this she whispered to her child:

—Here, my child, your place will be.
Listen carefully to me.
I will leave you here because
Danger's opening its jaws.
With these children nicely play,

364

just be quiet, and obey.
Not one Jewish word from you;
you no longer are a Jew.

Bitterly he pleads with her:
"Can't we stay the way we were?
Please don't leave me here alone."
And his tears come rolling down.
She bestows kiss after kiss,
but he's not assuaged by this;
still he argues: "No!" and "No!
I won't stay and let you go!"

So she lifts him in her arms;
with a voice that lulls and charms,
"Oh my son," she sings to him,
and he slips into a dream.
Now her grief flows unconfined;
and she leaves the house behind
full of worry, full of fright,
and retreats into the night.

Cold outdoors, a wind blows wild,
and a voice cries, "Oh my child,
to strange hands I've trusted you;
there was nothing else to do."
Talking to herself, she goes;
and outdoors a cold wind blows,
cold against her face, and wild—
"God, protect my only child!"

Strange house, full of folk. The boy's
motionless; he makes no noise,
asks for nothing, never speaks,
no one's heard him laugh in weeks.
Not of day or night he takes
notice; neither sleeps nor wakes.
Vassilka—a strange new name—
strikes his little heart with pain.

Mother roams about; she's grown,
like her son, as still as stone.

No one knows, and no one cares.
Waits and waits—too well compares
with Jochebed, Moses' mother!
for, abandoned as that other
to the mercy of the Nile,
she has left her only child.

Index of Poets